LANDSCAPES AND MEMORIES

JOHN PREBBLE was born in Middlesex in 1915, and spent his youth in Saskatchewan, Canada. He began his writing career as a journalist in 1934 and is now a novelist, historian, film-writer, and the author of several highly praised dramatized documentaries for television and radio. His previous books include: *The Highland Clearances*, *Glencoe*, *Culloden*, *Highland Regiments in Revolt*, *John Prebble's Scotland* ~~and The King's~~ s in Surrey.

JOHN PREBBLE

Landscapes & Memories

An intermittent autobiography

HarperCollins*Publishers*

HarperCollins*Publishers*
77–85 Fulham Palace Road,
Hammersmith, London w6 8jb

This paperback edition 1994
1 3 5 7 9 8 6 4 2

First published in Great Britain by
HarperCollins*Publishers* 1993

Copyright © John Prebble 1993

John Prebble asserts the moral right to
be identified as the author of this work

isbn 0-00-637460-3

Set in Linotron Imprint

Printed in Great Britain by
HarperCollinsManufacturing, Glasgow

FOR HARRY CLARK

List of Illustrations

Plate Section

Four generations spanning 150 years

The Rising Sun at Barnet

Henry Wood, maternal grandfather of the author

The author's parents on their wedding day

William Wood, the author's uncle, after emigrating to Canada

Prairie Locomotive, Canada, 1912

Sutherland in the early 1940s

Christmas dinner at Binderstrasse, 1945

The sergeants' mess, Hamburg, 1945

All photographs supplied by the author

May the Fifteenth

I am sitting on an old tombstone in the walled cemetery at Braemar and thinking, for reasons which may be clear later, of Lieutenant Leefe Robinson of the Royal Flying Corps. The westward approach to this small Deeside town, and to the granite massif upon which it clings, was melancholy but beautiful this morning, black earth and the grass newly green, white blossom on the roadside rowans. As I came across the river-plain from Tullich Lodge, the horizon beyond Ballater was dominated as always by the majestic escarpment of Lochnagar. Unbroken along the curve of its mile-wide crest was a wave-lipped cloud, turning in a slow cascade to the corries below and to a lower hill sweetly known as the Little Breast.

In the hope of seeing this unnatural cloud more closely, I delayed my call upon the graveyard and drove south-west from Ballater, by the flank of Lochnagar to Spittal of Glen Muick. A medieval bishop of Aberdeen built a hospice here, for the sick and for those enfeebled travellers in need of rest before taking the drove-road over the pass of Capel Mounth. Two centuries ago that redoubtable whisky smuggler, John Robertson of Crathie, would sometimes assemble his contraband caravan in the glen – men, horses, weapons and kegs of Lochnagar's dark malt. Later still, at an oar of the royal boat on Loch Muick, a kilted John Brown first caught the approving eye of Victoria. When I reached the Spittal the white cloud-wave was gone from the escarpment. Against the sky, where the land rises towards the pass, a line of red deer was climbing a gentle slope, elegant and stiff-legged. No more than a hundred yards behind, and as if in pursuit, was a file of soldiers, laden with field-kit and moving as soldiers will upon such occasions, slow-bent in a pace that anaesthetizes all pain and thought.

As I watched their dark figures turn at last in descent towards me, my nostalgic sympathy was distracted by a flock of chaffinches which rose from the woodland beyond the burn, mobbing the car and hanging on frantic wings before the windscreen. I offered these discriminating seed-eaters fragments of peppermint cream, placing them on the side mirror where some were taken and then discarded. The pleasure of being the attention of so much fluttering colour remained with me until the first Guardsman came over the wall with an oath of relief. Easing the straps of his equipment with his thumbs, and surrounded now by the departing finches, he moved away to a waiting truck. His presence seemed less eccentric than the behaviour of the birds. Soldiers are not strangers here, and in the past they have been more bloody in purpose than the young Guardsmen who came over the wall behind their section-leader, some cheerfully and some sullenly. The Royalist forces of James Graham, Marquess of Montrose, marched this way on an April day in 1645, in his *Annus Mirabilis*, his year of miraculous victories. He brought them by the drove-road from the Braes of Angus, over the Mounth to the Spittal and down the twisting glen to Ballater where he crossed the River Dee. Nine days later, far northward and within sight and smell of the sea, his army fought a Homeric battle, a slaughterhouse in the village of Auldearn. Highland and Irish clansmen defended its kail-yards and pigsties against the pike-men of the Covenant, and the Royalists' lieutenant-general, black-haired Alasdair MacColla, stood in an arrow-storm, his great sword hewing away the pike-heads that pierced his leather shield.

From the thought of that merciless encounter to the walled grave-yard in Braemar, to another clansman one hundred years later, almost unknown yet fighting for the same flawed cause in its final, disastrous battle. This small enclosure, between the town and its toy-box castle, is the resting-place of Peter Grant, known as The Dubrach from his home along the upper Dee, below the mounting stairway of the Grampians. I wrote about him briefly in my account of the visit to Edinburgh by George IV in 1822. The Dubrach was then in his 108th year, and was among the last, if not the last, survivor of Culloden, eighty-six years before. The last Jacobite, perhaps. In the first two decades of the nineteenth century no newspaper recorded the tenacious survival of any British soldier who had fought against the Rebellion. Grant had served with the Farquharson clan-regiment, and was made its sergeant-major following his courage in an earlier battle. Taken prisoner after Culloden, he escaped, but when and how, and from which stone cell or prison hulk, I do not know. When he could, he returned to Braemar, sometimes working as a tailor and a weaver until old age drove him south to the comfort of his son's farm in Angus.

When the King arrived in Scotland he was welcomed by some as if he were the Young Pretender come again, and he responded with a romantic affection for the Old Cause. In the euphoria of the event he gave Peter Grant a pension of twenty shillings a week, upon the recommendation of Walter Scott, it is said. With this security The Dubrach returned to Braemar once more, and died a year later. Three hundred men followed his coffin to the graveyard, having drunk – in valediction and a modest observance of Highland custom – four gallons of whisky before the lifting.

A reader in Braemar wrote to me, giving me Grant's correct Christian name. It was not Patrick, as some contemporary newspapers had reported. I was also told more about the man and where I might find his grave. Thus, on this May morning with rain returning in fitful gusts, I walked over the tussocked earth of the cemetery and found nothing. I took shelter, and a seat on a bench-like slab, in the lee of the Farquharson mausoleum. There another visitor, a woman in Red Robertson tartan, having asked me if she could be of help, told me to look at the inscription on the stone beneath me.

Erected to the memory of Peter Grant, sometime farmer in Dubrach who died at Auchindryne the 11th February 1824 aged 110 years. His wife Mary Cumming died at West side parish of Lethnot in Forfar Shire on the 24th February 1811 aged 65 years and lies in the churchyard at Lethnot.

As I sit upon the stone, in soldierly comradeship rather than disrespect, my mind takes its own wandering course. I like to move back into the past, or from it to the future, by familiar and sometimes familial steps. I follow signposts that direct me along my own expended years and from them, sometimes, to the wider past that has occupied much of my writing. That is the form and nature of this book.

And so, with indulgence, there is no incongruity between The Dubrach's headstone and my remembrance of the night that Lieutenant Robinson destroyed a Zeppelin over Potter's Bar. I undoubtedly saw this horrifying incident but I have no subjective memory of it. What I do remember is vivid enough, and it is of course what my mother saw as she stood in a North London street, holding me high in her arms and excitedly directing my infant attention to the night sky. Her recollection of the event was still strong in her ninety-first year when she wrote her autobiography, in two exercise books and a firm hand that gave no indication that her schooling had ended at the age of eleven. Her written account of the Zeppelin's destruction varied little from the version she had told me many times when I was young, but in committing it to paper she did not say that she had taken me into the street with her. I think she now believed it was shameful to have risked my life with her own. When I chided her for leaving me out of the story, she shook her head and smiled.

The raid had been on for some time [she wrote] and it was very quiet. The children were asleep in chairs and I went to the front door and watched the searchlights. They showed up a Zepp and it looked no bigger than a cigar. Then the lights left it, then picked it up again. That went on and suddenly I saw a red and green light behind the Zepp, and when the lights left it again the plane's lights went out, and we read afterwards that the plane dived under the Zepp. I called the neighbour's girls out to look. We were cheering. I could see the pieces dropping from the Zepp which had drifted, and it was very low and big and it seemed it would drop on us. It was coming straight down on the road. Then I realized it was men falling out. We didn't cheer any more. It seemed awful.

That memory has often answered its own recall during my life, but never so vividly as one February morning on the Maas. Crouched with others in the cold sunlight, I watched a great formation of American bombers moving eastward into the Rhineland, through puff-balls of gunfire. Here and there, one slowly turned away from its companions and then, on spiralling wings and quickly ablaze, became a scarlet petal falling to the snow.

In my mother's tenth decade she still had a clear and affectionate recollection of her maternal grandfather, James Clark, once a miller and later landlord of the Rising Sun in Barnet. 'A tubby Dickensian man,' she wrote, 'in heavy boots and very kind.' She was born in Barnet, 'on Palm Sunday 1884 in a little cottage by the brook', and she was christened Florence, for Miss Nightingale whom her mother admired. When she was a child in London, and a victim of consumption it was feared, she was returned by trap to Barnet to recover in the country air and the care of her grandparents. James

Clark was fond of her. He would sit her on his bar, with a small horn cup from which she drank fortifying porter. Although old, he was able to carry her on his shoulder to eat cherries in the orchard and watch the squirrels gathering filberts in the hedges. Sometimes he lifted her up to delight in his circling doves, as she would in time hold me to see a deadlier flight.

James Clark was born in 1813, eleven years before Peter Grant was taken to the graveyard at Braemar. Although certainly improbable, it would have been possible for them to meet and for The Dubrach to talk of his young manhood with the clans. And this could have been retold to my mother. She would have enjoyed my conjectural juggling with age and time, for although unschooled in it she had a keen sense of history and this, perhaps, compelled her to lift me to the sky that I might remember one of its terrible moments. Before the Victorian age ended she was already a working woman, a tweeny-maid at eleven in a Finsbury Park boarding-house, a factory-girl at fifteen in Bunhill Row. Although she believed that teeming age had been unfair, unjust and cruel to her class, she was proud of having shared its greatness, and of being part of its astonishing history. I think she would have understood how and why my mind found its way from The Dubrach's stone to her.

So strong is my wish for contact with the past, to hear a voice or see with another's eyes, that I have encouraged it within my own family when I could. In the course of a journalistic interview I was invited to bring my wife and children to tea with William Stone, the oldest resident of Albany, a gentle and dignified man, almost a centenarian and known as The Squire of Piccadilly. So far as I can remember his account of his life, it had never been necessary for him to work, nor had he ever thought it proper to describe himself as rich, but he did not believe privilege gave him licence to comment upon the behaviour of others, morally or politically. Wealth had protected him, longevity had preserved a charming, informative anachronism.

With the assistance of his butler, whom my son Simon first took to be our host, he presided over a tea party such as he remembered from his own childhood. A great round table was covered with lace-fringed linen, and laid with white porcelain, dishes of hot muffins and scones, crystal bowls of preserves, a large fruit-cake and silver terraces of sandwiches and pastries. He poured the tea himself, filling the pot from a kettle kept hot on a spirit-blue flame. He talked of the past with familiarity, and in faint wonder that it no longer existed. In his childhood, he said, a maidservant would take him down Lower Regent Street to the Duke of York's Steps, at the bottom of which a girl sold them cups of warm milk, drawn from a cow tethered in the Mall. In middle age he had been a guest at the wedding of the last Tsar of Russia. The butler was sent to bring a photograph of the event, a stone stairway on the outside of a large building, crowded with tiny figures among whom William Stone appeared only as a blurred image. He took it away from the table himself, carefully replacing it on a wall amid his many cases of iridescent butterflies. He had collected walking-sticks and canes from all over the world, from countries whose names, kings or presidents had been lost in the wrack of two great wars. He had also attended the funeral of Disraeli, and he told my son and my daughter Sarah how odd it had been to hear no sound but the harsh cries of peacocks when the cortège passed through the dark trees of Beaconsfield.

I envied his ability for such recall. My idiosyncratic methods of research, although properly deplored by some academics, have frequently brought me a deep empathy with the past, in Scotland particularly. But it seems to me, sometimes, that I know more about that beloved country's history than I can recall of my own life. This has been some compensation for the fact that ageing demands a price for survival, a loss or misting of memory that might be nepenthe, since remembrance is too often the recollection of sorrow. Although I can see and hear some fragments of my childhood with astonishing clarity, much more is gone, and I am conscious of the time I lost then in dreaming. Throughout my prairie childhood my mind was occupied with fantasies and inventions which prevented a healthy awareness of my environment. They were years of disappointment and relentless hardship for my parents, who had dreamt the emigrant's dream after the Great War and found only a nightmare in the Canadian West. Although I know this now, my memories are a series of innocent tableaux, timeless and beguiling, where despair sometimes masquerades as delight. I can see my parents sitting at a table, close together in the yellow light of an Aladdin lamp, counting and recounting a few copper and silver coins, an occasional dollar bill. I can hear the smooth slide of a carpenter's pencil on a wide wood-shaving as my father tried once more to balance debit and credit. Seen through a crack in the hessian curtain that hid my bed from the main room of our shack, indeed the only *room*, it could have been the subject of a Norman Rockwell cover for the *Saturday Evening Post*, a warming glimpse of small-town America. But the truth was more cruel.

There are other memories without this bitter irony. The return of spring after a glittering white and merciless winter, prairie-crocuses flowering miraculously in the dead grass and melting snow, the wing-beat of wild duck coming north in disciplined flight, soft rain-showers that covered the earth with small green frogs. In a seemingly unchangeable world – a world that had been buffalo-ground a short lifetime ago – we floated rafts of railroad ties on deep slough-holes, played hookey and went fishing bare-foot in frayed overalls and straw hats like Huck Finn. We crouched in the forge near the engine roundhouse and waited impatiently as the blacksmith bent horseshoe nails into our initials. We placed them on the railroad track out of town, waiting until the afternoon freight – a mile in length and occasionally driven by my uncle – had passed over them and changed them into paper-thin letters of silver. Burning to the touch, they had to be prised gently from the iron rail and were sometimes broken before we could carry them home. I placed mine in a cigar-box which I kept under the front step of the shack. This secret place was also used to hide a somnolent grass snake, an Indian arrow-head or a stone evocatively shaped, several tobacco-spitting grasshoppers of spectacular green, and once a meadow lark with a broken wing. This bird, as large as an English thrush with a black V on its yellow breast, did not flourish under imprisonment and pain, and my father gravely advised me to release it. Resentfully, I took it to the open prairie beyond the Presbyterian church and laid it where I had found it, beside our truant-path to the river. There, no doubt, it was devoured by one of the hump-backed coyotes which limped into our distant vision by day, or awoke us at night with their peevish howls.

Such memories, and others, would mean less were it not that they link me to Scotland and its past. The name of our Saskatchewan township was Sutherland, scarcely five years old when the first of my family, my mother's brother, arrived as an emigrant boy of seventeen. It was founded by a man of the same name whose great-grandparents were among the ninety-six young Highland men and women who came to the Red River Settlement in 1813. More than a thousand fearful or already displaced Highlanders had written to Lord Selkirk asking for land, for hope and opportunity in his prairie colony along the Red and Assiniboin rivers. The young pioneers he first accepted came from the parish of Kildonan in the county of Sutherland, victims of the Policy of Improvement by which this shire estate of the Marquess and Marchioness of Stafford, later Duke and Duchess of Sutherland, was inexorably converted into a great sheep-farm. Its Gaelic people were evicted or removed to coastal fisheries for which they had no practised skills. They were driven into colonial exile or abandoned to the slums of southern cities, their language, their culture and their oral history dying with them or with the dispersed generation that followed. I did not know this when I was a boy, nor was it known, I think, by the Scots-Canadians living in the township, not even our schoolteacher, Miss Campbell, whose romantic descriptions of a homeland she had never seen were so disturbing a contrast to the yellow prairie and cloudless sky beyond the classroom windows.

I first learnt something of the Highland Clearances a year or so before the War, and the knowledge became a small part of the fuel that was firing my political anger and partisanship. There was much in that dramatic and frightening decade to persuade youth that change – just, rapid and immediate change – was a desperate necessity, and this was not exclusively a reaction to the rise of Fascism. The passion we felt made me, like others, a member of the British Communist Party. My reasons for this decision were more subjective than I could have admitted at the time, and more Radical in an English tradition than Marxist in a European mould, though I became adept at the think-talk of the latter. If I am obliged to explain – and I do not think I always must – why I eventually left the Party, first in spirit and then in fact before the War's end, the answer is that it was probably for the same reasons that had compelled me to join it. Experience and a reflective reading of history were also teaching me that in the struggle for liberty and justice the cause is often more at risk from its leaders than it may be from its enemies. Frequently inept and always imperfect, the *human* nature of democracy makes it vulnerable to exploitation, and only a vigilant scepticism can preserve it from corrosion and self-destruction.

All Communist recruits in that Munich year may have seen an early flicker of their own particular warning-light, and by the same probability ignored it as I did. My political beliefs and my emotions, always interlocked, persuaded me that I should go to Spain, where the Civil War was nearing its tragic end. The proposal was derisively rejected by an organizer at the Party's headquarters, his half-smile inviting me to share his mockery of what he was saying.

Enough middle-class Communist intellectuals, he said, had already been killed on the Ebro. What the Party needed, now that the War was ending, was more working-class martyrs. I was told to continue as a member of my local branch, concerning myself with meetings, recruiting, the sale of the *Daily Worker*, and classes in Marxism-Leninism. I was also advised to exercise my professional talent with a clandestine group of Communist journalists who hid their existence under such pretentious titles as The Samuel Johnson Literary Society, and were never more active than when looking for new and undetectable meeting-places.

Until that moment, perhaps, I had never thought of myself as a middle-class intellectual. My roots as I knew them were deep in many generations of rural labourers, my father's people in Kent and my mother's in Hertfordshire and Essex. Class, religion and politics were never discussed in my home until in my aggressive adolescence I violently introduced them, to my parents' confusion and dismay. They were High Church Anglicans, and in childhood and youth I was well-schooled in that faith, going to church once during the week and twice on Sundays, and later serving its rituals in the red cassock and white surplice of an acolyte, choking in sweet smoke when I attended the censer during Stations of the Cross. Until she met my father, touching his sailor's collar for luck when she saw him outside the Empire Music Hall in Islington, my mother rarely entered a church, having a London factory-girl's impatience with the seeming irrelevance of religion. My father's influence changed that and, as it was for many of the Victorian and Edwardian working-class, their faith became a necessary strength in a hard life.

Their politics, in another sense, were also part of this need. My father's long service with the Royal Navy from the time he became a boy-seaman until the end of the Great War, the loss of his brother and friends in that struggle, attached him and my mother to the Tory Party, believing it to be the guardian and the manifestation of their pride in England. They were stubbornly steadfast in this belief, and it is in my mind that they gave their priests and their rulers better service than was deserved, although they would be grieved to hear me say that. Socialism, they thought, was an alien and a destructive creed. Although they believed this intensely, most particularly my mother, they had a great admiration for her brother, the emigrant who would become the locomotive-engineer of that mile-long freight. Before he left England, conflict with his drunken father compelled him to live alone, upon what work he could find, sleeping wherever possible with a covering of newspapers for warmth. During that time he became a Socialist, a pacifist and a trade-unionist, maintaining those convictions when he returned in the Great War as a Canadian volunteer, conscientiously refusing to fight but serving as a stretcher-bearer in Flanders.

My mother's recollections of her childhood were written without rancour, but with thankfulness that its deprivation had somehow been rewarded in later life. She was charitably generous in her memories of her father, whom I remember in his virile old age as stubborn, self-centred and sadly unlovable. His life had not persuaded him to be otherwise. He was a character from the time and the pages of *The Ragged-trousered Philanthropist*, a builder's labourer, an erector of some skill and a strong hod-carrier who could lift a thousand bricks a day to the layers who worked on the high scaffolding he built. When he could not earn enough for his wife and six children, which was most of the time, they were expected to forage in support. Thus my mother, at the age of eight or less, with one of her younger sisters . . .

Every Saturday my sister Annie and I had a big bag and went round the better streets and picked up coal and wood which the delivery man dropped, and we really walked a long way, sometimes not getting back till past dinner-time. Of course, if our bags got lots and were heavy, we came home pleased with ourselves, and had a piece of bread and dripping for dinner. There was no money coming in. I think our landlady was very good. She had to wait till Father got work, and as I heard years later, his money was only fourpence-ha'penny an hour, labourer's money. And long hours, six o'clock in the morning till six o'clock at night. When it rained, no work. When snow was on the ground Father used to walk to the Council offices in Caledonian Road, a long way from us, to try to get a few hours clearing the snow in the main roads, but he wasn't very lucky, and once he and two other men went to a better part some way from us and stood at a street corner and sang some old ballads. Father had a lovely voice.

The trouble in his trade was pay-day. It was drinks for the ganger, it was him who found the workers, so Father was late home, and often drunk. But never noisy or quarrelsome, like our landlord was. Poor Mum, do you know the only day I ever saw her eat a dinner with us was Sunday, that is if there was a dinner that day. Six children, how did they manage?

In my schooldays I could see little connection between the lives of my parents, their parents and grandparents, and the history I read so hungrily – textbooks of Historical England, the eighty-six appalling novels of G. A. Henty, the romantically absurd romances of *Ivanhoe* and *Quentin Durward*, the more intellectually challenging work of Macaulay and Trevelyan which I read too soon. There seemed to be nothing in these books that gave the lives of my parents, their parents and grandparents, purpose and nobility. In my last year at school, however, and through the guidance of a socially repressed but gifted history master, I began to hear bolder voices from the past, speaking with an unfamiliar clarity and muscular wisdom. The first came across five and a half centuries, the strange but in time understandable language of William Langland and *Piers Plowman*, an Everyman edition given me by the master. And from Langland to his contemporary John Ball, the rogue priest, the hedge priest, chaplain to and a leader of the Peasants' Revolt. The same master told me where first to find him, in Froissart's *Chronicles*, behind the names of kings, princes and earls, brazen trumpets and clanging armour. John Ball, said Froissart as if the name were sour in his mouth, was a crazy priest given to unauthorized and absurd preaching, particularly in the market-place after mass on Sunday. As the people came out of church he would gather them about him and say:

> My good friends, matters cannot go on well in England until all things shall be in common, when there shall be neither vassals nor lords; when the lords shall be no more masters than ourselves . . . Are we not all descended from the same parents, Adam and Eve? And what can they show, or what reason can they give, why they should be more masters than ourselves?

He was executed for such impudence, of course, and for his leadership in the Revolt. He died at St Albans, hanged and disembowelled while still living, his body then quartered. On that same July day a Cambridgeshire man was hanged for telling his tavern companions that John Ball was a true and good man who had been falsely condemned. Who now remembers the names of the king, the lords and masters who rode back into power over the mangled bodies of Ball, Tyler, Jack Straw and many of their followers? Who knows a single unselfish, ennobling word uttered by any of the victors? But the rough tocsin rhymes which John Ball sent from village to village, declaring that 'falseness and guile have reigned too long, and truth hath been set under a lock', have echoed in spirit through six centuries of succeeding struggles. Never more stridently, or expediently perhaps, than in the late 1930s when the Communist Party of Great Britain, declaring itself the political heir of men like John Ball, embraced a 'patriotic people's nationalism' as a tactic in the Popular Front and later, after some cowardly hesitation, in the war against Fascism.

To me, and many others no doubt, it did seem that the Party had lifted a standard so often raised in a valiant cause, and accordingly needed support. It spoke, or so it seemed, with the voice of that medieval peasantry, of the Levellers, the Radicals and the Chartists who followed. Here was an English history of which we could be proud, without the shame of industrial greed and imperial growth. Amid the hectoring dogma of Marxist-Leninist interpretations it was sometimes possible to hear the inspiring words and feel the heady emotion of great events untaught in our schools. The most relevant of these, at the beginning of the War, was the Putney Debate of 1647.

In the autumn of that year delegates from the New Model Army – footmen, troopers, junior officers and an occasional sturdy field-officer like Thomas Rainborough – met in the parish church at Putney to determine their rights and their future now that they had won the long war against the Royalists. The Agitators, as the most forthright of the delegates were known, were faced by an obdurate hierarchy, by Cromwell and his son-in-law Ireton, by the so-styled Grandees of Army and State. Such men believed, in Ireton's words, that property was 'the most fundamental part of the constitution', that it would be foolish to give landless men the power to vote against it. Before the Debate was abandoned – on the specious alarm that the King had escaped and was once again threatening the State – property, and the power it gave, became the nub of all argument. Rainborough, a courageous and short-tempered Leveller, set the tone of the Agitators' complaint. 'The poorest he that is in England hath a life to live as the greatest he.' Therefore, he said, any man who was obliged to live under a government 'ought first by his own consent to put himself under that government'. Another Agitator, a London tradesman who now wore an officer's yellow sash, placed the soldier's view more bluntly before the increasingly uneasy Grandees.

There are many thousands of us soldiers that have ventured our lives; we have had little propriety in the kingdom as to our estates, yet we have had a birthright. But it seems now, except a man has had a fixed estate in this kingdom he hath no right in this kingdom. I wonder we were so much deceived. If we had not a right to the kingdom we were mere mercenary soldiers.

Throughout much of the War I carried these words, or some paraphrase, on a slip of paper which I kept folded in my Army pay-book. They had a strong and immediate relevance to the time. My generation reached maturity with the bitter realization that there had been a political betrayal after the Great War. Many of us, like myself, who came of age before this second war began, did not have an opportunity to vote until we were thirty, and when it came we were determined that promises so glibly made to all soldiers in all history would this time be kept. Sometimes I lectured on the Agitators, when bored or idle officers allowed me to speak in their place, in the hour set aside for sanitized political discussion. I am not sure that what I said was more important than their conscientious explanation of parliamentary procedure or the wording on a ballot paper, but I had an attentive audience when I talked of such men as Robert Lockyer.

He was a trooper of Whalley's Horse, and had joined the army of Parliament in 1640 when he was seventeen, one of those 'honest men in buff coats' for whom Cromwell professed love until they challenged his authority. Lockyer was perhaps a Leveller in 1649; certainly he had been the political leader of his troop, a pious man, it was said, and much loved. In the spring of that year he was found guilty of mutiny in a dispute over arrears of pay, and was sentenced to death. The dispute was real enough, but it was his Levelling influence, and the Levellers' continued opposition to further military ventures by Cromwell and the Grandees, that made his execution inevitable. He was shot by a file of musketeers outside Old Saint Paul's churchyard, facing them without a bandage across his eyes. The exact site of his death is lost among the stone and glass canyons wherein another cathedral now stands with gathered skirts like a frightened nun.

Robert Lockyer's funeral was perhaps the most remarkable ever held in the City of London, and an indictment of the great men who had ordered his judicial murder. The crowd it attracted was later said to be the largest gathered for such an occasion until the funeral of Wellington. All who came, it seemed, were wearing green ribbons in their hats or in their hair, and many carried branches of fresh green leaf. Green, sea-green, the Levellers' colour, the colour worn by Englishmen in revolt long before it became an Irish song, before naval mutineers at Spithead and the Nore gave the whole globe a more sanguinary hue. Bearers from Lockyer's regiment carried him to his grave in Westminster, having laid his bared sword upon the coffin, dipped in his own blood and resting upon sprigs of rosemary. Six cavalry trumpeters led the procession, playing a silver-tongued farewell. Immediately behind the coffin were Lockyer's close friends, wearing mourning-capes and leading his horse in black housing. And then troopers from many regiments, hundreds it was said, even thousands, marching on foot, slowly and with great solemnity. Behind these a long, long procession of men and women. No general officer, not even Wellington, was *mourned* like this trooper of Whalley's Horse.

A month later, Oliver Cromwell surrounded the last militant Levellers in the village of Burford, twenty miles to the west of Oxford, stubborn men from six or seven regiments who had bitterly accused their general officers, '*You kept not covenant with us!*' The engagement was quickly over. The sloping main street was stormed at midnight, from north and south and with a brief flurry of shots. Although most of the Levellers escaped in the dark, more than three hundred did not and were imprisoned in the church. On the next day they were assembled upon its roof to watch the execution of three men against the wall below. It was Cromwell's mercy. It had been his angry will to shoot one in ten. Burford is now a tourists' centre, and a few who visit the church may find the name of one waiting Leveller, carved upon the stone of the font, *Anthony Sedley 1649*.

I touch my forehead in salute sometimes when the uncomprehending stream of traffic carries me over the Thames and past the old parish church of Putney. I have written the drafts of several books at an inn near Burford, and on those days when writing has been hard I have gone by lane and field to see once more that enduring church and its sad graveyard.

Such things were the substance of my emotional attachment to the Communist Party fifty years ago, and because of them I did not think I was as good a Party member as I believed others to be, but that is what it expected me to think. I have not suffered greatly from that long-ago affiliation. It has nagged at the mind of Authority, however, in the Army and among some employers later. It once brought me close to military imprisonment, but that was the more direct result of my activities at the time. It was certainly successful for a while in keeping me from the War itself, but in my journalistic career later its intrusion was more bizarre than menacing.

Like others who felt a need to take six khaki years by the throat and shake some understanding from them, I wrote a war novel, fitfully begun in Germany before demobilization and continued with therapeutic energy after my release. On the day of publication it was brought to the knowledge of the first Baron Beaverbrook. Not because he wished to read it, if ever he did, but because he was lunching with my publisher, that good man David Farrer, who had been one of his personal assistants during the War. Upon recommendation, therefore, rather than acknowledged merit, I was summoned that afternoon to Arlington House. After a short conversation which I have forgotten, I was offered and accepted employment on his newspapers.

This dissembling little man, whose mischievous or gnomic grin was the Devil's gift to the cartoonists he employed, was undoubtedly a great publisher, but he had a paradoxical weakness that would seem to deny it. He admired good journalists, indeed good writers in any medium, yet understood so little about their craft that he believed a man who could express his thoughts and feelings so well in writing would, of course, do as well with the thoughts and feelings of Lord Beaverbrook. The careers of many good writers were spoiled by remaining too long in the service of such sophistry. I was grateful later when happenstance saved me from this misfortune – that is to say, when an editor who had not been informed that I was joining his staff ultimately appeased his chagrin by discharging me.

Later that first afternoon I was suddenly recalled. Lord Beaverbrook was now standing before the broad window of his apartment, immaculate in blue hopsack and white linen. The trees of Green Park were behind him, and his large head was surrounded by an aureole of glistening light. It was a position, I believe, he frequently took when the sun was in the west. His conversation this time was even more brief. Two barked questions and a comment. Was I a member of the Communist Party? No, I said. Had I ever been a Communist? Yes, I said. This he considered for a moment only. Tell no one, he said, nodded a dismissal and walked from the room.

It was customary for a young writer to whom Beaverbrook was offering the world, if not ease of conscience, to play a minor and usually short role at his court. Within a week of joining his newspaper I was invited to Cap d'Ail, his Riviera villa. It had once belonged to the couturier Molyneux, and in 1948 it had not yet recovered from neglect and misuse during the War. I knew I was there to be tested, and since I was not sure that I would approve of his plans for me, I think I took a defensive position behind a polite and uncommunicative impassivity, sedulously cultivated during six years in the ranks of the British Army. Part of that military service had been as a mechanic, repairing and maintaining radio-location equipment, which Beaverbrook wrongly assumed made me capable of restoring the one ancient wireless set in the villa. He was anxious to hear the results of the Italian elections, telling me repeatedly, by way of encouragement and in sardonic humour, that he expected the Communists to win handsomely.

My work on the set, without enthusiasm or proper tools, was further hampered by two obstacles I regarded as insurmountable. The first was the wall of hills above Monaco, preventing or distorting reception. The second, of course, was that when I did get some audible response the report of the election was in Italian, which was understood by nobody in the villa at that moment. The set was placed on the table beside Beaverbrook at dinner, cracking and spitting incomprehensibly. When the word Communist was heard, as it was with depressing frequency, he sometimes glowered at me in suspicion, and sometimes grinned as if in impish knowledge of a secret shared.

Almost as unnerving as this was the discovery of mutual experiences in our childhood, separated though they were by more than thirty years. The swimming-pool at Cap d'Ail, unused for so long, was covered by a bright green scum, sometimes as smooth as billiard-cloth and sometimes broken into black whorls by the life beneath it. This consisted largely of frogs. Every evening as we gathered for dinner the croaking in the pool threatened the maintenance of easy conversation, and from the window in the moonlight I watched the scum moving and turning as another frog rose to the surface and to song. The noise greatly irritated Beaverbrook. On the second or third night he turned upon me. When I was a boy in Canada, had I ever caught bull-frogs? From slough-holes, I said, with torches as they floated to the surface. That, he said, is how we did it in New Brunswick. He called for his top-coat and for a powerful torch, and out we went to that rectangular lake of green. He pointed the torch at the water as I knelt and parted the scum with my hands. It was a waiting while and my fingers were numbing cold before the first frog floated upward, slack-limbed and black-eyed with stupor as it came into my hands. How many I caught, and threw from the cliff into the sea, I do not know, but on the following evening their lickerish wooing began again. Damn it, Prebble, he said, they've climbed the darned cliff. Out we went once more, and every night until he tired of this unproductive recall of our boyhood innocence.

Before I was abruptly returned to England, I was sent to find a story in Monte Carlo, at that time seedy and derelict, exhausted by a war that had destroyed its self-indulgent reason for existence. Beaverbrook talked of it as it had been twenty years before, a town of opulence and pleasure, of great characters, men and women. I was to draw comparisons with the past, form judgements, find a story with a beginning, a middle, and an end. I was driven into the town and left there, spending an hour or more in the Casino, gambling and losing the few francs he had given me. The others present at the tables were shiftless, ill-dressed and middle-aged, and the comparisons I was required to make were inescapable. I climbed the streets of the town, talking as best I could to those inhabitants who were willing to spare the time. The appearance of Monaco was a reflection of the faces in the Casino, dispirited and waiting for the past to resurrect itself. The only building that had been painted since the War's end, and which looked as if it were facing the future with some confidence, was the headquarters of the Monaco Communist Party, its woodwork freshly blue and red, a Tricolour and the Red Flag hanging in motionless harmony above its door.

This was the opening paragraph of my story, which I wrote that afternoon. Before Beaverbrook read it, he asked for my winnings at roulette, and when I told him there were none he said 'Dammit' very softly, and then 'Dammit' again. He read, and paused at the first paragraph. Was this the best way to begin my report? I thought so, if I were to make the comparisons he had suggested. There was no further comment and the story was published as I had written it, not so much for its merits, perhaps, as for my continued seduction.

I cannot say I ever liked this man. His generosity was calculated, and his use of power was accompanied at times by a childish spite which chilled any warmth. Apart from those boyish moments by the couturier's pool, my most vivid recollection of him is a hot afternoon on the sun-roof at Arlington House, where he lay brown and almost naked in a reclining chair. Here he summoned a leader-writer from Fleet Street or Shoe Lane and coldly destroyed the man's work and self-respect. This cat's-play of power was performed before a grandchild sitting at his feet.

In a brief exchange, on the first evening of our frog-hunt, he seemed genuinely interested in my boyhood in Canada, asking why my family had gone there and where we had lived. I told him what I knew of Sutherland's origins. Sure that knowledge of his Scots ancestry had made him familiar with the story of the Highland Clearances, I explained the connection between them and this prairie town. He nodded, but asked no questions. I believe he had never heard of them, and had no wish to be enlightened by me.

My own knowledge of the Clearances at this time was slender, largely based upon a book published in the late thirties, part of or in pursuit of a great deal of left-wing pamphleteering. Entitled *The Destitution of the Highlands*, it was a thin volume in absurdly inappropriate lilac boards, and was intended to fuel contemporary debate rather than illuminate the past. My copy was lost in the domestic movements of the War, and only later did I understand that it was not an original work but a reprint of some of the writings of Donald MacLeod, stonemason and valiant journalist from Strathnaver in the shire of Sutherland. He was born towards the end of the eighteenth century on his father's holding below the brown stub of Ben Rossal, where the River Naver turns quickly northward to the sea. From the beginning of the clearances in his glen until his death far away from the Highlands, he continued his tireless polemics against removal, eviction and the savage dispersal of man in favour of the Cheviot sheep. In this relentless fight he lost his wife and his home. He was hounded by Stafford's agents, brought before the justices, and finally driven into lonely exile across the Atlantic. The newspaper articles which he republished in 1841, and again in 1857, contain much that is factually inaccurate or unsubstantiated. They are also angry, and anger is said to obscure truth, even though that truth has provoked irrepressible rage. He was a contemporary of the events, an observer, and if academic judgement cannot accept his cry of pain as a diagnosis of the sickness, it is nonetheless evidence of injury. Anger and pain were MacLeod's strong motivations, and both speak defiantly from his *Memories*.

I am a Highlander, and must have revenge for the wrongs I have suffered. The revenge I desire is that these letters may be preserved for many a day in my native country, to keep up remembrance of the evil that was done to many an innocent individual, and among others to DONALD M'LEOD.

MacLeod's book, however abridged in the first version I read, shattered the romantic image I had of the Highlands and the Highland people. This had been conventionally created and was seemingly authenticated by a walking-visit I made at the age of twenty-one. Carrying *Kidnapped* in my pack, and travelling some of the way in the steps of Alan Breck and David Balfour, I never once asked myself where the people had gone and why. It seemed only proper that these lonely blue hills should be abandoned, an accusing testament to the tragedy of Culloden, I thought, and to the brutality of the English battalions who drove the clans into exile. The lilac book told me another story, and where culpability truly lay. I would like to think that it also made me think clearly about my own experience of property ownership, of extortionate rents and heartless eviction. My first employment, eighteen months after leaving school and an enforced idleness without dole which put my parents to despair, was with a firm of estate agents in South London. I was taken as a junior clerk upon proof that I was the product of what the agency wished to recognize as a public school, and that I could confirm this academic distinction by correctly pronouncing the word Belvoir. I was paid twenty shillings a week, less eighteen pence for National Insurance, and a further deduction of one shilling if, on the day I was required to dispatch the post, I could not balance the stamp-book. I never achieved this immaculate objective, and the manipulation of the book was one of the reasons why the Secretary of the agency was later asked to resign. Villain and victim, we left appropriately on the same day.

The agency's lucrative business was not so much in conveyancing as the profitable exploitation of the Law. Acting allegedly on behalf of clients – who were, in fact, one or more of the agent's kinsmen – it bought the freehold ground-rents of decaying property in Bermondsey, Rotherhithe, Bethnal Green and like slum districts. In some cases it was a single dwelling, more often a terrace, and sometimes a street itself. Once acquired, the property was then surveyed and Schedules of Dilapidation were served upon leaseholders and tenants. Rarely could either meet the financial burden imposed. On behalf of its client, the agency then offered to buy the leasehold at considerably less than its meagre worth, or to sell the freehold at substantially more. When the former was the result, the agency became the reluctant landlord of distressed houses, and was invariably laggard in fulfilling its own schedules. Junior clerks, such as myself, were used as rent collectors in these overcrowded, malodorous and crumbling streets, where hard-tongued women would call from an upper floor, compassionately warning me that the obscene stairs were not safe for me to mount, and throwing their rent from the window, a few shillings and pence in a twist of paper.

I remember the goodwill of the majority of those upon whom I called at the same hour of the same day each week. Some paid their rent of six shillings and ninepence, or five shillings and eightpence, as if it were a debt of honour. Others, more hostile, maligned the landlord but pitied me as a fellow victim of his greed. Those who had no money begged my tolerance with hostile faces. I carried the collected rent, small silver and coppers, in an old music case, riding the trams on an all-day ticket, the bag growing heavier with every street. I was never once threatened or robbed, or believed I might be. On occasions, although they were mercifully few in my case, the junior clerks were obliged to accompany an agency partner, the bailiffs and policemen, all those servants of the Law who were required to enforce the penalties of default, to evict the pauper in arrears, to abandon the sick and helpless to wayward charity. On such days, it seems to me now, it was always cold or raining, and sometimes both.

Walter Scott knew the reality of eviction and clearance. He wrote of them twice, once in an appendix to *Rob Roy*, and again much later in a letter to Maria Edgeworth. In the latter he raged against Highland lairds who were depopulating their estates to provide grazing for sheep, and he wished to God that the hanging of one or two would be a lesson to the others. In the most Highland of his novels he recalled the day when he had himself been an evictor, or more exactly the instrument of eviction. Some sixty years before this event the Stewarts of Appin, disputing the ownership of land upon Loch Voil in the Braes of Balquhidder, clashed in arms with the MacGregors. Two hundred men of Appin, under their chief, came down from the north and met the *Griogaraich* before the kirk at Balquhidder. This potentially murderous confrontation was resolved in single combat between Rob Roy and young Stewart of Invernahyle. Upon the first blood drawn – it was Rob Roy's –

the Stewart claim was maintained. Such honourable if impractical solutions no longer obtained at the end of the century. This time, when he wished to evict a family of MacLarens from the same glen on Loch Voil, another Chief of Appin went to Law and instructed his lawyer, Mr Walter Scott senior, to serve writs of removal.

Loch Voil lies in a glen below the Braes of Balquhidder, running east to west from the northward road to Breadalbane. It remains as it once was, I think. Oak and rowan, sycamore and birch march with the twisting road that leads to the lochhead. To the south across the water is a green glen, falling steeply from the bowed shoulders of Bhreac. At its mouth, not far from the shore, are patches of greener grass, a few unnatural stones and other enduring reminders of the MacLarens' holding of Invernenty. Upon his father's bidding, and scarcely more than a year into his law studies, Walter Scott came here to serve the writs, his awesome power reinforced by a file of Highlanders from the Black Watch. Scott was happy to have them and their sergeant marching beside his plodding horse. The MacLarens, he later wrote, were 'strapping deer-stalkers' and although attached to their land, and even to Appin himself, they had at first been agreeable to taking ship for America. But the threat of compulsion and the humiliation of eviction had touched their pride, and they were now refusing to leave. 'Such was the general impression,' said Scott, 'that they were men capable of resisting legal execution of a warning by very effectual means, that no King's Messenger would execute the summons without the support of a military force.'

It was Scott's first visit to that wild and evocative country of Balquhidder, indeed his first to the Highlands, and he later admitted that it had inspired his imagination. The Braes and the lochside below have a natural, unaffected beauty which is becoming increasingly rare in a land of hurried change.* The mirror-glass water holds the inverted image of its protective hills, an indistinguishable replica until a rising wind or the sliding fall of a water-bird breaks it into fragments. When I last passed along the lochside – admittedly in early spring before the coaches arrive like buffaloes at a waterhole, to see Rob Roy's grave in the kirkyard – I met no one coming from the west. The air hummed with the industrious energy of insects, and a hawk rose on motionless wings to the clean sky above

---

* But which now, I read, is to be improved by a property developer who wishes to build thirty 'holiday chalets' on the shore of the loch.

the Monachyle Glen. But the silence and the solitude are not the past surviving. Once there were townships, men, women and children. Then there were sheep. 'The MacLarens,' said Scott, remembering them as best he could in middle age, 'received their money and went to America, where, having had some slight share in removing them from their *paupera regna*, I sincerely hope they prospered.'

Scott's sympathy was undoubtedly genuine, as was the common belief that a chance of prosperity after hardship in a new world was worth the pain of being driven from the old. The anguish of eviction was rarely recorded by travellers from the south. *How came you to this unfortunate state . . . ?* was a customary question which privilege put to the poor, begging an answer that would not be too disturbing. In her bountiful journal of a Highland tour with her brother at the turn of the eighteenth century, Dorothy Wordsworth wrote a great deal about many curious things, but almost nothing about removal and eviction. Samuel Taylor Coleridge, who accompanied this inquisitive and enquiring couple on part of their way, was more sensitive. He was a sick man at the time, and his insight may have been sharpened by his own melancholy thoughts. When he met and questioned an old woman living alone by Fort Augustus, his manner and obvious sympathy inspired her answer. Within this space, she said, indicating the hills and lochside about them, and only a short time ago, there had lived one hundred and seventy persons. In every home there had been a man, woman, boy, girl and babe, and in almost every house there was an old man by the fireside. She could tell of the troubles before the roads were made, of brave young men who loved the birthplace of their fathers, whose broadswords they would swing and carry to the wars, marching to battles over the seas. And there had been many a good lass who had respect for herself.

Well, but they are gone, and with them the bridled bear and the pink haver, and the potato plot that looked as gay as any flower-garden with its blossoms. I sometimes fancy that the very birds are gone, all but the crows and the gleads. Well, and what then? Instead of us all, there is one shepherd man, and it may be a pair of small lads, and many, many sheep. And do you think, Sir, that God allows of such proceedings?*

* *bridled bear*, barley; *haver*, oats; *glead*s, kites, birds of prey.

It was not a question Coleridge could answer, or if he could he did not think it worthy of record. What comfort could this ailing Englishman, with a fine horse to ride and room and board at the end of the day, what reassurance could he give to a spirit so lost?

Three-quarters of a century later more powerful men, sitting upon a Royal Commission to enquire into the state of the Highlands, heard stronger voices from the residual Gaelic people of the mountains, their grief now strengthened by anger. The Commissioners travelled by steamship north-about the coast of Scotland, coming ashore in bay or firth with their clerks and interpreters, establishing their tables in chapel or schoolhouse. In the great volume of evidence taken this way in the summer of 1883, sometimes in literal translations of the Gaelic, a bewildered race speaks of neglect, injustice and betrayal. When the Commissioners came to Annat in Wester Ross, below the seamed face of Liathach and the dark sweep of Torridon's great trees, the evidence they were given was the more chilling for being heard amid some of the most majestic scenery in the Highlands. They listened to men who still lived on the Applecross estate, a wide holding that not only included the axe-blade peninsula of that name but also the long, green shore of Loch Torridon, its townships and sea-fishing. It had once belonged to a Mackenzie laird, whose right to it was now questioned by old men. In 1859, said witnesses, the estate 'came into the hands of Her Grace the Duchess of Leeds and the rule was in the hands of her gamekeeper'. She was an American from Maryland, and her 'gamekeeper' was Captain MacRa Chisholm, and neither was remembered with sweetness. But there was to be worse. The Duchess sold the land to an English peer who cleared it so effectively of its people that few were left to tell the Commissioners of their anger and sorrow.

Two of them were John Mackenzie and Roderick MacBeath, small crofters of Annat. In the name of others they brought the Commissioners a petition which began with a warning from Proverbs, Chapter Fourteen, Verse Twenty-five. 'In the multitude of the people is the king's honour, but in the want of the people is the destruction of the prince.' This they followed with another text, paraphrasing it in their own translation. 'Again, woe is pronounced against those who join house to house and field to field till they dwell alone in the midst of the land, and no place left for the poor to dwell in.' The petitioners wished the Commissioners to know that the lot of the people had grown no better since the English peer sold the estate to another, who had in his turn sold it again. There were few houses now in Annat where fire was kindled, but if the remaining population could get 'pasture for a few sheep, say a dozen for each family, or even half a dozen, it would be so much help'. Emigration would not necessarily free the people from the greed of landlords, this they had discovered.

> The young of both sexes, as soon as they attain puberty, make off to where they can best live, some of the young men go to trades, others emigrating to the colonies, whence cometh complaints, especially from New Zealand, that the insatiable and avaricious spirit which pervades the hearts of too many at home has gone abroad, even to that colony, where the land in a great measure is engrossed and monopolized by land speculators, buying up large blocks of the land from Government on easy terms and reselling it by auction in small divisions, at exorbitant prices, to the detriment of the people. Gentlemen, these enormities cry loudly for redress at home and abroad.

The chairman of the Commission, Lord Napier and Ettrick, teased an admission from Mackenzie and MacBeath that neither was literate and that they, like eleven others, had signed the petition when it was *read* to them. But it was none the worse for having been written by 'John Macdonald, a brother of a crofter in the place'; no one disputed the truth of it.

A cruel and relentless past to contemplate from this crusted stone in a Braemar graveyard, with the realization that redeeming texts have not greatly improved the nature of man. History, or my interest in it, hangs in repetitive loops where the end is sometimes indistinguishable from the beginning. I came to Peter Grant's stone, a tangible remembrance of the waste of Culloden, from another site eight centuries older. Thirty miles to the east of Braemar, where the valley of the Dee widens to the lowlands of the shire, a branch road leads northward to the village of Lumphanan, its name a garbled corruption of the Gaelic for Saint Finian's church. It was once a changing-halt on the old coach route from Aberdeen to Huntly and Inverness. When steam replaced the motive power of a four-in-hand, the village became an important station on a railway that curled its way northward before coming down again to the banks of the Dee. The rutted stage-road now lies beneath a metalled surface, and nothing remains of the railway but low embankments and discreet cuttings, abandoned to the growth of birch and rowan. The most important event in Lumphanan's history, however, predates the earliest record of its name by half a century. It was here that Macbeth died.

On a hill-slope to the north of the village there is a tumbled cairn. It is perhaps prehistoric but by tradition it marks the spot where Scotland's most maligned king was struck down with most of his shield-wall, destroyed by a vengeful army that included Norman-English mercenaries from the court of Edward the Confessor. Macbeth is now believed to have been a good king, as the phrase may go, or as any king was good in that part of Scotland he called his realm. Whether or not he murdered Duncan, he was not the hell-hound whom Shakespeare created from the lies of Holinshed and thereby from Hector Boece. He reigned for seventeen years in comparative peace, visiting Rome and giving generously to the poor, thus earning his reputation for piety. Nor was he troubled by a nagging wife, I think, even though her simple-minded son by an earlier marriage had a better claim to the crown than he.

Since nothing so long ago can be believed with certainty, the place of his death is of course disputed. He is also said to have been killed, and beheaded, on another hillside to the west of the village, by a steading overlooking the green Peel of Lumphanan. Stunning though this great, wind-whispering earthwork is, the cairn to the north stirs my imagination more. It is truly no longer a cairn but a shallow pit, filled with an untidy mass of boulders and surrounded by a dry-stone wall, much broken. From this wall, or beside it, grow some fifteen trees. Most are beech, the rest are elm, sycamore and ash, and never at rest.

If Peter Grant's battle was an end to the direct line of Scotland's kings, it might be said that its beginning was here at Lumphanan. Macbeth was the nation's last mountain-king. The man who took his life and crown had a Saxon wife, a daughter of the Athelings whose English throne the Conqueror had usurped. Margaret and Malcolm Canmore made Dunfermline the centre of their realm, and under them Scotland took its first resourceful steps out of the darker ages. There should be no silence about the cairn, perhaps. In the whispering leaves that shelter it there is remembrance of shield-wall and regicide, of dynastic murder and brief Renaissance, flowers of the forest and the busy bayonets at Culloden, and an ageing pretender drinking himself to death in exile. Popular folklore of the thousand years in which kings and the king's enemies fought savagely along this placid valley is now lost in the enduring memory of the German queen who brought it bourgeois respectability in her railway train. She built her faery castle by the rapid water of the Dee, picnicked in glens where Montrose marched, and from her Gothic window she studied Lochnagar's dark crest with a water colourist's eye as she 'strengthened' her claret with some of Mr John Begg's 'remarkably fine old whisky'.

April the Twenty-sixth

T his morning there are bright sequins on the wind-broken firth below Drummossie Muir, and the warmth of spring is heavy on the air. Where the flagship *Gloucester*, fifty guns, once rode at anchor with the rest of Admiral Byng's squadron, there is only a small tanker coming through the narrows at Chanonry Point. Today, not the sixteenth, is perhaps the proper date to recall the battle fought upon this moor. The adoption of the Gregorian Calendar in 1751, which persuaded some honest fools that their lives had been summarily robbed of ten days, makes the cruel weather of that mid-April appear harsher still when moved on to its last week, although a Highland winter can indeed persist well beyond its considerate term. On a June morning in Strathtay I once awoke to an astonishing landscape. The air was warm, but birch and rowan leaf were bent beneath the weight of snow, and the braeside was white from a skyline of blue to the river's black run. At Culloden on April the sixteenth, 1746, the east wind was cold, blowing sleet into the faces of the clans as they watched the first red line of the enemy rise into view a mile away. It is customary to think of such weather as the Hanoverians' ally. But a British soldier, marching fifteen miles and more through bog and lochan, might have argued that cold sleet upon the face would have been better than water dribbling beneath his collar and freezing his spine from the nape of his neck to the small of his back. Having experienced both I could not state a preference, and am mindful of what one private of the Royals wrote on the following day. 'It rained very sore as I ever seed, both hail and rain and strong wind. Strong on our backs and the enemies face.'

Thirty years ago, on such a kindly April morning as this, I came again to the battlefield, to see it with fresh eyes and imagine it, if I could, as it might have been on that Wednesday in 1746. I made notes which I have still, written in the lee of Leanach cottage, sheltering from occasional showers that moved across the face of the sun.

> In April heath and bracken are dry and dead . . . rich chocolate and coal-black, and the coarse grass is bleached yellow . . . To the south the hills are treeless, as perhaps they were in 1746, sleeping under a pelt of brown . . . the valley floor of Strath Nairn a rich green . . . From the English position one can look south-west down the strath to the hills beyond, blue, brown and black according to the weather . . . Ahead is the Great Glen, a rolling thunder-cloud of dark hills . . . snow-capped . . .

I should not have written 'the English position'. The mistake is common, even wishful perhaps, and upon the moor I have sometimes heard a schoolteacher grasp at the wandering interest of bored pupils with declamatory references to the *English* being here and the *Scots* there. Of course it was the last battle of the last civil war in Britain. There were four Scots regiments in Cumberland's army, and a cloud of Campbell militia from Argyll. Indeed, in Bliadhna Tearlach, this Year of Charlie, there were more Highlanders gathered against him (however reluctantly) than appear on the muster-roll of his own army. The small contingent from Clan Chisholm was commanded by Roderick Og, the youngest son of its chief and still a boy. Across the moor, six hundred yards to his front, were his two brothers, subalterns in the Royal Scots. The Earl of Kilmarnock, alone and lost in the smoke of the battle, wept as he surrendered to a British battalion. His son, an officer of that regiment, held his hat before the old man's face, to hide the tears of shame.

When I made those preliminary notes, the heathered cairn and monolithic gravestones at the centre of the field were held in a dark enclave of alien timber. The trees have now been cut back and the view to the north, to the Moray Firth and the rise of the Black Isle beyond, is as it might once have been. Also visible, at one point, are the roofs of a new housing estate called Culloden, on a braeside where Hawley's hurrahing dragoons rode down in pursuit, killing with pistol and sword. Major-General Henry Hawley probably deserves the name of Butcher more than Cumberland. His soldiers certainly called him The Hangman. He erected his gibbets along the line of the Army's march, from the Lowlands – where he was shamefully beaten by the Jacobites at Falkirk – to Aberdeenshire and the heights above Inverness. Red-faced and shouting oaths, he rode over the field when victory was won, urging his men to kill, and if there were doubt that life still existed, to plunge with the bayonet nonetheless. Laggard officers were subjected to the same abusive encouragement. *'Damn you, Shaw, do you mean to preserve the life of a rebel?'*

Today I came to the moor by the old road from Nairn, along the backbone of the ridge. Cumberland's fifteen battalions of Foot, assembled in three columns and flanked by cavalry, marched along and on either side of this road, twice forming line-of-battle as they came within sight and sound of the enemy. The road is metalled now, of course – no longer wheel-rut, pot-hole and broken rock – and much of the bogland on either side has been drained. But if the eye is lifted to the sky and to the challenging mountain-rim of the horizon, if there is sleet in the air and despair in an aching body, some recall of that distant April morning may be possible. I believe the outcome of the battle was inevitable, long, long before the deep, drubbing advance of infantry drums was heard by the waiting clans. They had learnt nothing, been taught nothing by their victories and their mind-spinning invasion of England. Their strength and their only advantage was, as it had been for centuries, their superb courage in one headlong charge. The men they were now to face had been taught a new discipline, however, enforced by the cat and rope where necessary. Three months before, in Edinburgh, Cumberland had issued detailed orders, changing the customary method of firing so that his soldiers might receive and repel those terrifying swordsmen. Each infantryman had already been trained to thrust his bayonet at the exposed under-arm of the clansman attacking his comrade on the right, and to trust his left flank-man to do the same service for him. The new orders were to prevent the charge from reaching the British line, or to weaken its terrible impact. Some of the Pretender's army, said Cumberland, were mere 'Lowlanders and arrant scum'. Only the Highlanders were a danger.

The sure way to demolish them is, at three deep, to fire by ranks diagonally to the centre, where they come, the rear rank first, and even that rank not to fire till they are within ten or twelve paces; but if the fire is given at a distance, you probably will be broke, for you never get time to load a second cartridge, and, if you give way, you may give your Foot for dead, for they being without a firelock, or any load, no man with his arms, accoutrements etc., can escape

35

them, and they give no quarter; but if you will but observe the above directions they are the most despicable enemy that are.

It is not always easy to visualize the battle when looking across the moor. This morning, a friendly sunlight glistens on the dead heather and rain-bent grass. When the wind drops to a sigh it is lost in the hum of the motor road along the firth, the ceaseless throb below where Inverness is slowly growing into a small metropolis. It is even more difficult to believe that the fury and carnage involved so many children, some lying in the heather and watching as their kinsmen plunged through the smoke, others bearing arms and advancing with a clan-regiment. Fifteen of these boys were taken prisoner, and the mind may guess at the numbers never recorded. All were under the age of sixteen, and most were fourteen. The youngest was John Johnston, who was thirteen, not a soldier but described on the prison roll as 'a servant to a French officer', probably one of the Scots Royals, mercenaries in the service of Louis XV. The boy did not long survive his capture. Before he could be tried and sentenced he died in an overcrowded room of the Tolbooth at Inverness. John Wilson, fourteen, a surgeon's assistant with Ogilvy's Regiment, remained alive until he was sent to a prison hulk on the Thames, and there he died. Alexander Mather, fourteen, was the son of a baker in Brechin, one of three brothers serving in Ogilvy's second battalion. It may therefore be concluded that they were not pressed men, as many were in that regiment, but eager volunteers. Alexander was taken at Montrose, four months after the battle, and was said to have escaped or been released in consideration of his tender age. Such concern did not help other children who disappeared into the darkness of rotting imprisonment or anguished exile in the Americas.

A young boy who may have been with the Jacobite army later joined a Highland regiment of the Hanoverian crown. If he enlisted voluntarily, and was not pressed, it could have been from a desperate longing to wear his traditional dress once more, 'the kilt high above the knee, and the sword-belt on shoulder, and the slim sharp broadsword with its three flutings'. The words are from his own verse. Having no remembered name, he is called 'an unknown Badenoch poet'. He composed a moving lament for his people's past and for those now soldiering in far distant garrisons.

If our lead had not been exhausted
the English would not have been victorious
in a cause as hard as the blows of a fist.
But since they have got the upper hand
they have miserably and
wretchedly dispersed us
and sent us out of the kingdom
to King's Fort in Good Hope:
to a strong fort
with a slab of rock for a billet.

But we were brought up
in the cold high mountains,
where the antlered stag was plentiful,
high would he lift his head.
Salmon in the rivers,
hares from the cattle-grazing
where there were many herdsmen,
tending the calves:
where there were beautiful girls
in gowns and well-shod,
with eyes bluer than blae-berries,
and cheeks lovelier than roses.

Why, he asked, were he and his friends not left alone to enjoy life
as their fathers had done? Had it been so they would not now be
'young men grey-haired'.

This literal translation of the Badenoch's verse, and many others',
was made for me by my friend Rory Mackay. He was a lawyer
of Inverness, a Gaelic scholar and historian, perverse radical and
Highland nationalist, a man of many talents – writer, carpenter, a
lover of folk music, an untiring source of knowledge about his
mountain people, and a loyal friend. He came to my defence when
Culloden was published, at a time when it was thought by some
that this Englishman was being too presumptuous. He helped me
with advice, translations and introductions when I was writing *The
Highland Clearances*, and later publicly derided a modern defender
of them who had foolishly declared that I could not understand
Scotland and its people because I had not 'got a drop of Scots
blood'. Rory was a descendant of the Glenalladale Macdonalds, and
although he disliked the wearing of the kilt by most Scots who did

so, he wore it himself in defiance and because true Highlanders, 'our people' he said, had been too demoralized by its proscription after Culloden and could not return to it when the ban was lifted thirty-six years later. On the occasions we met he would talk emotionally or mockingly of his country's history, and always with new information and advice, as if I were a fire he wished to keep re-fuelled. Over a dram, and with raw humour, we talked of service life in the ranks, his own with the Air Force and mine with the Army. My last clear memory of him, before his death, was his approach down Union Street on his way to his office in Inverness. He was wearing the kilt, his eyes smiling owlishly behind the thick lens of his glasses as he walked through a strutting regimental pipe-band which was entertaining tourists in the middle of the street. He said nothing, but when he reached me he lifted a hand towards them in despair.

The first draft of my account of Culloden and its aftermath was written, as other books were, at the Old Swan in the Oxfordshire village of Minster Lovell. The inn was always quiet, and my exclusive preoccupation with a typewriter was generously tolerated. The room I customarily had looked across serene fields, sometimes under green leaf and sometimes cut to a yellow stubble. At dusk I walked by the reedy water of the Windrush where the swans went downstream like ghostly frigates in line-ahead. When I came to write *Culloden* I was given another room, smaller and dark, with only a corner window for light and air. It was August, and all day I heard the mechanical murmur of hay-cutters turning and re-turning on the hill-slope beyond. Because of their industry the room was filled with midges, flecks of torture that clung to the sweat of my face and body. I wrote little that satisfied me. I slept uneasily, my mind painfully involved with the past, not with this battle alone but with violence more recent, and only yesterday it seemed.

In March 1945, on the plain before Xanten and in days of unnatural sunshine, we waited to cross the Rhine, its waters hidden from us by a smoke-screen laid by the Pioneers. This pulsing fog was more than fifty miles in length, we were told, and sometimes a canister would fail, or a gust of wind would lift the skirt of the screen, exposing the tree-lined road on our bank. The responsive sigh and thud of mortars would then explode along the slender poplars, filling the air with fragments of wood and floating leaves until the smoke came down again. I know this was a brief period, a few days only, but in retrospect it seems a long and thoughtful interlude between our thunderous arrival at the Rhine and the great leap across it. I remember the daffodils that flowered on the raw earth of broken trenches, the splintered trees in sudden leaf. The medieval town of Xanten, now a shell, had been defended with extraordinary ferocity, sometimes by boys of the Hitler Youth who had been sent, it was said, to stiffen the spirits of the exhausted Wehrmacht. On the day the smoke-screen first gave us some security, and while leaning against the wheel of a truck, I wrote to friends in England, describing things that would later disturb my mind in that small, suffocating room in Minster Lovell.

Germany will never forget this invasion. Nor must we. The Germans have such a reputation throughout Europe that a child like my little Dutch friend Elly Jacobs can pass her finger across her throat and say with a bright but old smile 'Is good for Mof !' There is little compassion in the way we think and talk of the Germans, whether the speaker is eleven-year-old Elly, or the Canadian driver of the bull-dozer who stopped his work to pull our truck from the mud. He was chewing gum methodically and there was three days' beard on his chin. He was burying German dead, soldiers and cattle. Burying them in one great ditch. 'Hell,' he said, 'this baby wasn't going to dig two holes.'

He was an infantryman of the Chaudières, the Canadian regiment that had been engaged in such bitter fighting before Xanten, and perhaps he too was dead before the War ended. The remembrance of the bodies he buried, young men in green or field-grey sliding down with the sand-red earth, must have been recalled to my mind by the thought of the boys in the Jacobite army, and the men of the Royals pulling kerchiefs over their mouths as they turned from killing to the digging of mass graves.

Elly Jacobs, whose name I linked with that Chaudière, was one of the children we had fed and warmed during the winter, in Heldendorp near the Maas. They should not have been there in the forward area, but their families had refused to join the long columns of refugees who moved from the front when snow and ice stabilized the line. There was no safety or security for those who chose to remain, no food, no civil authority, no one but us.

Elly Jacobs. She sits with us, swinging her legs in their black, darned stockings as she sings the Dutch parody of Lili Marlene.

I first saw her on Christmas Day. She is a thin little girl with hair hanging down her shoulders in plaits, tied at the bottom with narrow orange tapes. Her face is thin with a terribly beautiful pallor, and there are dark crescents under her eyes, the ugly bruises of malnutrition. Her hair has no lustre, and her hands, as she grasps yours and begs you to swing her round, are thin, and the flesh offers no resistance to your fingers. Until recently, in some of the most bitter weather I have experienced, Elly had no coat and no gloves, and no shoes that protected her from the snow.

She comes to sit with us, swinging her legs in their black, darned stockings as she sings the Dutch parody of 'Lili Marlene'. She searches inside the little oilcloth bag she always carries, taking out her black powder, sucking it from her fingers. At first, we thought it was dirt. We told her that we didn't think it would do her much good. But it was medicine, she said. She had a pain, and she rubbed her stomach. The medical officer at the advance dressing-station had given her the powder to stop the pain. There are always children in the ADS, and the RAMC treat them for sores, for burns, for cuts, for sickness. There is no civilian doctor, there are no medical supplies for children.

Such small casualties are often forgotten in the arrogance of victory. One of the most impressive scenes in the television documentary which that gifted man, Peter Watkins, made from my book, was not of the fighting on the moor, but a candle-lit group of officers in Inverness that evening. As I remember, it was a fixed shot, with no panning and few close-ups. The central figure is Cumberland, young and fat, smirking in response to the flattery of his companions. It was upon such a self-satisfied evening that some of the battalion officers formed The Culloden Society, 'in grateful remembrance' of the battle and the defeat of the most unnatural rebellion against their royal Commander's father. Membership was at first limited to twenty-five, the Duke of Cumberland's age, but increased with his years. The Society dined once a year on the anniversary of the battle, which was celebrated in great style, and this convivial practice continued as long as Duke Billy himself was alive. A medal was struck for its members, of both gold and silver I believe, but certainly one costing the wearer ten guineas. He was obliged to wear it, hanging from his throat by a pink and green ribbon, when going into action, confident in the knowledge that if it were lost it would be replaced by the Society. It was elaborate in design, and in the classical spirit of the age. The head of the victorious Duke appeared on one side, and upon the other was the figure of Apollo triumphing over a dragon.

Vanity and euphoria are part of the triumph in a soldier's life. In that small room of the Old Swan, with the night too hot or a mind too restless for sleep, I worried about the style and nature of the book I was writing, and I sought some guidance by reviving memories that had been quiet for fifteen years. I remembered foolish things made important by their solacing triviality. The music of Glenn Miller coming from the open turret of a tank in the great assembly area near Arromanches. Hearing it again with nostalgic pain many weeks later at Deurne, this time from a tank emblazoned with a black bull on a yellow field, moving slowly forward in the diffused light of our ninety-centimetres. The music of Glenn Miller cut short by static, by urgent, incomprehensible voices. Silence and then the muted clank of a dixie striking a bayonet scabbard, white faces going up the line, and salt in the mouth. And later the incredible knowledge that we had entered Germany.

41

It seems as if we are always laughing. We live in high spirits. Six years of war to reach this . . . and small things but full of such significance. Taffy standing by his 15cwt, a long, scarlet Nazi banner falling from his hands and trailing in the pine needles. And all he can say is 'Look at it now!' Or Jimmy the Cook, top-hat on his head, long black overcoat about his ankles, a white tape-measure round his neck as he cooked our meals. Or Slim, his orderly, with a German policeman's helmet shadowing a walnut face, nonchalantly lighting petrol-fires with a cigarette lighter . . .

All day the noise battered at our ears. The Vickers clearing the woods of German stragglers. The barrage that began at midnight and lasted until dawn; the hot blast of 5.5's fifty yards from us, firing over our heads and taking away our breath.

Bright flowers blossoming along the ridge as the flame-throwers went in before Xanten . . . The wood so full of fox-holes, and in each a German soldier, bent over, with his dead face in the light earth. Prisoners coming back, grey as the dust through which they pulled their feet, and the green woods filled with graves.

Every house its copy of *Mein Kampf* . . . black-bordered mourning-cards for sons or relatives killed on the Eastern Front . . . every house its top-hats . . . its jars of edible snails . . . its portrait of Hitler . . . Nazi uniforms, insignia and papers hurriedly buried in the gardens . . . Winter has passed and spring has brought us to the west bank of the Rhine.

It is sometimes difficult to recognize myself as the man who wrote that. Only rarely nowadays do I remember him, his first awareness of the sick smell, the sweet smell of decaying dead among the pine needles where we waited for the crossing. Or the bird-song so rich, unaffected by the enemy's shells passing overhead, their hasty flutter like turning skates on ice. All now seems frozen in melodrama or comedy. Before the smoke was laid, and while Xanten still burned, three Canadians came up to the woods, riding farm-horses, with cradled weapons in their arms and driving two or three hundred prisoners before them like herdsmen on the plains. And again, from somewhere in the trees, from the blue wood-smoke fires of our waiting army, the beguiling and deceiving sound of *In the Mood*.

In such a way, their brutal way if you wish, the men of Cumberland's battalions, quartered in Inverness or tented on Castle Hill, also had their rough euphoria and hope of absolution. Save for recruits and replacements hastily enlisted for the suppression of the Rebellion, they were veterans of Flanders. Before leaving for that cockpit, or after returning from it, they would have been encamped on Barham Down to the south of Canterbury. Here, for centuries, English armies had been mustered for the unending wars against France. And for as long as this, if not longer, the village of Barham was the home of my father's people. Regardless of my birthplace, in that Edmonton street during the Great War, I like to think that I too am a Man of Kent and thus a descendant of the Jutes. The earliest record I have of a probable ancestor is a William Preble and his wife Joanna in the early decades of the fourteenth century. One hundred years later, another was happily pardoned for his involvement in Jack Cade's Rebellion.

The poverty or brevity of the records make their lives, century by century, seem uneventful. They lived in a small triangle of villages to the south of Canterbury – Barham, Denton, Wootton and others. Now and then they became small yeomen, but more often they broke the earth and herded stock for others. Being Men of Kent, born east of the River Medway, they were by custom and perhaps by law recognized as free men, exempt from serfdom. Their ill-defined but stubbornly held liberties made them natural recruits for any revolt against the tyranny of crown or government, and their last rising against such intransigence was a hedge-riot in the years following Waterloo. After the Reformation it was perhaps natural that many should become Dissenters, and my collateral ancestor Abraham Prebble fled from persecution to America in 1636, to the Old Plymouth Colony. There his descendants prospered, as his brother Robert's did not in England. Barham church-yard contains many of their graves, most with headstones long since mouldered and unreadable. Among them is my great-great-grandfather John, who was born sixteen years before the death of Peter Grant. He lived to be photographed in his ninth decade, in a brass-buttoned jacket, stout breeches and leather gaiters. His arm is about the shoulders of a young child in a sailor's blouse and collar, my father John William. The old man was a land-worker, Lord Kitchener's ploughman when that great man lived at Broome Park to the south of Barham. The position of his grave in the churchyard is a rare honour for a labourer, and I conclude from it that his employers considered him a worthy man. It is on the north side, and the headstone faces south, that the sun may fall upon it and preserve it from the corrosion of moss.

Despite the omnipresence of soldiers on the Down, none of my ancestors, so far as I know, felt obliged to enlist, not even in Howard's 3rd Foot, later the Royal East Kent Regiment and known as the Buffs from the colour of their facings. At Culloden, Howard's men were on the right flank of the second line, and there took some of Clan Chattan's furious charge when it broke through the front. Later the Buffs were employed in the burning and harrowing of Lochaber, the driving of cattle and the relentless pursuit of fugitives. In idle curiosity rather than enthusiasm I have studied the muster-rolls of the regiment for this year, as far as they exist, and found no man of my name. The inn at Barham is The Duke of Cumberland, but this is not surprising, for two royal princes of that title were each a general in his father's army. Which is remembered here is not clear, for the sign has little resemblance to the victor of Culloden or to his grand-nephew, the one-eyed, sometime insane, and certainly the most hated of all the hated uncles of Queen Victoria. The identification is of no importance now, and perhaps meant little to the thousands of soldiers who have taken ale here. Some, however, men of Highland regiments, may have seen the irony of it. With satisfaction, I hope, for the ale was said to be good.

Three of the battalions that went from Barham Down to Culloden – Bligh's, Sempill's and Munro's – later became known as Minden Regiments. On the first day of August in 1759, as part of a brigade of six British infantry regiments, they marched in good order against a French army deployed before the Hanoverian town of that name. Forming line as they emerged from a wood, and firing one volley only at ten paces, they broke the charge of eleven squadrons of French cavalry. They then reloaded and marched on to fire a second volley, this time dispersing twenty-two squadrons. In the characteristic mood of men in good spirits, or to sustain their courage as they advanced, they plucked roses from a village garden and thrust them into their hats. On Minden Day thereafter, the men of these regiments have worn a rose, choosing its fragrant purity to commemorate their pride in that fierce conflict.

Bligh's 20th eventually became the Lancashire Fusiliers, and it was a field-officer of this regiment who affected my military life to a marked degree, and to my occasional despair. I have forgotten his name, as if my memory wished that to be lost when so much else should be remembered. In the ranks he was known as Wingy,

44

having lost an arm in the Great War. Recalled to service, he was now the commander – reluctantly, I suspect – of a battery in an Anti-Aircraft Training Regiment in North Wales, to which I was sent upon conscription in 1940. My first memory of him is his resolute march down a steep incline from the Officers' Mess, through the regimental lines to his Battery Office. He wore a well-tailored service dress of dark barathea, and I do not think he ever wore a battle-tunic. Upon his breast were the colourful ribbons of his youthful service, the first of them being the white and deep purple of the Military Cross. He was stern-faced and uncommunicative, and never once did we see him smile. He did not look at the men he commanded, or through them, but *into* them, and this with no indication of approval or dissatisfaction. On this first occasion, I was returning to the barrack-room from a ceremonial guard, with belt and shoulder-straps loosened for the first time in twenty-four hours, my collar undone, and my helmet pushed back from my forehead. It was early evening and I did not expect to meet a sergeant or an officer. When he saw me he halted, tucked his cane beneath the stump of his arm and returned my fumbling butt-salute with the abrupt lift of a gloved hand to the peak of his hat. It was then, I think, that I noticed the red rose almost obscuring his Fusilier badge. I was still staring at it when he retrieved his cane and smartly touched every offending item of my appearance, the last being a ringing rap on the rim of my steel helmet. He spoke without emotion. 'Battery Office, Gunner. Tell the BSM why he is to place you on a charge.'

Considering his later influence upon my life it is perhaps odd that these are the only words of his I clearly remember – apart from the customary 'Will you accept my punishment?' when I appeared before him on that first charge. It was not easy then to endure his apparent hostility, and it is perhaps too easy to understand it now. His terrible memory of war was that great conflict twenty years before. Training recruits now for what might become as great or even greater slaughter was an awesome responsibility, and there could be no weakness of emotion, no time for tolerant compassion. His dreams, and perhaps every waking moment, must have been peopled by the dead of his youth, whose faces, no doubt, he daily saw when he looked at us.

It is chance, of course, but there is an irony in the way soldiers of this man's regiment have occupied my thoughts and my work. The most famous, no doubt, is James Wolfe, whom I was taught to revere as a boy in Canada. As a result of Miss Campbell's passionate admiration, my day-dreaming by the railroad track was occasionally filled with images of the young general, dying dramatically in the arms of a Highland soldier, or sitting in his barge below the Heights of Abraham and close to tears as one of his officers quietly recited verses from Gray's *Elegy in a Country Churchyard*. Wolfe served on Hawley's staff at Culloden, and two years later, at the age of twenty-two, he was gazetted major and given command of the 20th in Scotland. He had little sympathy for his men, and nothing but contempt for Highlanders, and was ready to sacrifice some of his regiment to justify a salutary slaughter of Clan Macpherson.

A more agreeable member of the 20th was Michael Hughes, a weaver by trade and a volunteer in Bligh's regiment. He took to soldiering in 1745 with patriotic concern for his country and a stout Protestant desire to resist the ambitions of a Catholic pretender. He wrote an honest and articulate account of his life in the battalion, at Culloden and during the punitive occupation of the Highlands, and when his service was over he went back to weaving, preferring it to any other trade. Had he chosen to be a regular soldier, rather than a volunteer for the duration, there would have been no discharge but death, disablement or old age, and he might well have walked through the Minden rose-garden with his comrades of the 20th. But he went home to his weaving, to write his *Plain Narrative* for the entertainment and instruction of his friends. I read it when I was working on my own book, and I wished I had known of it during those days long since when I hated the Lancashire Fusilier who was my Battery Commander.

The training I was given in that early summer of 1940, and later helped to give others, was hard and unrelaxing in the haste to turn reluctant conscripts into soldiers. We were almost all aged twenty-five, and it was said that we were perhaps hostages to fortune, having been conceived at the outbreak of the Great War, and must therefore be of special quality. In my case, part of this endearing assumption may be true, for I was born in the June of 1915. My father, a Naval Reservist, was recalled to service two weeks before the August weekend that changed the world. In September before he went to sea in the *Royal Scot*, he was given a brief leave from which I may date my conception. He parted from my mother and my sister at Holborn Station, and the brave pain of the separation was deep in my mother's memory.

When we got there it was crowded with sailors and their families. We were allowed on the platform, no charge, and oh dear the way some of the wives were creating. Most were crying, but we walked up the platform and waited for the guard and his whistle. Jack kissed us both and leaned out of the carriage till we were out of sight. I turned, and there were women flopped down in faints and noisy weeping. Well, at the thought of whether I would see him again, I too shed a tear, and a man said to me 'Now, now, what do you think your husband would do if he saw you like that?' I smiled and said 'Hop out of the train, I expect.' He said, 'You know, I did admire you sending your husband off with a smile. Are you sure you're all right, or would you like a little brandy?' 'Oh, no, thank you, I'm all right now.' It was kind of him.

Our Troop Commander was a lieutenant of the Welsh Guards, aged nineteen. Why he had been sent to train us, as an honour or as punishment for some transgression, we did not enquire or speculate. For thirteen weeks he did what he could to kill us or break our spirit. That he did not succeed was due to our stubborn refusal to let him see that he had in any way got the better of us. And that, of course, was how he wished us to respond. Nonetheless, the individuality and unconscious spirit we had each brought from civilian life were systematically debased by aural and physical humiliation, by merciless stress, by the pain of noise, by relentless obscenity and demoralizing ridicule. Coincidentally, and almost gratefully, we learnt to act instinctively and immediately in response to any order, to accept a corporate identity superior to our own and be jealously loyal to it. We were not persuaded by argument or precept, since they invite disputation. There was no time and no precedent for anything but desperate haste and the crudest of compulsions, vigorously approved by an authority whose greatest fear was that when the enemy's invasion came, as it must, the British Army would not have the morale to resist and repel it. And thus the cleaning of floorboards with a toothbrush, the scraping of fresh paint from woodwork and its repainting, the repetitive loss of small privileges, group punishment for one man's fault, the waking of twenty-nine men in the middle of the night to hear and deride the homesick whimpering of the thirtieth. The miracle is that I remember no man who shared this life with me as an automaton, but each as a clearly defined and different human being.

There were exquisite punishments which had been refined long before the days when Bligh's men, or Sempill's, were marching in Lochaber and the Rough Bounds.* Hesitation in response to a command given on the great drill-square of Kinmel Camp could bring a barking order to double about its 800-yard perimeter with a nine-pound Lee-Enfield held straight-armed above the head. A stumble clumsily hidden, or a slackening of pace, could provoke another screaming order to repeat the run. A section that fell behind in the sweating, hating competition between troops would be collectively punished by an hour's ceremonial foot and arms drill in field-service marching order, back and side packs weighted with sand from the fire buckets. But this, I believe, the young Guardsman ordered without sanction from the Battery Commander, for the junior NCOs showed an unusual sympathy for our bodies and minds when the ordeal was over. We were taught to catch a rifle flung at us from five paces. A painful fumble was punished by an immediate perimeter run. We learnt to perfect the three movements of the Present Arms while facing a wall, its rough-cast surface three inches from our bodies. Too wide a swing of the rifle in the second movement tore the skin from our knuckles. A flinch, a strangled obscenity, and the order was repeated, an inch closer to the wall. If we thought the mad and handsome zealot from the Welsh Guards was exceeding his authority, as perhaps he was, we had no appeal against it, for occasionally we were watched impassively by that one-armed Lancashire Fusilier. When he came to the square during these drill exercises, we were ordered into line and came to the Present, a salute he acknowledged with a quivering leather glove. Never that alone, however. Before he left there was always one man, too often myself, at whom his accusing cane would be pointed.

As the thirteen weeks approached their end our health improved; we could now eat the uneatable in the cookhouse, and our anger was a potent, motivating energy. We were determined to triumph over anything the Troop Commander devised. There was an intense, impassioned struggle between us. He enjoyed and encouraged this, as did his senior NCOs. They were instructors on the permanent staff, sergeants and lance-sergeants, long-service men and recalled reservists who had entered the Army after the Great War, too old to be sent on active service now but dedicated to the belief that we should fear them more than we might the enemy.

* An old description of the districts of Knoidart, Morar, Moidart, etc., roadless and inaccessible to the north-west of the Great Glen.

Our forced marches, twice and occasionally three times a week, became longer, and the miles were meaningless when the last four or five were conducted at the double. In the beginning, when unfamiliar boots produced blisters the size of old pennies, we learnt not to go to the Medical Room. To report such injuries, we were told, was a chargeable offence in the Guards, where men were expected to take good care of their feet. What was proper for the Brigade should be no more than expected from Gunners of the Royal Artillery. After every march this smiling boy would slowly pace the aisle between our beds, where we lay with naked feet extended, and ask whether there was any pain when his prodding cane touched our yellow, ballooning flesh. And of course there was not.

There was perhaps an intelligent madness in such behaviour during that hot summer of 1940. The nation was alone, a scorched timber on the edge of a European conflict that had burnt itself out in one brief and astonishing conflagration. We were there, our Lancashire Fusilier surely believed, to be properly trained, and when we died, as we surely would before the year was out, it would be with the least discredit to our instructors and the maximum damage to the enemy. I suppose we understood this, but we were too exhausted to care. Exhaustion is an old companion of the military man, cementing friendship and reinforcing pride. Edward Linn, of the Royal Scots Fusiliers, was proud of the goodwill among his comrades when they approached the field of Culloden. And no wonder, he told his wife, 'considering the fatigues we have undergone this winter by hunger and cold and marching day and night'.

We knew that goodwill towards the end of our training. The forced marches, now made at night sometimes, were along the high ground of the Elwy Valley. They began in summer's late dusk as the blue wall of the Conway range grew darker, and the air was thick with the scent of meadow-sweet in wayside ditches. Before dawn there was the taste of blood from bitten lips, the stink of sweat, and of urine from the fool ahead who had not relieved himself when warned. There was that impossible blessing some of us possessed, the ability to sleep on the march, right and left flank-men closing in to support your unconscious body. Bombardiers and lance-bombardiers, in lighter equipment, sometimes moved along the line to take the rifle of a stumbling man, and we hated those who carried two or three as they marched beside us. This mercy the Troop Commander permitted, because it was a Guards' tradition, good sense in encouraging interdependence, or because he did not know what he would do if we all stopped and refused to march one pace more. But we did not, we soldiered on, singing obscene songs at his back, sometimes increasing our pace to make *him* march more quickly. Approaching the Main Guard gate upon our return, we came to attention at the slope, pace after pace in immaculate time as if we believed in this and everything else we were enduring. And perhaps we did. The alternative would have been the escape chosen by one man in every intake, it seemed, to go with a rifle to the ablution hut, to sit in the only isolation allowed us, and there blow out his brains.

The eternity was at last ended. Thirteen weeks of field-training and trench-digging from infantry manuals published in 1916. The use of rifle, Lewis gun and grenade. Mentally stunning, barking instruction in the operation of sound-detectors, searchlights and light anti-aircraft weapons. Bayonet practice of comic ferocity, the sweat and loneliness inside the small world of a gas-mask. And always foot-drill, eyes weeping from the dust and reflected light of the great square. The merciless public scrubbing of the perversely unwashed, the humiliation of the nervously incontinent. The white and purple ribbon on the Fusilier's tunic reminding us that whatever we hated now could be remembered with affection in the obscenity that might come.

The Battery was told that it would shortly leave for an undisclosed destination, the identification of which occupied desultory conversation after Lights Out and the lowering of the black-out boards. At last we were given a free weekend, to sleep, to sit in the Gaff and see the films we had seen almost weekly, to get drunk, to write long letters, to visit Rhyl for the last time. I cannot remember this deserted holiday resort with any pleasure, but it was sometimes the only escape from the suffocation of the camp. There were abandoned chalets along the front, concrete dragon's-teeth, barbed wire and railway lines in the wash of the tides, green with seaweed or red with rust. There was always darkness in the town, it seemed – dark streets, and dark figures colliding in the black-out. And at its centre was a crowded bus station, seething with khaki figures. I wrote something about it in one of the little reviews which flourished then. It seemed to me sometimes that they were designed to prove that sensitive intellectuals understood the truth of soldiering far more than the ordinary squadee. What I wrote may perhaps be proof of that uncharitable criticism.

The High Street was full. Its noise, the flashing of torches, the high screaming protest of girls' voices, came as a sharp shock to the soldier after the silence of the beach. The noise and the crowd thickened as he made his way to the bus station. There, lighting the long queues with red pin-points, the cigarettes glowed, and voices were singing

> There's an old mill by the stream,
> Nellie Dean,
> Where we used to sit and dream,
> Nellie Dean . . .

Torchlights shone on the cap-badges. Eyebrows, or the sharp tip of a nose, the dip of a side-cap, would appear suddenly here and there along the length of the queue as a cigarette burnt up between the lips of a smoker. The soldier found the end of the queue. The dog followed him until someone trod on it, and then it yelped its disappointment and trotted away. The soldier did not see it go. He did not know it had followed him from the beach. He took his place in the queue. 'Hullo,' he said, 'Got a fag?'

The anonymity here is contrived, and perhaps unsuccessful. But lost, indistinguishable in khaki, uniform in dress and experience, we feared and distrusted our anonymity. The friendships we made were a defence against it, and we believed they should be unbreakable, and worthy of a group manifestation whenever possible. There was a public house in Rhyl opposite the bus station, a hundred yards and more from the front where the Irish Sea washed in upon the shingle and the anti-tank obstacles. The bars of this small house were selective. Officers drank here, warrant officers and sergeants there, bombardiers and gunners in the Public. The divisions were meaningless, but were rarely ignored. There was also a small room upstairs, used for celebrations, recognitions of promotion or achievement, but more often for farewells.

We came there to celebrate the end of our training and our departure. Our drill-sergeant, whom we were now able to forgive in our euphoria, joined us briefly, it being the custom, he had told us, to buy him a drink upon such an occasion. He was a short, red-faced man with very light, close-cropped hair, and when he wore his best battle-dress, as he did this evening, his stripes were carefully chalked, and there were ball-bearings in the bottoms of his trousers, above his gaiters, to improve the hang of the cloth. His soldiering, in Coastal Artillery, had begun after the Great War, and was mostly spent in India and Mauritius, from which he had acquired some obscene and some Kiplingesque wisdom. He was virtually illiterate. By that I mean that although he could read and write, and had passed the elementary educational tests necessary for his promotion, he was unable to express his thoughts verbally or in writing. In my callow beginning as a soldier I detested him. My profession, my lingering transatlantic accent, and perhaps my thinly disguised dislike, offended him, and he had the power and opportunity to make me suffer. He did this often, and I can still hear his barking, hysterical voice coming across the square as the rifle above my head became heavier, sweat blinded my eyes and my feet turned to lead. But the hostility between us, so mercilessly cultivated on his part, was changed in a single extraordinary moment.

I stood one night outside the Main Guard, stiffly to attention at the Slope, aware that my silhouette could be clearly seen from the Adjutant's office and thus I could not relax. The drill-sergeant, who was Guard Commander that night, came out to me. Helped by the darkness, and perhaps by the fact that I could not move in response, he began to explain his marital problems. He had an affectionate but complaining wife, who was also jealous and thriftless. He was unable, in his letters, to assure her of his fidelity and persuade her to be satisfied with the allowance he made from his pay. All this said, without asking for my comments, he returned to the guard-room. But he had only gone to fortify himself with a cigarette and shortly came out again, placing the extinguished stub in his field-dressing pocket. Could I, he asked, compose a loving letter to his wife, explaining his point of view? I did so later in the week, dictating it to him slowly in his small, tobacco-smoked room at the end of the barrack-hut. He did not refer to the matter again, but now, when I was the object of a particular tirade of his humiliating abuse, one of his lashless eyelids would be lowered briefly.

He did not remain long with us in that upstairs room, timing his stay to within the contradictory limits of familiarity and regard for rank. He took our teasing and laughter remarkably well. Before he left he cleared his throat for a solemn caveat. 'There's only one thing I want to tell you shower, one of the best mobs I've ever trained. And that is . . . apart from good luck, of course . . . Remember, when you leave a unit, all debts and friendships are cancelled.'

Once he was gone, and as if upon a theatrical cue, the Troop Commander arrived, politely knocking on the door with his leather-covered cane. He was in field-service dress and was carrying his Guardsman's cap, an assurance of the informality of his visit. He accepted a gin and tonic, bought a round for us, and then said goodbye without affectation, saying that he was proud of us. Now, so long after, I hope he did not hear the suppressed but derisive laughter when he left. I suspect that he truly despised us, for we were not Guardsmen, and neither was he in this camp. He had not told us that he was himself leaving, to join the special service unit from which came the Commandos. I saw him again, months later in London, in battle-dress, his sleeves ablaze with formation signs. His young face was now disfigured, and its deluding arrogance was sadly intensified by the scars. He did not recognize me as I saluted him, and there was no reason why he should. He returned my salute with the same casual precision as the Lancashire Fusilier, and there was the ribbon of the Military Cross on his tunic too.

I did not go out with the Battery. I was retained, given a lance-bombardier's stripe and told to hold myself ready for posting to an OCTU should a selection board consider me suitable for a commission. This was what the earnest organizers of the Communist Party had urged me to secure if possible. The need for experienced officers among the membership was essential for the revolutionary situation which, it was thought, would follow victory over Germany. I do not think I believed this startling, if not risible, improbability, and far from working to secure a commission I had been told, on my second day in the Army, that I might be kept in the camp as a junior instructor until I was sent to an OCTU. This may explain the cool, watchful eye of the Lancashire Fusilier, and his obvious belief that I should experience and survive the worst that a training-camp could require of a soldier.

My friends, and my debts, left on Monday, down the Rhuddlan road with the unbowdlerized words of 'Bless 'em all!' shouted from the tailboard of every truck. I have never heard from any of those men whom I knew so intimately, nor have I any certain knowledge of what happened to them. A year or so later I was told, with what truth I do not know, that many had been disembarked at Singapore and sent forward into the hands of the advancing Japanese.

April the Thirtieth

I come to Kintail as often as I can, from the Great Glen to the sea, and never more happily than on a late afternoon such as this. On the lower braes of Glenmoriston the tawny plaid of last year's bracken is already flecked with green, the water of Loch Cluanie holds a blue sky upturned, and the melted snow of winter runs musically from every rock-fall. At this hour the cowled heads of the Five Sisters are red-gold in a westering sun, and the gorge of Glen Shiel below them is darkening rapidly. It was the old Highland way to think of any group of mountainous hills, held together in a primeval embrace, as sisters three, or five, or seven . . . These stone women, standing at the gateway to Kintail with their backs turned to the Atlantic winds and their wide skirts fringed with scree, have no feminine names. Each is a *sgurr*, the uninspiring English for which is perhaps 'high cone or hill'. Thus they are the Conical Hills of the Stony Place, of the Black Chest or Coffin, of an Arrow, a Mountain Spring, the origin of such names long gone with the men and women who once lived here. One alone fits the splendour of them all in the warmth of the sunset, *Sgurr na Morachd*, the Hill of Majesty.

Kintail is the oldest land-route to the Isle of Skye, and the only one until the coming of road and rail. It is a knuckled fist, a green peninsula between two sea-lochs, Carron and Alsh, and its Gaelic name describes it well – *ceann t'sail*, at the head of salt water. Visitors in the long past were often less impressed than I am when I come once more to the most noble landscape in Britain, but some travelled by wretched roads or tracks, with no certainty of dry lodgings ahead, and no confidence in the goodwill of the inhabitants of so remote and wild a district.

Thomas Pennant, the peregrinating naturalist, came here by sea in 1772, aboard a handsome cutter of ninety tons. From her deck, at the mouth of Loch Alsh, he was content with a distant but picturesque view of an amphitheatre of mountains, including 'the country of Kintail', and was naturally more excited by the sudden appearance of two whales ahead, and 'the *jets d'eau* from their orifices'. A year later, Johnson and Boswell travelled by Glenmoriston, a bold and brave venture for both of them, and it is a pity the Doctor was in so contentious a humour as they approached Glen Shiel. He deflated his companion's enthusiasm by calling the tallest Sister a 'mere protuberance', but, as I have always been quick to add when quoting him in this context, his journey to Kintail was wearisome for a man of his age and health, and he was out of patience with Boswell's chattering. Drinking frothed milk from a wooden cup at the now lost village of Achnashiel, he warmed a little toward its people, in whom he had seen 'a very savageness of aspect and manner'. When he wrote of this day in his *Journey* there was even a note of admiration. More than a century before, he said, almost all the clansmen of Glen Shiel had been killed in Montrose's campaigns, but their widows, 'like the Scythian ladies of old, married their servants and the Macraes became a considerable race'. Apart from this approval, the Doctor was firm in his classical distaste for a landscape that was 'incapable of form or usefulness, dismissed by nature from her care, and disinherited of her favours, left in its original elemental state, or quickened only with one sullen power of useless vegetation'. Standing upon the timbered heights of Mam Ratagan today and looking across the quiet water of Loch Duich to those grieving gentlewomen of Kintail, I am obliged to agree that there could have been nothing so useless in the neighbourhood of Lichfield or Gough Square.

In 1803, James Hogg was robbed as he lay abed in the squalid, slated inn at Invershiel, by a skilful rogue no doubt, for he complained that he was kept awake all night by drunken Highlanders, male and female. He lost no money – that he had placed in his waistcoat which he then used as a pillow – but six letters of introduction to Highland gentlemen were taken from his coat, and with them the hope of better accommodation than the inn at Invershiel. The houses of the glen, he noted, were mostly deserted and in ruins, but the braes were well stocked with sheep, Cheviots such as he had recently seen in Glengarry where he had lodged with Thomas Gillespie, the rough and ambitious grazier from the Lowlands. The sight of a wide sheep-walk, where once there had been that abundant but short-lived renascence of Clan Macrae, undoubtedly impressed Hogg, for he was not only a renowned, versatile and gifted writer, he was also foolishly pleased to be known as The Ettrick Shepherd.

The first *true* road to Kintail was marked for later engineers by the buckled shoes and iron hooves of an English army in 1654. Four or five hundred miles from their own green and placid shires, these Cromwellian soldiers followed the old trails of the cattle-drovers and sometimes the coffin-paths by which the bodies of Norse kings and Celtic chiefs were brought to the headwaters of Loch Linnhe. There at Corpach, the place of corpses, they remained overnight on the tidal shore, and in the morning were taken by galley to their tombs on Iona.

The English soldiers of the Protectorate were marched to the far waters of Kintail by Lieutenant-General George Monck, Cromwell's commander-in-chief in Scotland. Their campaign has interested me and inspired my admiration since I first read of it in the General's blunt report to his master, the Lord Protector, in London. Although they fought no spectacular battle against the Royalist clans, their dogged invasion of a wild and unknown terrain was a military triumph, and their relatively mild pacification of the mountains has been obscured by the systematic brutality of Cumberland's dragonnade a century later. From this largely neglected period of Highland history has come the beguiling notion that the natives of the town of Inverness speak the finest English to be heard in the British Isles. This claim, it is said, was first made by Daniel Defoe in his *Tour through the Whole Island of Great Britain*, published in 1726, and repeated fifty years later in Samuel Johnson's *Journey to the Western Islands*, but the contention is weakened by their exact text. The people of Inverness, said Defoe, 'speak perfect English, even much better than in the most southerly provinces of Scotland', but he would not say, as others did, that 'they speak it as well as at London'. Johnson's reference was made without comparisons. 'The language of this town,' he wrote, 'has long been considered as peculiarly elegant.' Whatever its quality, both men were agreed that it was a legacy from the English Occupation during the Protectorate, and Johnson thought there had also been a fleshly inheritance. 'The soldiers seem to have incorporated afterwards with the inhabitants, and to have peopled the place with an English race.' One half of this observation must be undeniable.

English cannot have been an unfamiliar tongue, however. Inverness was the only seaport of any consequence in the Highlands. It had no direct road-link with the south, and it had looked outward from the kingdom long before the Union of the Crowns. As early as the Middle Ages, English seamen and merchants would have given the town its first experience of their sibilant and insistent speech. A decade of English military occupation made the knowledge and use of it a daily necessity, but it is hard to understand how the townsfolk acquired an elegant diction from tutors who spoke in the different voices of their English shires. Mrs Sarah Murray, who travelled the Highlands by a well-sprung carriage in 1796, was more particular in her praise than Defoe or Johnson. She was entranced by the English she heard in the town. It was unlike any other in the Highlands and was 'extremely insinuating', she said, using a word that has now been bludgeoned out of sensitive use.

> I could almost say bewitching; neither has it any resemblance to Lowland Scots in idiom, being very pure English, accompanied with a sort of foreign tone, which is very pleasing; in short it is like broken English proceeding from the soft voice of a beautiful female foreigner, taught English purely and grammatically.

No longer, I think. The speech of Inverness has sadly changed, even in the fifty years since I first heard it, four hundred miles from that town – the soft and precise voice of an ATS driver talking pleasantly in the darkness as she took us home from a cold night-deployment above the Conway Valley. And surely no part of Scotland today would believe it must be gratified by English praise for the English it speaks.

The first soldiers of the Protectorate came to Inverness in 1651, one thousand men of Colonel Fitch's Regiment, their deep wooden drums making the pace of their march from Aberdeen. Four months earlier the young king Charles II, recently crowned at Scone, had taken a Scottish army into England and to its decisive defeat at Worcester. The Severn was dark with Royalist blood, and the ditches before the eastern gate of the city were filled with Highland dead, five hundred and more from Clan MacLeod alone, it is said. After a sharp and determined campaign, sturdy siege and brief resistance, George Monck imposed Cromwell's rule upon southern Scotland. In the mountainous north, 'that frightful country' as Defoe would later describe it, there was no immediate acceptance of the Protectorate. Here Montrose had gathered much

57

of the courage and fury that brought him his year of miracles, and although his dismembered body was now displayed in the principal burghs of the country, the defiance of some clans under Royalist generalship was still a threat. To subdue all hostility, English soldiers were to be garrisoned in the Great Glen, with a most powerful fortress on the river's mouth at Inverness. The building and governing of this was now the duty of Colonel Thomas Fitch.

His regiment arrived on a hoar-frost day at the close of the year, coming down the brae to the white bank of the Ness. The buff jerkins and scarlet coats, lifted pikes and slanting muskets, greatly alarmed a town that was only now learning of the death or transportation of neighbouring clansmen, Frasers and Mackenzies, who had gone south to Worcester. Yet it submitted to the rule of the English without resistance, protest, or even serious complaint. In time, and after some final bloodshed, all the north of Scotland, according to the Presbyterian minister of Wardlaw, was willing to be 'demure under a slavish charm, submitting their Voluntar unvoluntar [sic] necks to the present swaying yock wreathed about their necks until Almighty God bring us Post Nubila Phoebus, light after darkness, and order out of confusion'. Clumsily expressed, perhaps, but it conveys a philosophical surrender to irresistible force. Although Fitch's regiment had been newly formed for service in Scotland, many of his men were old campaigners. Some had served in the New Model Army and all were certain that they were the finest soldiers in Europe. There was also an enlisted God upon their side, and his word was preached to them by Mr Gosle, an Independent of extreme religious faith. James Fraser, a young divinity student who later became that Minister of Wardlaw above, was outraged by the presence, appearance, and religion of the Englishmen.

Collonel Thomas Fitch and his regiment came down to Scotland, marched through Aberdeen in December, a rude, rageing rabble of a Sectarian new regiment, running down men in the streets, I being myselfe there at the time, witness of their extravagancies.

When the English were finally in control of Inverness, another strongpoint was established at Inverlochy, sixty miles down the Great Glen in the shadow of Ben Nevis. The command of this garrison, its fort when built, and the governorship of Lochaber about, was given to John Hill, the ablest of Fitch's young captains. Promoted to Major upon this appointment, he governed with sympathy and discretion, making friends rather than enemies of the Lochaber chiefs, particularly Ewen Cameron of Lochiel and Alasdair MacDonald of Glencoe. When the end of the Protectorate came, he surrendered his command to these fierce companions, and on his way northward to Inverness he may have looked back along the run of the River Lochy to see the smoke of his burning fort. He returned to Inverlochy thirty years later, a widower with two spinster daughters in London, and with orders to rebuild the fort and govern Lochaber once more, this time for the new monarchy of William and Mary. It was in his green-panelled office, within the south-east ravelin of the fort, that he finally signed a cautious letter requiring two companies of the Earl of Argyll's Regiment to obey the King's order for the slaughter of 'that sept of thieves', the little clan of his friend Glencoe.

I long wished to learn more about this tortured officer who was betrayed by his duty and by the great men who placed its terrible weight upon his back. He was the only man of authority who showed compassion for the survivors of the Massacre, and he defended himself honestly before a Commission of Enquiry called by a king upon whom responsibility for that bloody act must finally rest. When he was relieved of his post in Lochaber, Hill rejoined his daughters in London, knighted in empty honour, poor in pocket and sadly embittered. 'I think you begin to forget me,' he chided a Highland friend who was lax in corresponding, 'or to think I live too long.' In the closing years of his life he disappears from record, but now I know a little more about its beginning than I did when I wrote my account of the Massacre.

Serendipity, that happy faculty so named and defined by Horace Walpole, has been a good companion in my work and has come again to my aid, if tardily. In pursuit of another matter at the Public Record Office, and of course by fortunate chance, I discovered a letter of 1680 in *State Papers (Domestic)* referring to John Hill as the 'agent and actor' for the Countess of Donegall in Ireland, where he served after the Restoration. With this unexpected knowledge to guide me, it was not difficult to find that the first Earl of Donegall, in the early years of the century, had married Dorcas, daughter of John Hill of Honiley in the county of Warwick. She died in 1630, but it is clear that even fifty years later the Donegalls felt an obligation to her kin, for I believe the Governor of Lochaber was her nephew or, less likely, a much younger brother. The Hills were thus small gentry, an untitled class that had risen and prospered under the Tudors. His Highness the Lord Protector, Oliver Crom-well, had such roots, as did many of his officers who were, as he described his own condition before the Civil War, 'living neither in any considerable height nor yet in obscurity'.

Whatever it was in the seventeenth century, Honiley is certainly obscure now, on a by-road to the west of Kenilworth and below the great flank of Birmingham, but it was a human settlement at least eight centuries ago when its felicitous name was first recorded, the wood where honey is found. I went to it on a still afternoon in August, believing that in its Norman church there might be tablets or a hatchment in memory of John Hill's family, even his own tomb. There is no village, only some scattered houses in an open landscape that seemed cruelly deserted on a hot and insect-humming day. The Norman church – as once there must have been – is long gone, and in its place is another, built in the eighteenth century by an Improving squire, I suspect. There are no hatch-ments, no headstones, no trace of John Hill, soldier of the Protec-torate. His memory must therefore survive in the printed word, in the gateway of his garrison now used as the entrance to a Highland cemetery, and in any compassionate thoughts that may be aroused by a change of light, the darkening of the sun in Glencoe.

There is also nothing left of 'Cromwell's Citadel' in Inverness except its clock-tower, absurdly enduring on the carseland at the mouth of the river and surrounded by oil storage tanks. Some stones used in the construction of the fort do survive in the fabric of older buildings in the town, notably in Dunbar's Hospital on Church Street. Built after the Restoration as an infirmary, it is now a rest centre, but it has also been a school, a library, and housing for a fire-engine. In 1751, when it was a grammar school, Major James Wolfe took lessons from its mathematics master to relieve the tedium of his second tour of duty in the Highlands. This I learnt in later life, but in my boyhood, when Miss Campbell's knuckled hand drummed Canadian history into my bowed head, I was occasionally and confusingly reminded that the Great Hero of Que-bec, as she called him, 'was not too proud to be a schoolboy even when he was a man'. Unfortunately for this precept, the Major's studies only deepened his boredom. He told his father that he was now perfectly stupid, having 'algebraically worked away the little portion of understanding that was allowed to me'.

The fortress of Inverness, 'a most stately sconce' in the opinion of the Minister of Wardlaw, was built upon land civilly purchased from the burghers of the town. One shilling a day was paid to all Highland labourers in the ditches and on the walls. So popular was this employment, said Fraser, 'that all the country people flockt in to that work, and hardly could you get one to serve you'. Fitch's soldiers also worked as builders, and willingly enough it may be thought, for in addition to their daily pay of ninepence they received as much or more for labour upon the citadel. Five years were needed for the final completion, and when it was finished the cost, as is the way in fiscal matters, was probably more than double the £30,000 Colonel Fitch had originally required from the Council of State in London.

The brief existence of the Citadel began with barrack-houses along the river-bank, built of bricks and timber. From these it slowly grew into a classical pentagon of stone, much of which came from the deserted abbeys and religious houses along the Moray Firth, mute and eyeless since the Reformation and now, by this military rape, hastened towards picturesque ruin. Surrounded by a moat large enough to float a sea-going vessel, and approached by a stout wooden bridge only, the citadel was built to withstand any conventional attack by artillery, mining or infantry assault, but since none of these sophisticated skills was practised by the clans, and in the absence now of any threat from a foreign fleet, its main purpose was to warn and intimidate a subject people. Its inclined walls were as high as a three-storeyed house, and the barracks within – built of English brick, English oak and Scots pine – could accommodate twice the strength of Fitch's regiment. No one entered the fort without astonishment and wonder. Once across the Blue Bridge and through a gateway surmounted by the carved stone of the Commonwealth's arms, the great clan chiefs, who came willingly enough to their brief and comfortable imprisonment, were conducted through a vaulted gallery, seventy feet long and walled with pikes and drums. In the heart of the fortress there were stables, stores, a hospital, granary, armoury and magazine, lodgings for strangers and a long tavern for the garrison. On the highest floor of the four-square keep was a chapel, well furnished with a stately pulpit and seats, said James Fraser, and above it was 'a brave clock with four large gilded dials and a curious bell'. The highest point of all was a staff upon which flew a great standard, its silken colours enfolding the restless wind from the sea and hills – Saint George's Cross of England emblazoned in letters of gold with the word 'Ebenezer', meaning 'The Lord hath helped us'.

So involved were many Scots in the building of the Citadel that it became a venture from which all might prosper according to their wish. Thus a gentleman of Clan Fraser, a renowned kinsman of its chief and once a captain of the Royal Lifeguards, provided much of the fort's indigenous timber from his red forest above Loch Ness. All Englishmen were soon welcome in the town, not only soldiers from the garrison but traders and merchants from the south, apothecaries, surgeons and physicians. In the euphoria of the Restoration, James Fraser could still write with admiration of the town's departed masters. 'It were a rant not to relate what advantage the country had by this regiment,' he said. They had brought 'such store of all wares and conveniences' that the cost of them was little more than it was in England, and a pint of claret could be had for a shilling. Although he rejoiced that the Restoration had brought an end to 'prosperous wickedness' it did not diminish an earlier compliment, the greatest ever paid by a Scot to the English. 'They not only civilised but enriched this place.'

The building of the Citadel and the establishment of garrisons in the Great Glen began before the final suppression of Royalist resistance in the mountains. In this, the last struggle of the long civil wars, the decisive initiative was taken by the English, who marched into the unknown hills without doubt of final success. Even those familiar with the Highlands today, beyond the boundaries of its roads, might find it hard to imagine the difficulties faced by George Monck and his soldiers. Ahead of them as they marched from Perth was an angry sea of mountain waves, rolling northward and northward yet. Something of that remote and trackless past endures in the great massif of the Grampians, the desolation of Rannoch, the threatened flow-country of Sutherland and the cathedral heights of Wester Ross, where there is sometimes solitude and ceaseless wind, sometimes the stillness of hostile heat, but never a need for man's imperfect presence. Such a land, offering no compromise to those who invade it, must have persuaded the Commonwealth soldiers that they were not only pursuing an elusive enemy but also challenging all the admonitory terrors in the Old Testament.

From his reports it is clear that Monck had no doubt that when he began his campaign – 'as soon as grasse may be had in the Highlands for the Horse' – he would shortly find the Royalist forces. These, four thousand it was said, had been mustered under the command of John Middleton, once a pikeman in a regiment of Scottish mercenaries and now the King's last Captain-General in the field. 'We shall draw up close to them,' Monck told the Lord Protector,

> . . . and so we do hope we shall keep them close up together, or inforce them all to go into Caithness or Sutherland again, where we hope to destroy them in that country.

His campaign lasted six weeks and two days, fewer than three thousand Horse and Foot travelling five hundred miles – remarkable even for soldiers who were trained to march for thirteen days before being granted the mercy of one to rest. Monck had none of the advantages which would sustain Cumberland's bloody invasion a century later – a strategic framework of military roads, established garrisons, and the constant support of warships in the western lochs. From first light until mid-day in yet more narrow glens, Monck marched his men through the worst of a Highland summer – hot, humid and insect-plagued. Braesides at dawn are glissades of dew-wet heather. At noon the air smokes above treacherous ground which could embrace a stumbling man or faltering beast. And at all times the mountain floors are scattered with a scree of rippling stones, ready to break the legs of dragoon horses and give no peace to any exhausted body stretched upon such ground at night. Not once was the enemy seen in so much as company strength, only a tartan swirl or broadsword gleam on a hillside where a scouting clansman watched the march below.

Monck was not untypical of Cromwell's generals, but he was among the best that the anvil of these harsh times was required to forge. He was a Devonshire man, born into a landed family whose conceit was that it had Plantagenet forebears. He was roughly devout, with more ease of conscience than other soldiers of pious persuasion, for he believed in God's sanction for his killing trade. 'The profession of a soldier,' he said, 'is allowed to be lawful by the Word of God.' This dogmatic claim, for which there is certainly justification in the Scriptures, saddened and perplexed Captain Fereday, the good non-conformist padre of Kinmel camp who once refused to be chairman of a debate which I had proposed upon that timely assertion. More pertinently, Monck was perhaps in advance of many of his age and rank in his claim that a general officer should always consider himself subordinate to the civil power. When the

Protectorate was disintegrating after the death of Oliver, he pledged the soldiers of his Scottish command to the lawful authority of Parliament and declared his unswerving opposition to 'the slavery of a sword government'. Rapid events turned this principle upon its head, for it was his sword and his regiment, the Coldstreamers whom he brought to London, which cowed the squabbles of Cromwell's heirs and brought the Stuarts into their own again.

It was said that Monck was admired and loved by his men, but this was also said of Wolfe, and of most commanders until literacy and popular printing gave the soldier a reflective voice. We can never know the thoughts of the General's veterans when a grateful king rewarded 'old George, honest George Monck' with a dukedom, but if there were indeed an affectionate regard it could have been due in part to his economic expenditure of their lives and to what they knew of him as a man in this would-be egalitarian age. He was an uxorious husband and was said to have ignored all other women after his marriage to his mistress, Nan Ratsford, although some said it was because he was more afraid of her than he was of a whole army. The rank and file of his command undoubtedly approved of her, for she was a laundress at the Tower, the widow or deserted wife of a perfumer. She would, of course, die a duchess and be buried in Westminster Abbey with her husband, but her mother, gossips said, had been a famous barber and street-walker of Cheapside, and her father a farrier in one of Monck's regiments.

The little army the General took into the mountains was conventionally composed of pikemen, musketeers, horsemen and dragoons. Their clothing, equipment and arms, compared with the lightly clad swordsmen of the clans, now seem ridiculous, and it is almost impossible to believe that men so handicapped could survive more than a week in those inhospitable glens. The steel-tipped pike was officially eighteen feet in length and although experienced commanders often shortened it to thirteen it was still a heavy and awkward weapon to be carried over rough ground, always rising and ever descending. The cumbersome weight of a musketeer's matchlock was further increased by a dragging bandolier of metal or leather tubes, each containing powder and ball for one charge. A pikeman's head was contained in a steel cap, the musketeer's topped by a broad-brimmed hat, one unbearable in heat and the other a purgatory in drenching rain. Dragoons wore back- and breast-plates, which Monck had re-introduced, and however useful they might have been for withstanding a sword-stroke or the sighing impact of a spent shot, heat and humidity turned them into cruel ovens.

Each soldier carried a week's supply of bread and cheese in his knapsack, and sometimes part of a bivouac tent on his back. The ration was his principal sustenance, and old campaigners afterwards boasted that they had conquered Scotland as well as Ireland on Cheshire cheese and biscuit. The total weight of a foot-soldier's burden at this time was in excess of sixty pounds, the heaviest ever carried by a British infantryman. The archers and spearmen of medieval wars were lightly laden. Sixty pounds was the most carried by Wellington's men in the Peninsula, and by the Great War the load had been reduced to forty. Only the dedicated sadists of Kinmel, and other training-camps no doubt, insisted that we learnt to march with back- and side-packs, water-bottle, bayonet and rifle, weighing fifty-six pounds in all. One man and sometimes two in every section also carried the extra burden of a canvas bandolier, its pouches full of ammunition clips or weights to simulate them. I remember our foolish and perverse pride in such loads, for this was the hot summer of 1940 when the earth seemed burnt beyond rebirth and the sky trembled with the sound of bombers moving upon Merseyside. I did not know, not then, of the march made by the pikemen and musketeers of Monck's army, and not until I saw the land itself could I have come close to an understanding of their forgotten achievement.

Their daily march was never less than ten and frequently more than twenty miles. A map tracing their turning, sweeping northern advance gives a chilling indication of what they encountered – high escarpments and narrow glens, swift rivers, wide lochs and desolate bogs. From Perth they marched to Loch Tay in Breadalbane, following routes the Romans may have taken, and beyond Kenmore they turned by the curve of Schiehallion's breast to a broad strath of lochs, its water-run drawn from the western Moor of Rannoch. At Kinlochrannoch they marched eastward, following rumour and report to the Braes of Atholl, past the Murrays' dour castle and northward again over Drumochter's saddle to the valley of the Spey. But here they were told that Middleton was gone into the west again, gathering clansmen from the country of the Glengarry Mac-Donells. Monck followed by Loch Laggan and the River Spean, a green valley meandering between the tall heights of the Moy and Ardverikie forests. To these Englishmen it was perhaps no more than another hostile glen and thus unlovable, but here and there along the weary column of march a soldier may have responded to its serene beauty and felt shame for the black smoke of burning townships from Lagganhead to the Braes of Lochaber. Ten days after leaving Perth, the General at last halted his army, in the heart of the Great Glen where the River Spean runs rapidly down to the Falls of Mucomir. The burning continued. 'Being the first bounds of Clan Cameron,' Monck told the Protector, 'and they being up in armes against us, we began to fire all their houses.'

In the clenched fist of this great land-fault, where Montrose recently came out of the winter hills to destroy the Campbells, scouts from that wounded clan told the General that Middleton had now gone into Kintail, northward beyond Loch Arkaig and Loch Quoich. The English continued their unflagging pursuit, over the braes of Glengarry towards Glenmoriston and the blue skyline of Kintail. In the last days of June, the heat of the day is rarely sweetened by compassionate rain, and there was nothing to sustain the spirits of the English but the occasional burning of 'a gentleman's house'. The wind on their faces as they drew closer to Kintail must have had the same salt taste which always welcomes me when I come by Loch Cluanie to the first Sister. Monck's forage officers took what they could from the forbidding land. Five hundred cattle and sheep belonging to the hidden people of Glen Shiel were taken up and brought to the night-camp on Loch Duich and there butchered before dawn. The news brought to Monck was that Middleton had gone northward from Loch Alsh, round the brown flank of Ben Killilan to Loch Monar and Glen Strathfarrar, and thus could soon be at Inverness and thence to the valley of the Spey. Speed in pursuit now became imperative, but for one day more the General allowed his men to rest. The black stains of their fires, the print of their shoes and the steam of their horse-lines would soon disappear, but they became part of the violent and saddening history of this lovely ground. Here had come Dalriadic Scots from the south and Ireland, Norsemen from their kingdom in Outer Isles. A medieval king of Scotland built the first castle on Eilean Donan in Loch Duich, to give himself a base for an assault on the Hebrides. A more lasting stronghold on this island was later held by the Macraes until English frigates destroyed it on a May evening in 1719. It then remained a ruin until its reconstruction in this century. The biscuit-box castle that now stands on Saint Donan's isle also masks the faded memory of the longboats once beached beyond it at the mouth of Loch Long, waiting to take an unwanted people to the emigrant ships and thence to the western sun.

Monck marched his army up the shore of Loch Long and into a country no force such as his had ever entered. Here wind and rain can seem incessant, distance and height are lost in bewildering mists. There could have been no sign of an enemy recently gone, only the scars of haste by the water of a burn, broken grass on a lower brae. 'In all this march,' Monck wrote, 'we saw only two women of the inhabitants and one man.' No others wished to invite his attention, or perhaps the story told to Samuel Johnson was true – all the men of this district, Macraes and MacLennans, had been lost in the wasteful triumphs of Montrose's year of miracles.

In the wildest part of the high ground, which Monck confusingly called 'Glenteugh in the Shields of Kintail', he turned his army to the east. The order was probably given a day's march beyond the head of Loch Long and below the northern flank of Killilan. Another day and the earth became a terrible enemy as the column stumbled into a spongy morass that stretched for five miles. 'So boggie,' said Monck, 'that about 100 baggage horses were left behind, and many other horses were bogged or tir'd. Never any horsemen (much less an armie) were observed to march this way.' It was the closest Monck's soldierly report came to pride in his men, and to directing that fact to the attention of the Lord Protector.

The exact route which he took to Glen Strathfarrar is now impossible to determine, but a memory of it survives, not in the mind of man but in a name. North-eastward from the thundering fall of water at Glomach there is a stretch of open ground, scattered with bright lochans and surrounded by crouching hills. This was the boggy land, and to the south of it, below the steep rise of Aonach Bhuidhe, is a narrow glen, its swift water fed by a score of noisy streams. The burn is called *Allt coire nan eachd* – the stream of the corrie of the horses.

The English came out of the hills of Kintail to Strathglass, and moved eastward now in great haste, forty-five killing miles to Inverness and the news that Middleton was away south into Atholl with his four thousand men. Once across the Spey, Monck left Morgan's brigade to watch the Braes of Mar and took the rest of his army into Atholl. He went on to Tayside, pursuing Campbell rumours westward along its pleasant waters, well into Argyll and the head of Loch Awe. Finding nothing, he turned about, coming into Breadalbane by Glen Lyon, that winding valley of good grain, hermits' cells and eyeless castles. There he was found by a rider who told him that on the day before, and on the high pass of Dalnaspidal, 'Colonel Morgan has met with Middleton's Horse and routed them.'

It was the undramatic end of the Royalist threat, driven into exhaustion and submission, and time would soon forget Monck's Highland march, its hardships and its courage. He turned now to the military government of this kingdom, so successfully from the point of view of those who believed it necessary that he declared 'a man may ride all over Scotland with a switch in his hand and £100 in his pocket, which he could not have done these five hundred years'. Whether that was a true boast or not, within five years of the Restoration of the monarchy and a Scottish Parliament a wayfarer complained that the kingdom was now 'so pestered with highway men, robbing all travellers, that there is no safe journeying'.

In the second week of April 1662, two years after the return of Charles II, the remaining English soldiers left the Citadel of Inverness with their weapons, drums, colours, wives and children. James Fraser recorded this event with honest emotion. Never a people, he said, left a place with such reluctance.

> It was even sad to see and hear their sighs and tears, pale faces and embraces, at their parting farewell from that town. And no wonder; they had peace and plenty for 10 years in it. They made that place happy, and it made them so.

But when the last fading drum-tap was heard from the road to Nairn there was great haste to remove every trace of the English occupation. All the country about, said Fraser, was called into the town to demolish the Citadel it had built. 'I saw it founded. I saw it flourish. I saw it in its glory, grandeur and renoun, and now in its ruins. Now the fragments of the Commonwealth breathes out its last gasp.' Before they left, and in what was certainly a personal and symbolic gesture, the English soldiers began the work by demolishing the sentinel turrets on the walls. The people then destroyed the Main Gate and the Blue Bridge, filling the moat with stones and bricks from the tumbled walls. The arms of the Commonwealth were broken, and to cries of 'God save the King!' its red and white standard was replaced with the yellow, scarlet and blue of the monarchy. Year by year, century by century, all tangible evidence of a now shameful occupation was demolished and distributed among the growing town. Even the great governor of the

Citadel, it seems, became as much a ruin as his abandoned garrison. A few years later, in England with a friend, James Fraser saw him and unkindly rejoiced at what he saw.

> Coming one day from London Bridge, we remarked Thomas Fitch, once governour and colonel to the English regiment at Inverness, whome I saw in grandure and state there. We spy him in a privat lane, most dejected; all alone, but he knew us not. These happy changes hath brought such snakes to skulk up and down the city obscurely and in disguise.

Great times must sometimes be made greater yet by what men wish to see, a supernatural event which throws an unnerving shadow across the face of rational truth. In the town of Ayr, the Commonwealth arms above the gate to its renowned citadel were covered during the years of the occupation by a sturdy thistle of prodigious size, growing there from a blown seed. This was taken by many people to mean that Scotland's prickly flower must in time eclipse Saint George's cross. Such imagery is irresistible to one not tightly held by the hand of academic discipline. When I wrote my account of Culloden and its aftermath, it seemed proper to close it with the report of a vision seen by twelve witnesses in a valley to the west of Aberdeen, not long after the defeat of the Jacobites. Two armies were observed in silent conflict, one dressed in scarlet and the other in blue beneath a Saint Andrew's saltire. Twice they fought, rallied and fought. When the blue army at last triumphed, the vision passed.

There were such visions or thought-inspired dreams in Germany too, and they flourished in the rot of its unbearable devastation. The weeks following the May surrender on Luneberg Heath were a time of physical and emotional exhaustion, and I have no strong recollection of harmony and goodwill. If they eventually came, more in fear of a greater peril in the east, it was after my friends and I were gone from the petrified forest of Hamburg's awesome ruins. The dark gulf between enemies, or between victor and vanquished, dominated the mood of my letters home.

> Outside Osnabrück our truck pulled over to the soft shoulder where we watched the German Army on its homeward march through the relentless rain. It was as if all these men had but one face, young

and old, fat and miserably thin, one face drawn to a sharp and hungry point by the jutting peak of a Wehrmacht cap, dusky skin immobile in its shadow. Little knots of women and children moved along the shuffling column, coloured pinafores and blonde hair wet, clutching at a grey sleeve, calling a shrill question.

In Hamburg now they say two million Germans will die from starvation next winter. It is impossible to think of them in such numbers, but sometimes we watch those who share our tram-ride to the Dammtor station, who work for us in the billet, or the print-shop on Grossebleichen-strasse. Who will have the cigarettes or coffee to survive the winter? Who will starve? The Wehrmacht tailor who repairs and presses our uniforms in return for white bread? The old compositor with the bushy Bismarck moustache? Will one be Karlheinz, the boy with yellow skin and bruised eyes who hid in an attic for most of the war to escape conscription? Or his mother who sits in her empty café, eyes closed, rocking to the music of an accordion and the sentimental voice of a drunken singer?

> Deine Liebe, meine Liebe
> Die sind bei mir gleich,
> Jeder Mann hat bur ein Herz . . .*

Man has one heart only. It isn't enough.

I remember the district of St Pauli during the first winter of peace in Hamburg, an area to the west of the bomb-raked docks and a ribbon of parks now ugly with black snow and the stumps of long-burnt trees. The inhabitants of St Pauli lived underground, as did many people of the city, in caverns below the hills of brick, stone and bodies yet to be recovered, the stacks of isolated chimneys rising above them in an obscene mockery of the Nazi salute. The main thoroughfare of the Reeperbahn was even then unsavoury, out of bounds to us and patrolled by recently enlisted red-caps in noisy jeeps. But we went there in civilian clothes. These we borrowed on a cigarette-rental from the relations and friends of Mama LeMoult in whose requisitioned apartment our sergeants' mess was quartered, and where we kept her safe from a Military Government which would have evicted her.

In the smoke-filled cacophonic cafés of St Pauli we were immediately recognized as British soldiers. With an occasional drunken

---

* Your love, my love / They are the same to me / Each man has only one heart.

exception no one abused us or even made us unwelcome. Discharged officers of the Kriegsmarine or the Luftwaffe, ageless in heavy coats stripped of insignia, were anxious to talk to us. It was the humour of some to taunt us amiably, telling us that 'The hot sun of democracy will soon turn all Germans brown.' Those who doubted our grasp of current events in the past decade would explain, with nods and shrugs, what was meant by brown. But some older men, or greyer men, talked of omens, persistent sounds in the night sky, an attested vision of young Germans marching arm-in-arm across Luneberg Heath. Much of this was the maudlin result of the spirits we brought to the café, and the *angst* of the time, but some wished to interpret the omens and visions for us. Soon there would no longer be a need for military zones and the Allied occupation. The meaning of the young men marching with entwined arms was clear. Germany would be united again, one people, one government and one flag. Sometimes this was whispered with a nod of caution. Sometimes it was shouted boldly that it might be heard above the stamp of military boots, each keeping time with the singing of a red-haired, black-haired, yellow-haired girl who stood alone in the smoke, wrapped in cardigan, scarf and gloves.

> Unter der roten Lantern von St Pauli
> sang mir der Wind heut' zum Abschied ein Lied.
> Ay-ay . . . ay-ay . . . ay-ay . . .*

We did not believe in the visions or the prophecy. They were absurd, of course.

* Under the red lamp of St Pauli / the wind sang a farewell song for me today /
  Ay-ay . . . ay-ay . . . ay-ay . . .

May the Sixteenth

On this day in 1746 an advance brigade of Cumberland's victorious army – three battalions of Foot and six companies of kilted militia from the Campbell glens of Argyll – came here to the head of Loch Ness and pitched their weathered tents on the river-meadows below Borlum Brae. A week later, amid spiteful showers of rain, the Duke joined them with ten more battalions and three detachments from his regiments of Horse. This menacing column left Inverness with some reluctance, for the town's citizens had been eager to buy the loot which the soldiers gathered from the battlefield and from their oppressive raids upon neighbouring estates – plaids and laced waistcoats, hats, bonnets, blankets and jewellery, as well as bags of meal from the granary at Culloden House. The trade on the Rialto Bridge, said Michael Hughes, was nothing 'in comparison to the business that was done by our military merchants . . . And while our highland fair lasted, if a soldier was seen in the streets of Inverness the good wives and lassies would certainly run after him to buy a plaid. As we sold them very good pennyworths we had customers in plenty.'

At the same time, to stiffen the soldiers' discipline and concentrate their minds for the long march here to the heart of the Highlands, thirty of their comrades were executed, found guilty of desertion during the campaign. But for a card, looped about his neck and bearing his name, each man hung naked upon the gibbet, his clothing now the property of the hangman.

No other army invading these remote and beautiful mountains had been so powerful, so arrogantly proud of itself and so intent on remorseless punishment. Twelve days before its victory at Culloden, its royal commander had made his purpose clear to his father's first minister. 'Don't imagine,' he told the Duke of Newcastle, 'that threatening military execution and many other such things are pleasing to me, but nothing will go down without it in this part of the world.' Three weeks later, flushed with triumph and the flattery of his sycophantic staff, the young man thanked God for making him the instrument of victory, but if every Jacobite had been killed in the battle, he said, such was the nature of the soil in Scotland that the seed of rebellion could easily sprout again. 'All the good that we have done has been a little blood-letting which has only weakened the madness, but not at all cured it.'

Such language from punitive commanders, conceived in contempt and delighting in the exercise of murderous hate, is depressingly constant in history. Ordering the winter campaign of 1868 against the Cheyenne Indians, General Phil Sheridan told an enthusiastic Colonel Custer how to deal with a people he customarily described as savage butchers and cruel marauders. 'Destroy their villages and ponies, kill or hang all warriors and bring back all women and children.' When Custer's troopers returned from their indiscriminate slaughter of Black Kettle's people by the ford of the Washita, some of them carrying the scalps of Indians they had killed, General Sheridan publicly complimented their Colonel upon his gallantry. In Africa, during the same period of imperial chivalry, the inept Governor of Cape Colony urged his superiors towards the military humiliation of the Zulu king Cetewayo, declaring that the renowned bravery of his terrible impis was 'the courage of drunkards and wild beasts, infuriated and trained to destruction, and once cowed they will not rally'.

There can be little doubt that many of Cumberland's officers and men believed the Highlanders to be savage beasts and therefore, in that harsh summer of reprisal, they could be savagely treated without offence to a Christian conscience. The Duke now had the approval of the King, his father, said Newcastle, 'his authority to do whatever is necessary . . . no general rule can be given'. This was confirmation of a common wish. The people of the Highlands, said a captain of Foot, writing in his tent by the dark water of Loch Ness, 'are deservedly in a most deplorable way, and must perish either by sword or famine, a just reward for traitors'. In London the civilized aphorist, Lord Chesterfield, advised Newcastle to starve Scotland, place a price upon the heads of Highland chiefs, 'and let the Duke put all to the fire and sword'. There were, of course, humane if ineffectual voices against this thirst for redemptive blood, but in the mountains the use of terror was accepted as a practical philosophy by the redcoat patrols who harried the glens for fifty miles about the Army's encampment, 'burning of houses, driving away cattle, and shooting vagrants'. Michael Hughes and his

73

comrades in the 20th 'did great execution amongst those who were still in arms, obstinately refusing to submit and accept of pardon'. He had a soldier's respect for some of those vagrants who would not kneel or wear a blindfold when they were shot, but his *Narrative* says nothing of the worst atrocity for which his regiment was remembered in the folk-history of Knoidart. The 20th had a new commander now, Lord George Sackville, a short-tempered dandy much in pain from wounds received at Fontenoy twelve months before. He was proud of the shot-holes in the scarlet coat he wore that day, and sometimes wore now in challenging pride. Perhaps his men admired his arrogant courage and his wound-shrunken leg, and when he wanted revenge for the theft of his baggage by marauding MacDonells they obligingly gave it to him at the next township. The women were first raped, it was said, and then held to watch the bayonetting of their men. In what I can recall from the writings left by the officers and men of this bloody army, there is no expression of compassion for the vanquished and no mercy for the terrorized. None was shown, I think, except by the patrolling clansmen of the Campbell militia – which should be remembered by those who like to perpetuate an absurd and theatrical antipathy towards that name.

The suffering experienced during the Rebellion, and the dragonnade which followed its defeat, was diligently recorded then and later by the Episcopalian clergyman Robert Forbes, later Bishop of Ross and Cromarty. He filled ten manuscript volumes with accounts written by those involved in the great event, all patiently gathered, subjected to clarification where needed, and recorded with little editorial comment. He called this remarkable work *The Lyon in Mourning or, A Collection (as exactly made as the Iniquity of the Times would permit) of Speeches, Letters, Journals, &c. relative to the Affairs, but more particularly the Dangers & Distresses of / / /.* The broken sentence ends with those sloping strokes, but their meaning was implicit and was added when the manuscripts were fully published – ... *Prince Charles Edward Stuart*. Forbes was a Jacobite, of course, and was on his way to join the Rebellion, almost before it was begun, when he was arrested and imprisoned for ten months. The *Lyon* is thus partisan in sympathy, but not therefore in purpose. Declaring his love of truth, 'let who will be either justified or condemned by it', Forbes was willing to record any act of humanity shown by the victors. If there are not many such incidents in his book the fault is not his.

Nonetheless, the *Lyon* is viewed with hesitant caution by academics who distrust its great weight of subjective evidence, and may perhaps be more unnerved by their own unexpected emotions than by the narratives which arouse them.

The original ten volumes of the *Lyon* contained more than three thousand manuscript folios. They were bound in black leather and the title-page of each volume was edged with the same mourning colour. Inside the boards of some were relics of the Prince and his disastrous visit – blue velvet and buckled silk from his garter, a scrap of the gown he wore in his fugitive role as Betty Burke, pieces from his tartan waistcoat, red velvet from the basket-hilt of his broadsword, and wood from the eight-oared boat that took him by moonlight and storm-blow to Benbecula in the Outer Hebrides. Most of these small items, sad detritus of high hopes and sullen despair, were rotted or lost when the complete text of the *Lyon* was published by the Scottish History Society in 1895, one hundred and twenty years after the death of Robert Forbes. My first acquaintance with it was in the last year of my schooldays when my thoughts and my imagination were idling in that deceiving doorway between dreams and reality. I read it in the British Museum beneath the awesome dome of the Library. I had early abandoned the bold reason I gave when applying for a reader's ticket – a proposed biography of Titus Oates – and I do not think I took out another book during that first year, going infrequently but eagerly from Hammersmith to Bloomsbury to read more pages of the *Lyon* and make copious notes long since lost. I remember endless afternoons of cool green light, the scratch of pens, footsteps moving softly, an occasional cough, or a yawn like a suppressed cry of pain far across the Reading Room, crusted ink-wells sunk in the brown wood before me, and the blue covers of the *Lyon* opening upon a terrible agony.

It was a coincidence, of course, but it could now seem providential that in this same year my parents bought a copy of *The First World War – a Photographic History*.* The book was handed to me on a Saturday evening, when my weekend homework was concluded and thrust at last into my satchel. I was given no explanation for the gift, then or later, and no encouragement to read it. They were perhaps exorcizing some of their haunting grief, and wished

* It was indeed so described as the *First*, six years before the beginning of the Second. In those inter-bellum years it was more often called The Great War or The World War.

me to know the obscene price paid by their generation for the eternal peace that was to be enjoyed by mine. This may have been Lord Beaverbrook's motive in publishing the book, a prescient argument in support of his later insistence that there could be no *Second* World War, even when German divisions were turned towards the Vistula. Now, at the close of this murderous century, we have become accustomed to the photographic face of war, and familiarity with the image weakens a necessary hatred of the reality. Yet I still remember the youthful shock of disbelief when I opened that book on the kitchen table, a numbing sadness on seeing the blurred figures of so many dead laid side by side, row upon row and awaiting burial. I was angered by the caption in bold-face sans beneath this picture, and was too young to see its irony . . . *Name? Rank? Regiment? Number?* On the following page a fleshless skull in a German helmet slept upon a muddy parapet: . . . *Ich hatte einst eine schones Vaterland, es war ein Traum.** I do not know what deep effect these books had upon a mind already entrapped in melancholy by Henry Williamson's *The Flax of Dream,* but I do recall my shame in realizing that I was the miserable heritor of such men, that I would have neither the spirit nor the courage to endure the sufferings described in the *Lyon* or pictured in the Photographic History. I allowed this to become an inconsolable dread, and it was a long time before it released its hold upon my mind.

My decision to write about Culloden and its aftermath – made on impulse during an hour's visit to the battlefield in 1959 – may have been influenced by the *Lyon,* buried in my memory for twenty-six years. Certainly I returned to the book almost immediately, acquiring my own copy from an antiquarian bookseller in Edinburgh, Ian Grant, whose help and friendship I would later cherish. I read each volume again before attempting any other serious research, accepting my publisher's opinion that while the book might be worth writing I could not expect it to have more than a limited appeal and a less than satisfactory sale.

I came again to the Highlands as soon as I could, my first long visit since the mid-1930s. I was resolved that wherever possible I should see the mountains, the waters and the bleak moors where the events I wished to relate had occurred. I did not fully realize that clearance, sheep-walks, road-building and afforestation had

* 'Once I had a beautiful Fatherland . . . it was a dream.'

greatly changed the face of this magic land, but what I saw stirred my mind and my heart, and once I understood the chronology of change I was able to draw closer to the past. On or about the April anniversary of the battle I came here to the centre of the Great Glen, following the victors' line of march along General Wade's military road, by the lochside for much of the way and then climbing steeply from Foyers to the leaning grass on the high braes of Stratherrick. At the eponymous hump-back of Whitebridge I placed an open hand upon its arching stones and felt, I thought, the vibration of a battalion's march, breaking step and passing dry-shod over the wild water of the Fechlin. Such physical contact with the land soon became essential to any satisfying re-creation of its past.

Although little of the book had taken shape in my mind at this time I had already composed its opening words and they would remain unchanged. This is an obligatory practice with every book I write, and is not uncommon with other writers, I think. Until those first words take an uncompromising form I cannot continue with any confidence and resolution. They are a hand-hold, a storm-stay for the inevitably troubled and sometimes dispiriting course ahead. On this occasion they were written with sudden inspiration in Edinburgh, on the flap of a notebook in the timeless tranquillity of the reading-room at Register House. This building was so long in construction that it was derisively called the finest pigeon-house in Europe, since only the birds seemed to be making any use of its uncompleted rooms. But it is one of Robert Adam's greatest works, a magnificent filing-cabinet for the archives of his countrymen, who have since spoilt its noble prospect from the North Bridge with a monstrous hotel and an inappropriate equestrian statue of Wellington. I like working here more than in any other public record office, and it has constantly rewarded my affection. On that first day, as I read the Duke of Cumberland's daily instructions to his soldiers, I knew that my book must begin with the cold spring morning when the battalions were aroused for their westward advance to Culloden.

The drums did not beat Reveille. The Army was to march at five o'clock that morning, and so it was awoken in its tents by the long roll of the General Call to Arms.

As I came here to the head of Loch Ness, by the old military road on that long-ago day, I could not see the hills as the soldiers had

77

seen them, the lower braes glistening with relentless rain and the peaks hidden in a leaden mist. An April sun welcomed me, glowing in the fiery orange of deer-grass and dead bracken. But knowledge stirs the imagination, and I tried to share the march of that remorseless army, plodding head-thrust into the rain, hating the land and hating its people upon whom a terrible vengeance must fall. Most of the foot-soldiers can have seen little but the rain-blackened shoulders of the man to their front, the heavy red cloth further stained by the grease or tar of a sodden pigtail. Pausing on the loch-shore by Foyers, before taking the stiff rise to Stratherrick, I thought of their waiting halt at this point, at ease upon their arms and watching the Duke as he drank brandy at the door of The General's Hut. This solid house had been built more than a decade before to serve as George Wade's headquarters, and it survived well into the next century as an inn of varying quality. Samuel Johnson described it as 'a house of entertainment for passengers . . . not ill-stocked with provisions'. The rain may have lifted when the soldiers reached the high ground at Whitebridge, for here the wind can blow hard when it wishes, turning the mist into long grey folds, rolling in and out of the corries. Standing on the weathered arch of Wade's bridge and feeling the marching vibration of its stones, I can see the approaching platoons, every man beyond blame or honour now but soldiering on through eternity and evoking the memory of others I recorded only yesterday it seems, at dusk on a roadside beyond Venlo.

Infantry going up to the Maas. White faces as they lay by the roadside sweating, and tartan flashes on their sleeves; one reading a book as he rested. A book? I wish I knew its title. Infantry. Life-belts over their Bren pouches, and always the smallest man carrying the Piat or the Bren. I remember one, he stuck out his tongue at me as he passed, and even when his face was no longer distinguishable I knew he was still sticking out his tongue. He was pushing a little cream-coloured perambulator in which were stacked three rifles, a Piat and a loaf of bread.

The valley floor at the lochhead, where the advance brigade set up its lines, lies between two rivers that feed the deep water of the Great Glen. The Oich comes north-eastward from the loch of its name, and the Tarff from the south, white water in a steep gorge five miles in length. On the western wall of this wild hill-cleft

Wade's roadmen built another of their remarkable highways, fourteen years before the Rebellion and linking the Great Glen with Rannoch, Taymouth and the Stirling Plain. The peninsula of bottom-land created by the rivers is now covered by the little town of Fort Augustus. There are the tailored greens of a golf course where the yellow tents of a dozen battalions once stood. The water of Thomas Telford's noble canal runs beside and sometimes within the River Oich towards the great gates that release it into Loch Ness. Children now play where the Duke granted his men the pleasure of horse-racing, and vastly enjoyed the sight of eight camp-women competing for his prize of a fine holland smock, riding little galloways 'with their legs on each side of the horse like men'.

There was a defence-work upon this ground for eight hundred years. Strategic advantage was thus combined with the humiliation of a defeated people's spiritual faith, a tactic effectively exercised by Hernan Cortes, Phil Sheridan, Garnet Wolseley and almost any commander who saw himself as the instrument of imperial destiny. For this was holy soil, and the Gaels continued to use its old name until they were gone with the memory of it. It was first called Kilchumein in the seventh century – *Cill Chuimin*, the church of the pious monk Cummin, seventh Abbot of Iona, also known in another variant spelling as *Cumuine Ailbhe* or *Finn*, Cummin the Poor or Fair. What endears him to me is the claim that he was the author of the first book to be written in Scotland, or at least the first so known. That is not all. A writer who has been obliged to ask the Law to defend his copyright against theft must feel a warm sympathy for the Abbot Cummin. His simple narrative of Saint Columba's life was frankly plagiarized by his successor Adamnan, the eighth Abbot of Iona.

In the Middle Ages the iron rule of Norman-Scots built a fortress upon the holy spot, a keep of wood and earth, forty yards by thirty and protected by a moat ten feet wide. Thomas of Thirlestane, the King's tenant who was master here in the thirteenth century, is said to have destroyed the last of the MacWilliams, stubborn men who combined lawless behaviour with insolent claims to the throne of Scotland. The only survivor was an infant girl who was ultimately battered to death in the market-place of Forfar, far from the Great Glen. The English chroniclers of Lanercost Priory, more inclined to delight in the misfortunes of all Scots, were sufficiently moved by this event to declare it 'somewhat too cruel'.

During the Cromwellian occupation two companies of Thomas

Fitch's Regiment and a troop of Horse manned a garrison at the lochhead, protecting the vessels that came from Inverness with supplies for John Hill's command at Inverlochy. Its defence-works, built between the river-mouths and probably on the stump of Thirlestane's castle, were enlarged into a modern military fort by General Wade in the third decade of the eighteenth century. When it was completed – and with unconscious prescience – it was named Fort Augustus in honour of the King's third son, William Augustus, Duke of Cumberland, then aged eight. Although impressive in appearance, with sloping walls, a deep moat, and gun embrasures dominating the water and the glen, it did not long withstand its first serious assault. A month before Culloden it was attacked by a Jacobite force, some clansmen and three hundred Irishmen, mercenaries in the service of the French. These wild geese from the regiments of Dillon, Rooth, Bulkley and Clare took the fortress after a siege of two days, and pillaged its contents with a ferocity that astonished their own commander. After an unsuccessful attempt to repeat this triumph at Fort William, they marched up the Great Glen to join the Prince at Culloden.

The fort remained a military station for more than a century after the Rebellion. Johnson and Boswell dined here with its agreeable governor before going over the northern hills to Knoidart and the Isles. Twenty-five years later that lone and intrepid traveller, Sarah Murray, admired its white-painted walls and was thrilled by the thunder of her carriage wheels upon its drawbridge. But she was disappointed with the garrison, a few old Invalids with ancient firelocks whose morning exercises before the Governor's breakfast window were 'quite a burlesque of soldiery'. In 1867, when the garrison was reduced to a corporal's guard, the government sold the site for £5000 to the Catholic chief of the Frasers, once a wayward Jacobite clan. He gave it to the Benedictine Order, and what little is left of Wade's fort may be found in the north-west corner of an abbey subsequently built in imitation of Early English and Romanesque styles of beguiling incongruity.

There is nothing in the town to recall the old garrison, but in the Queen's Collection in London there is a fading water colour of Cumberland's great encampment. It was painted by his young secretary, Thomas Sandby, a topographer and draughtsman who lived beyond this exciting year of battle and bloody suppression to become the first President of Architecture to the Royal Academy, of which he was also a founder-member. All is seen in his pleasing sketch – the great trench of hills and untroubled water, the broken walls and roofless gables of the fort, the tented lines of the battalions laid out like toys in a Victorian nursery. In the left foreground there is the customary contrivance in such military scenes, giving perspective and scale to the whole. A group of gossiping officers watch the passage of a monstrous cannon across the front, a siege-piece too great to have been moved by its team of thin and jaded horses. By the south-west ravelin of the fort is the canvas, turf and wooden cottage which the Campbells built for Cumberland's arrival, cutting its pine and oak with their broadswords.

They made a pretty place for the Duke to reside in [said Michael Hughes] with handsome green walls. They built a fine hut with doors and glass windows, covered at the top with green sods and boughs so that His Royal Highness resembled a Shepherd's life more than that of a courtier.

The young commander was greatly pleased by it, and indeed by the whole country about the fort, declaring with unconscious irony that it was 'a diamond in the midst of hell'. It was here in his sylvan bower that he was brought the severed head of Roderick Mackenzie. This red-haired young man, the son of an Edinburgh jeweller, was said to resemble the Young Pretender, a fact which he selflessly exploited when he was surprised by a redcoat patrol in Glenmoriston. Resisting its challenge, he was shot, and died crying 'You have killed your Prince!' For a while at Fort Augustus it was believed that the head brought to the Duke was indeed that of Charles Edward. Alexander Macdonald of Kingsburgh, who was briefly a prisoner there, was asked if he would recognize the head of the Pretender. He said that he would, if it were on a body. And if it were not? In that case, he said, I will not pretend to know anything about it. He told this story a year later to a group of Stuart sympathizers in Leith, and added that if he had recognized the head he would 'not have made them a whit wiser'. The pickled relic went south in Cumberland's baggage to London where its royal provenance was disproved, but it is part of Jacobite legend that the young man's sacrifice gave the heather-prince enough respite from pursuit to ensure his eventual escape. And perhaps it did. A cairn and a teak cross mark Mackenzie's grave in Glenmoriston, as close to it as memory can be certain, not far from where the little river Doe comes musically down to the valley floor at Ceannacroc.

I first read this story sixty years ago in the *Lyon*. Bishop Forbes repeatedly and without much success asked his informants for a full account of the incident, 'a thing earnestly desired', he said. What little he did record inspired me to write a short story loosely based on it, the first I submitted and the first to be accepted for publication – in the *Boy's Own Paper* for the astounding fee of nine guineas. It was typed inexpertly and laboriously on a machine that was almost as old as the century. My parents hoped it would be worth the fifteen shillings they paid for it, but it did not survive my assault upon it, a disaster I concealed from them while the euphoria of my literary success lasted. Quite properly for my conceit, it was a long time before anything else I wrote was published.

On my visit to Fort Augustus in 1960 I spent some days dreaming, along the waterside in the shadow of the Abbey or sitting on the gate-arms of Telford's magnificent locks. Time was endless, later enabling me to fuse factual knowledge with an imaginative recall of the past.

Although the Rebels had used nineteen barrels of powder to demolish the fort and the barracks, it was found that there were still some rooms, cellars and stables that could be used as kitchens to prepare fitting dinners for the Ducal Shepherd and his staff. The curious soldiers, picking over the stones, found something else. In a well or cistern to the rear of the barracks were the bodies of nine soldiers, their white gaiters green with slime, and their red coats rotting. An officer, writing home to London of this discovery, said that 'they were drowned by the rebels after having been made prisoners; that the bodies were then floating, and that rebel prisoners brought in by Howard's that day were set down by the well to view their own cruelty.'

I cannot be sure that when I first read the officer's account, in the *Scots Magazine* for 1746, it touched a key of personal memory, but I was aware of it when I wrote that paragraph in the small room at Minster Lovell. Sixteen years before, in a sun-rich summer, I was in pursuit of the British Second Army, then moving rapidly towards the Belgian frontier. I travelled by truck, and briefly along a broken railway towards the fallen bridge at Rouen, riding an open flat-car with fifty other men, bronzed and half-naked, drunk with exhilaration during the daylight hours and with calvados in the cooling dusk. I had no clear idea of where I wished to go, where I might be allowed to go, only that I must find a unit that would accept me before it was realized that I was in Normandy without authorization, and that as far as Regimental Records knew I was still cleaning greasy pans in a mess-tent at Cooksbridge. The warmth of that remorseless sun can be recalled now and then by a summer's heat, and with it the scent of pitch melting between the timbers of the flat-car. When our lame and shell-shocked train moved at all it was slowly, through a benign landscape. In the yellow-white fields of wheat there were bold tricolours of cornflowers, daisies and poppies, defiant confidence in the liberation we were bringing. My emotions responded to this with tears, as they would again later when I lay beneath a lorry in Nijmegen, sheltering from sudden mortar-fire with a Dutch child beneath each arm. A moment before, they had greeted me with *their* national colour, a garland of orange marigolds into which I now pressed my face and wept with love and fear.

Half-crazed by the heat of the open flat-car, and unable to sleep, we ripped up some of its floorboards and burnt them, boiling brackish water to make tea from a foul mixture of dried milk and fly-speck leaves. We received no rations for sixty lingering hours, and a sun-blackened Highlander, naked except for his underpants, webbing belt and a red-hackled bonnet, yelled his fury at the sky, coupled with an unqualified approval of Joseph Stalin. Becalmed near Lisieux and its basilica of glistening pearl, we watched in disbelief as a convoy of German prisoners, shuffling down from the sound of guns, was served with white bread and hot M & V. Those of us who leapt from the train for our share in this bounty were driven away by Field Security Police, swinging their Stens like scythes.

I remember nothing that occurred after this. As if it were an episodic film, there is a jump-cut in my memory to a Reinforcement Holding Unit somewhere to the south of Abbeville. I came to it at night by a long, long Flanders road, a straight and taut marching-road that had served two thousand years of wasting wars. The RHU was on a hill-top, or perhaps only a gentle rise in the highway, a nineteenth-century house, a modest château of grey stone, its mansard roof of black slates crowned with wrought iron, and the shards of its broken windows reflecting the spasmodic glare of gunfire to the east. As I dropped from the truck, and looked up to this brooding silhouette, I was reminded of the Maupassant stories which had been obligatory study during my matriculation year. I was sure the old house must have been a Prussian headquarters during the occupation of 1870, with Uhlan horses and pennoned lances in the decayed stables where we now laid out our bedding. The thought was not inappropriate. Not long before I arrived, three days at the most, it had been hastily evacuated by the Germans, by the Waffen SS or the Gestapo it was said. It was now full of confused and truculent British soldiers, each hoping to escape from it as soon as possible or to devise a useless but seemingly essential duty which would keep him there until the War's end. I remember nothing of the officers who commanded this anarchic chaos, only a young padre who had been given the derisory post of Recreation Officer. He was ignored by all, but in the only unavoidable contact we had he made me the unit librarian, with a wistful assurance that books must soon arrive to give substance to the office. I abandoned the post and his unflagging enthusiasm two days later, joining a convoy moving into Belgium, pulling myself aboard the last truck and thus avoiding any question about my intentions.

That morning something monstrous had been discovered in the stable-yard of this unhappy building. Like the redcoat men at Kilchumein, 'picking over the stones' of the ruined fort, soldiers here took the wooden top from an old well. Its rim was crusted with blood, and in the deep, wet darkness below skin-white bodies moved in uneasy death. It was presumed that they were men, and perhaps women, of the French Resistance, but I was gone before any explanation was given. I took the horror with me. In time it slipped below the surface of my memory until its recall in the room at Minster Lovell.

Their brutal deaths had occurred suddenly in the panic of their captors, and were thus denied respect. The belief that a condemned man should be given time to compose his mind before surrendering his life, and to comfort those who must grieve for him, did not survive into this century. The noble and the gentle-born among the Jacobite prisoners in 1746 were encouraged to turn their execution into a theatrical performance and sometimes, as in the case of Simon Fraser of Lovat, to make it the subject of black humour. The commonalty whose lives were ended on the gallows at Carlisle, Penrith or Kennington died without histrionics, but were mostly allowed a proper time to prepare themselves. Two young friends, Jemmy Dawson and Thomas Chadwick of the Manchester Regiment, were condemned on the flimsiest evidence. Chadwick, a tallow-chandler from Stafford with a fine singing voice, was said to have played the church organ and sung 'The King shall have his own again!' when the Jacobite army passed through Lancaster. On the night before they were hanged on Kennington Common, they sat together with their fathers, weeping in a hand-clasped circle. 'Our time draws near,' said Chadwick at dawn, 'but I feel in good heart.' Robert Forbes disapproved of a ballad celebrating the death of Dawson, although he included it in the *Lyon*. It described the feelings of the young man's sweetheart as she watched his heart being torn from his breast. 'Not fact,' said the bishop, 'for Mr Dawson never saw her before she had come to glut herself with the bloody scene.' James Cockburn was a stocking-weaver from Glasgow. How he came to serve in the Jacobite army, perhaps under duress, and where he was taken prisoner, are both unknown. He survives in the simple nobility of a letter he wrote from the Tower of London.

> Dear Children – should it please God I be taken to Himself I leave you two of my stocking-frames. Let me entreat you to imitate your grandfather in his valuable talents of honesty and probity for this truth will always be found the best policy.

But to make preferential comparisons between the deaths of such men and the manner in which those poor victims died in the well to the south of Abbeville is obscene. Despite its respect for the grisly proprieties it allowed the men it condemned to death, society's reaction to the Rebellion was merciless and calculated. It was also stiffened by a Christian rectitude which, quite wrongly, we would perhaps despise as hypocrisy. In 1752, now commanding the men of the 20th in Scotland, Major James Wolfe believed himself morally and politically justified in his plan for the slaughter of Clan Macpherson. The first requirement, he told a friend, was to capture its chief, Ewen Macpherson of Cluny, who had been hiding in a cave since the Rebellion. A minor figure in Jacobite history, Cluny survives immortally in one of the most vivid chapters of *Kidnapped*, wherein Stevenson describes him 'seated by his rock chimney, watching a gillie about some cookery. He was mighty plainly habited, with a knitted nightcap drawn over his ears, and smoked a foul cutty pipe.' For all that, said Davy Balfour, he had the manners of a king. An invention, of course, for who knows for sure what Macpherson looked like, but it is a more agreeable picture than the villainous traitor whom Major Wolfe proposed to murder, with all his clansmen if necessary, and that by a callous and ignoble trick.

> I tried to take hold of that famous man with a very small detachment. I gave the sergeant orders in case he should succeed and was attacked by the clan with a view to rescue their chief *to kill him instantly, which I concluded would draw on the destruction of the detachment* and furnish me with sufficient pretext (without waiting for any instructions) to march into their country *ou j'aurais fait main basse, sans miséricorde*. Would you believe that I am so bloody?

No, I would not have believed it, not six decades and more ago when my admiration for James Wolfe was directed by Miss Campbell's firm prejudices. Sitting at a polished desk in a Sutherland schoolhouse, and under the influence of her didactic reverence, it was easy to admire that tortured invalid, his pinched face, cleft chin and over-long nose jutting beneath a black tricorne. That portrait, in our green-covered *History of Canada*, remains clear in my mind, recalling the acrid smell of chalk. Miss Campbell's interest made me her favourite board-monitor, with the duty and privilege of standing beside her, duster in hand, as she wrote. She used the round, cursive and characterless script once common among North Americans, and it was probably a disappointment to her that I never mastered it. I took my style from my father's handwriting, though I was never able to match the artistry of his Victorian loops and interwoven curls. It is not difficult to imagine myself standing by that schoolroom slate. It stretched from the window to the far wall, and at the end of lessons for the day I was obliged to clean it until it was without ghostly mark or lingering dust. I can see my hand passing over her writing, her maps with neat hatchments in coloured chalk, one sweep of the brush and its whispering return erasing the words 'James Wolfe, Conqueror of Canada, 1727–1759'. This happened once only, no doubt, but memory gives it a continuance, as if each week her hero's achievements required Miss Campbell's devoted acknowledgement and our dutiful 'Amen'. Below his name, his title and brief span of years, she wrote a list of martial triumphs, his own and those he had shared, among them 'Laffeldt, Louisbourg' and, most properly capitalized, 'QUEBEC – THE PLAINS OF ABRAHAM'. She did not include Culloden in this roll, and even now I would not guess at her reasons for the omission.

The favourite story of her hero was of course traditional, frequently and sometimes inaccurately told. A cloudy night and no moon as the British Army moved slowly up the Saint Lawrence River, oars muffled and scarcely any sound but a quiet voice reciting Gray's *Elegy* before the young general's barge set off. The challenge from a sentinel on the shore of Pointe St Michel, answered in French by a captain of Fraser's Highlanders. An unopposed landing and then a spectacular climb up the cliff to the Heights of Abraham, the lead taken – in Miss Campbell's proud narrative at least – 'by those brave Scotch Highland men'. She told this story when our summer-jaded spirits needed encouragement, and never more so, she thought, than on Dominion Day.

Although Miss Campbell had never been to Scotland she spoke of it with an intense pride. Undoubtedly it was in these childhood years that my interest in the country formed its first imaginative roots, if only because all that she told us about that far land of mist and mountain was in so great a contrast to the familiar world about us – the wide and treeless prairie, our clapboard township crouching close to the earth, sidewalk planking on stilts above the snow of winter and the black thaw of spring, the mournful whistle of my uncle's freight coming in from the west, the howl of a plaintive coyote at dusk, and the clang of the trolley-car on its rocking journey across the wild grass to Saskatoon. I owe much to that stern but conscientious woman, and even today I can clearly see her pale and lightly freckled face, her red hair drawn taut into a bun at the nape of her neck. She was the first of my teachers to encourage my interest in the drama of history, and if this was sometimes enforced by the black strap which hung by a pink tape on the back of the schoolroom door, I could bear her no lasting grudge. Remembrance of her faded as I grew older in another country and another age, and for a long time it was forgotten. It has returned since I began to write this book, and the clear memory of her voice, retelling the story of the Plains of Abraham, has reminded me of a small but bitter irony that I should have recognized thirty years ago when I was preparing my account of the Clearances, particularly the final eviction of the people of Knoidart.

This is the most remote, the loveliest of all the Rough Bounds, the mountain peninsulas and deep-blue sea-lochs that form the mainland littoral of the Sound of Sleat. Knoidart was once held by the MacDonells of Glengarry, a clan of wavering loyalties and constant courage, a reservoir of warriors for the dynastic quarrels of Scotland and lastly for the Highland regiments of an imperial Britain. Three gentlemen of the clan, kinsmen of its chief, were officers in Fraser's Highlanders, those 'brave Scotch Highland men' so affecting to Miss Campbell's suppressed romanticism. To complete their companies in the regiment they enlisted men from their own lands, and some of these surely survived to tell their grandchildren of the dawn scramble up the cliff from Pointe St Michel to the French-Canadian village at the top. In their old age those children could have seen the irony which escaped me when I wrote of their eviction from their homeland.

In 1853 the seventeenth MacDonell chief of Glengarry was a minor whose affairs were in the hands of a determined mother and pliant trustees. To realize some of the young man's meagre inheritance, and to finance his insane ambition to become a cattle-rancher in New Zealand, the last parcel of his ancestors' wide lands – the blue and beautiful mountains of Knoidart – was sold to a Lowland ironmaster and coal-owner who now wished to increase his fortune with mutton and wool. The four hundred men, women and children who were all that remained of the fifteen hundred who had once been Glengarry's clan-folk in Knoidart, were thus evicted and soon replaced with sheep. The little townships of Inverie, Sandaig, Doune and Airor were all cleared, the dry-stone walls of the cottages torn down, and the roof-trees burned. Those people who accepted Josephine MacDonell's offer of transport to the New World or Australasia were carried by boat from Loch Nevis and thence across the bronze waters of the Sound to an emigrant brig waiting in the lee of Isle Ornsay. Money for their reluctant passage had been supplied by the Highland and Islands Emigration Society with which Mrs MacDonell had made all arrangements before writs of eviction were served.

The lawyer and journalist Donald Ross, a passionate critic of Clearance, came to Knoidart later that year, taking a boat to the mouth of Loch Nevis because snow had closed the mountain tracks in the east. He heard the story of the eviction from those who had refused to leave, sixteen families who ran into the hills, hiding until the factor's men were gone. They were now living along the shore-line in great destitution and hopeless despair, sustaining life with dulse and shellfish. He reported each case as he heard it, describing the woman who fought so fiercely with her evictors that they had to strike her hands with their sticks to release her hold on the doorpost of her cottage. At the approach to each cave or hovel where the obstinate survivors were facing winter, he called the old Gaelic greeting, 'Hail, good-morning to all here!', and was answered with responsive courtesy, even by those whose makeshift homes had been destroyed four times by Josephine MacDonell's factors in an attempt to drive them out. Ross raged against the evictions in the *Northern Ensign*, appealing for food, clothing and justice, and recalling the shock he had felt when his boat turned into the mouth of Loch Nevis.

> As far as the eye could see, the face of the strath had its black spots, where the houses of the crofters were either levelled or burnt, the blackened rafters lying scattered over the grass, the couple-trees cut through the middle and thrown far away, the walls broken down, the thatch and cabers mixed together, the voice of man was gone.

By the summer of the following year, the remaining people were driven out by hunger and despair, and by officers who could no longer be resisted. Those who had sailed on the emigrant ship, and had not died of cholera or typhus during the ocean passage, were now settled on the other side of the world, the pain of their home-sickness deadened by the harsh labour of a new life. The name of the little brig that took them away from Isle Ornsay teased at the edge of my mind when I was writing *The Highland Clearances*. The response came tardily not long since, with my thoughts of Miss Campbell. I remember her profile in dusty sunlight, her voice clear and emphatic as she turned now and then to complete her map of the great engagement on the Plains of Abraham. I saw the chalk move from the crooked ascent of the Heights to draw a neat representation of a village and a *fleur de lys* to identify it as a French outpost. From here had come the sentinels so easily deceived by the Highland captain, and here the first shots of the battle were fired. She wrote its name in small blue capitals and pronounced it in three distinct syllables – SILLERY.

Some of the older men cleared from Knoidart, approaching the emigrant ship and seeing that same word *Sillery* below her stern windows, may have remembered it from their grandfathers' tales. What they felt, I could not guess, but I hope it gave the thought of their exile some reassurance rather than bitterness.

May the Eighteenth

Mid-stream now across the Sound of Sleat to Armadale, and the mouth of Loch Nevis is on the starboard quarter of the ferry. Beyond the curving wake of the ship, this is one of the most magnificent sights in the Western Highlands, particularly towards dusk on a spring day. Darkening hills form a steep channel for the silver water, hooded peaks rising to the rock of Sgurr na Ciche, distant but not diminished beyond the hidden lochhead, the helmet of a king above the shelter of his shield-wall. Yesterday, from first light until dark, remorseless rain beat upon the road from the Great Glen to Mallaig, and the white-sand shores of Arisaig were grey, soiled by a dragging mist. Today the sun has blessed the noble hills of Knoidart. Storm-clouds may be thickening above Loch Hourn to the north-east, but against their deep and dramatic blue the last golden daylight on the braes of Nevis can lift the most dispirited heart.

Of these two sea-lochs, Nevis and Hourn, I have a greater affection for the first. Two centuries and more ago, Thomas Pennant was told that its name meant Lake of Heaven, an inaccurate translation, perhaps, yet closer to the truth than a scholar's notion that it may derive from the Gaelic *ni-mhaise*, without beauty. Pennant also translated Loch Hourn as the Lake of Hell, making two of a pair no doubt, but on a red-sky evening of smoking cloud, seen on high from the Glengarry road, it is infernal enough for those who first named it to have likened it to a furnace. There is no road to Loch Nevis-head. Rough tracks through the mountains are its only entrance and exit by land, old droving-trails and raiding-paths that went by Dessary and Loch Arkaig to the Great Glen and the garrisons at Inverlochy and Kilchumein. Even Cumberland's relentless patrols did not penetrate this far. The harrying of Nevis-side was done by landing-parties from warships in the Sound, one of which was aptly named *Terror*.

The sea-lochs of the Rough Bounds and all the western coast

were once rich in herring, schools so bountiful that in the eighteenth century Dutch fleets harvested great numbers by superior drift-nets, each vessel with sails furled, head to the wind and moving with the tide. On the narrows of Loch Carron the traveller John Knox was astonished by the fish that *tumbled* before the bow of the ferry, sometimes leaping from the water for a yard or more. This extraordinary sight was not enough for his companions. They amused themselves by shooting the herring as it flew above the water.

From its beginning, at least three centuries since, fish and the men who fish were always the principal reason for the existence of that small, squalid and lively township of Mallaig, clinging to the eyebrow of the Morar peninsula. Ninety years ago, the West High-land Railway finally drove its iron track towards Loch Nevis, through the narrow defiles of the Bounds and sometimes carving granite or metamorphic rock as if it were clay. The terminus of this brave little line was Mallaig and a proud station that has long since lost its original dignity. It was built a few yards only from the spot where the fugitive Charles Edward came ashore from Skye on an early morning in July, sick with dysentery but within the caring protection of The Mackinnon and boatmen of his clan. Once the line was completed, Mallaig became a flourishing ferry-point for the long stride across the Sound of Sleat, and the first passenger train to the south carried travellers from the Long Isle in the Outer Hebrides. During the town's richest years, fish-trains left its har-bour a dozen times a day. The air was thick with smoke, steam and the smell of a kippering factory. Oil-yellow fish-boxes were piled in battlements and castellated towers along the quay-side line, encircled by black-back gulls, those coasting scavengers so beloved a century earlier by the aquatint master William Daniell. Mallaig's great days still lingered when I first saw it more than fifty years ago, stepping from the Fort William train and wishing I had money to spare for the ferry to Skye. Its decline began when the great herring-schools abandoned the sea-lochs, but it has retained some of its old character. It is still Mallaig of the fish but it is also Mallaig of the ferry, of the tourist and the heedless car. It is a water-gate to the blue saw-teeth of the Cuillins, to the small islands of the Inner Hebrides, riding at anchor on a summer sea. And it still smells. Most properly, it still smells of sea-water, seaweed and sea-fish.

In the stern of the ferry this late afternoon, with an Ordnance map snapping at the wind, I look back at Loch Nevis. I know from the map that it is shaped like an arm bent at the elbow, and that what I see from the ferry and could mistake for the lochhead is only the green bay of Inverie, below its muscular shoulder. The rest of it thrusts south and east into the mountains, its fist striking at the great head of Sgurr na Ciche. I was wrong to suggest that all who look at Nevis from the sea can have their heart and spirits lifted. The evicted people of Knoidart, coming down the Sound in the *Sillery*, would have seen the last of their glen at this point. If they sailed at night and saw nothing, the darkness must have deepened their despair. But if they left on a morning tide when the sun's light touched the fire-black ruins along the loch-shore at Airor, Doune, Sandaig and Inverie, that pain would have been greater still.

The *Sillery* was one of twenty-nine emigrant ships which left for North America in the autumn of 1853. Conditions aboard them all were probably no better than those described by a *Times* writer in the following year, although Parliament had passed three Acts to improve them and was now considering a fourth.

> The emigrant is shewn a berth, a shelf of coarse pinewood in a noisome dungeon, airless and lightless, in which several hundred persons of both sexes and all ages are stowed away, on shelves two feet one inch above each other, three feet wide and six feet long, still reeking from the ineradicable stench left by the emigrants on the last voyage . . . Still he believes that the plank is his own and only finds when the anchor is up that he must share his six feet three with a bedfellow.

Compared to this, my parents, my sister and myself travelled to Canada in luxury after the Great War, although we shared a cramped, eight-berth cabin with four strangers, deep down on the water-line of the SS *Montcalm*. Almost all I remember of the voyage is an early morning of heavy weather, a child's eyes opening upon the porthole as it dipped into a green sea. I was too young to be aware of my parents' sadness. They were proud of England and were not leaving it by free choice. They were not driven out by eviction and cruel landlords but by poverty, unemployment and the harsh disillusion that followed the Great War. When my father left the Navy, two months after the Armistice, he received a gratuity of £100 and £20 in prize money. It was immediately placed in the

Post Office Savings Bank, and almost all of it was subsequently expended on the Atlantic passage, the long days of a railroad journey to the Saskatchewan prairie, and the first month's rent of a two-roomed shack in the township of Sutherland. Until the decision to emigrate was reluctantly taken, my father found some employment as a casual labourer and, more steadily, as a porter for a provision merchant by Smithfield Market. He worked from seven in the morning until six or later at night, sixty to seventy hours a week, and much more during the last days of the month. For this he received twenty-six shillings a week. Their rent was eight shillings and sixpence, but my mother added to their income by knitting crochet-work for infants' clothes, at one shilling and sixpence a dress, by which she earned another six shillings. My father was retained on the Fleet Reserve after demobilization, receiving three shillings and sixpence a week, and this was used to buy clothes. His duties in the Market were simple but heavy, emptying horse-drawn vans that came from the docks, carrying provision loads of a hundredweight and more upon his back. Writing carefully in her exercise book sixty years later, my mother was able to remember this with remarkable restraint.

His poor hands used to get cut from nails sticking out. His coat would get torn. We used to buy second-hand coats etc. for work. He always looked tidy, with clean shirts, and always his tie on . . . One week in a month they worked late, until the last van from the docks, and Jack had to run all the way to Liverpool Street station from the Market to catch the 12.25, the last train to our home in Edmonton. Consequence was, we overslept one morning, and he couldn't catch the 6.20 train. When he got his money that week from Lovell & Christmas, he got sixpence docked for being more than fifteen minutes late.

I was so mad. I didn't tell him but I wrote to the Chairman of Lovells and told him how many hours my husband had worked and what time he got home, and was fined sixpence, and that's after four years protecting ships to bring food to Lovells. No firm would have been in business now if it hadn't been for the men who served. Well, he sent for Jack and told him of my letter and said it was unique, and asked Jack if he was in a union. Jack said no, the union men had been round but he didn't want to join. The boss said, you'd better join, and we will be a union firm. They still didn't pay overtime. I was glad I kept my crochet job.

Encouraged by letters from her sisters who had already gone to Canada, and despite warnings from her wiser brother, my mother was convinced that this young country would give us a more rewarding life. My father was less certain but was persuaded by her high-spirited confidence. Their hopes were dreams only. The Dominion, and more despairingly the prairie provinces, were already sliding into the great depression which would swallow most of North America before the end of the decade. The first words my uncle said to my mother were 'Whatever made you come here, Flo?' She remembered them, and would repeat them with a wry smile in later life, not with bitterness but in memory of a caring man. There was never more than manual labour for my father in Canada. He had been a sailor for most of his life, serving with courage during the Great War. Adaptable though seamen were, he had none of the skills needed by the great wheatlands that surrounded us, and there were more than enough immigrant boys from the Barnado homes for the cheap drudgery of the farms. The first work my father found, with my uncle's help, was in the engine-house of the rail-road, crouching in the bowels of the long, black locomotives, chipping corrosion from their boilers. He went from this choking work to labour with the road-gangs, plate-laying and maintaining the tracks on the prairie, raw-skinned in the heat of summer and more than once frost-bitten when he rode with the snow-plough along the path of a retreating blizzard. To supplement his meagre wage – he began with fifteen dollars a week – my mother sold magazine subscriptions during our first winter, knocking on doors, plunging through drifts of awesome snow. It was well known as work for the desperately poor and was regarded as charity-begging, even by those who compassionately placed orders for magazines they did not want. She earned fifty cents for each yearly subscription she obtained.

Some people were suspicious they wouldn't get the books, but one time I said I was Billy Wood's sister and I was just out from the Old Country and I lived on Ninth Street. Come in, said the woman, and she sat me in front of the kitchen stove and put my feet on it, and she was so excited. Yes, she'd have both books and what part of the Old Country? She gave me coffee and then said, Have you got a heater in your shack? I said, no. I'll give you one, she said, it's out on the prairie and I can't get rid of it. Tell your man to come and carry it, she said. I think it was two dollars I earned that day, and a heater. We put it near the front door, leaving room to open the door, and the pipes went across the room to the chimney, and what a blessing that was. It was nice to look at too. I don't know what we would have done without it.

My father never felt easy with such generosity. Perhaps he thought it implied his failure as a husband and a father. He would not blame anyone else for the misfortunes he shared with many others on the prairie, but he was not happy that my mother was obliged to work as well as keep house. In the spring of the following year he went south across the Saskatchewan border to Chicago, in the hope of finding better employment there. He was offered work but was told he must first apply for American citizenship. Unwilling to surrender his British identity, and hurt by the suggestion, he came back to Canada.

After some years of unequal struggle my parents decided to return to England, helped by the High Anglican vicar who had married them in Shoreditch, and who now offered them work as caretakers of his church-hall in Earls Court. I was thus suddenly and most miraculously transferred to a strange world. Coming ashore from the *Montcalm* at Liverpool, I was deafened by noise and bewildered by so many people, none of whom appeared to be smiling. In the train to London I sat with my face against the window, staring incredulously at a rain-wet land, so green and so many trees. I can still see the engine's white smoke beyond the glass, rising and falling in its steeplechase gallop across hedgerow and field. In London I was taken underground to a brown train, twisting like a snake as it came out of its hole, with clanging gates and warning voices between the carriages. The walk from the District Line station in Warwick Road to the church-hall seemed endless, each hard flagstone striking cruel blows at my feet as I dragged the bag I had declared myself strong enough to carry. In a terraced crescent dominated by the neo-Gothic structure of Saint Cuthbert's Church and its less ambitious Hall, I was sure the red-brick houses were about to collapse upon me. I stopped several times to ease the weight of my small burden, and I was later told that I asked again and again if the dusty plane trees along the kerb were real.

Before we had our supper that evening, in the deep basement of the Hall, my sister and I were taken into the church for Evensong, to pray in thankfulness for our safe return to the Old Country. I thought it was the largest building I had ever seen, larger than the Berini family's tall clapboard in Sutherland, larger than the engine round-house and our three-storeyed school. Certainly, in my inaccurate judgement, it was as great as the turreted magnificence of Saskatoon's proud hotel, built on the river-bank like a Rhineland castle when the frontier was still a vibrant memory and the buggy and the box-wagon were the most common means of transport. The church was more modest than this, of course, but I was over-awed by its self-indulgent architecture and unnerved by its oppressive interior. The air was heavy with lingering incense, the smell of brass-polish and hot candle-wax. Beyond a great rood-screen of pale wood was the gleam of golden thread and white silk, the richness of stained glass above the High Altar. A red lamp burned for the presence of the Sacrament in the Lady Chapel, and about the walls, as I looked sideways from my bended head, I saw horrifying paintings of the Road to Calvary. The service was conducted in a nasal chant by the curate who had shown us the Hall that afternoon. His long fingers, which had rested upon my head for much of that time, were now lightly clasped before his laced surplice. They were orange-yellow with nicotine. He had been a pilot in the Royal Flying Corps, and only much later did I understand the connection between that and his enslaved addiction to Woodbine cigarettes.

That night, on the top floor of the Hall where there were two bedrooms for our use, I was unable to sleep. It was not only the trains immediately below that kept me awake. It was the thought of that implacable church and its obvious disgust for me, for all those sins I had yet to commit, for the undeserved absolution I might receive in Father Croom's confessional. I had learnt this day that God was not the old gentleman to whom hymns were sung in Sutherland's plain wooden church. He was not an unseen but friendly neighbour in whose service my mother baked pies for church socials and performed splendid comic roles in amateur theatricals. He was truly The *Lord* God, and, in a phrase that was still employed with effect, he was a cut above the class to which we belonged. That day, I think, the painter was loosed from its mooring and my faith began a slow drift into non-belief.

For a time, life in the Hall was a constant wonder to a mind still held in thrall by the prairie. In design it had been influenced more by William Morris than by the medieval masons whose work was caricatured in the bricks and stones of Saint Cuthbert's Church, to which it was physically joined. It contained a large auditorium with a professional stage for dramatic societies. It was used by cat clubs and the breeders of pedigree rabbits for their annual shows. Its stout flooring was also excellent for noisy Caledonian Balls on Scotland's euphoric anniversaries. Watching the dancers from the bay of a minstrel gallery above, I heard the pipes and saw tartan in swirling motion for the first time, and was curiously aware of being both an outsider and yet at one with it all. I suppose the influence of Miss Campbell's fierce pride of race had something to do with that.

On weekdays the main hall and the disused gymnasium beneath it were let to a school of mime and dancing, ancient Greek in character or invention and much inspired by Isadora Duncan. My mother's catering supplied homely fare for its hungry pupils. When I came home from school her kitchen, next to the gymnasium, was often full of robust young dryads in pastel gossamer, all talking at once in bird-song and unaware that the candour of their classical costumes filled an awakening mind with disturbing melancholy. Whether my mother sensed this or not I cannot say, but she would sometimes send me away to a room on the second floor 'to sit and watch, remember, so be quiet'. Locked for most of the week, the room was used on two afternoons by elderly ladies of the parish who came to maintain or make the rich vestments worn by Father Croom, his curate Father Langton, and any visiting clergyman. Chasuble, stole, amice and maniple, rochet and cope, all were explained to me by the gossiping women as they plucked at gold thread and silken cloth, handling rich stones with less care than I guarded my bag of glass alleys and clay marbles on the playground of St Matthias' School. On late afternoons, the sun from the lancet windows consumed the vestments in unnatural fire.

Victorian England endured in this quiet garden crescent. Old men and women, whom I would now regard as my enviable juniors in age, maintained the virtues, the truths, the prejudices and practices of their earlier years, all within the security of their High Anglican faith. I was adopted by some of them – that is to say I was regularly invited to take afternoon tea with them, for no reason that I could understand, although I went dutifully when told, and sometimes with pleasure. I did not realize that they were bereaved, lonely, and perhaps frightened by a changing and inhospitable world, and that I was a receptive audience for their nostalgia, an innocent who could marvel at their lost world. If it was thought necessary to explain my presence to another visitor, I was 'the caretaker's boy from the Hall, you know'. Only one of these sad, bigoted but kindly people can I now remember with any clarity, although her name is momentarily forgotten. She was fragile but erect in posture, and held a silver-topped malacca cane even when seated. Beneath her grey hair her face was heavily powdered, its startling whiteness relieved by a faint blush on each cheek-bone. She was always dressed in mourning-black from her shoulders to her ankles, the cloth falling in graceful, complimentary folds, its solemnity sometimes softened by a twist of mauve chiffon at the throat. More often than not she wore a large brooch of jet, at the centre of which was a small brown photograph of a man's head. The mantelpiece of her room, the white shelves and the piano that was never played, were covered with silver picture-frames, rectangular, circular and heart-shaped. Although they must have contained the likeness of many people in her life, it seems to me in recollection that there was but one in all of them, the man in the brooch. His largest portrait was in a central position on the piano, portly and middle-aged and wearing an officer's belted jacket, cavalry breeches and boots. His wide-brimmed Yeomanry hat, a white puggaree about the crown, was effectively displayed on a bamboo chair beside him. The man she mourned had not died in the Great War like so many in the other houses where I was invited to tea, but on the veldt in South Africa. She must have spoken of him often, for I was there to listen, but I can remember nothing.

Spending so much time with her and with others was perhaps unwise for an impressionable mind, but I cannot let myself believe it. I had come from Canada to a noisy, unheeding land and to a rough school where teachers and pupils were often less than tolerant of my knickerbockers and strange accent. I was perhaps no more understanding of them. Unable to answer when challenged to 'Say something in Canadian!', I lost my first fist-fight in the playground because – mindful of similar confrontations in Sutherland – I waited for my tormentor to place a chip upon his shoulder and invite me to knock it away before either of us could fairly strike a blow. The doors to those few houses in Philbeach Gardens took me from an inhospitable present to a more sympathetic if sometimes awesome past. It was often an immediate past remembered by surviving voices, and the uneasy murmur of Flanders' guns sometimes disturbed the tranquillity of the afternoon.

A discovery in the Hall transported me at once to a more distant time and a wider experience of thought and emotion. At the end of the gymnasium was another locked door which I persuaded my father to open. The room beyond was dusty and cobwebbed, ill-lit by a high barred window at pavement level. It was largely filled with ageing equipment, dumb-bells and weights, ropes, netting, boxing-gloves, a torn vaulting-horse and broken parallel bars, nothing of lasting interest to me. But in cardboard boxes, on sagging shelves and in piles along the wall, were the remains of what had once been – before the Great War and before the beginning of the century – Saint Cuthbert's Parish Lending Library.

It was a wondrous and providential discovery, although it was some years before I realized how fortunate I was. Most of the books had come from the estates of dead parishioners, or from others who found them an encumbrance in genteel poverty, and they were thus catholic in range and quality. I am now able to say that in my adolescence I studied, page by enthralling page, an original catalogue of the Great Exhibition of 1851. I read the Sherlock Holmes stories in their first published form, string-bound copies of the *Strand Magazine* beginning in 1890. These, I remember, were tied in a bundle with the first volume of *Punch*, 1841. In an old shoe-box I found some of the green-covered, fortnightly parts of *Pickwick* which appeared in 1837. These were my first reading of Dickens, although the story of Scrooge and his admonitory visions was told every Christmas by my mother. There was a complete if mildewed collection of Dumas' Musketeer novels, including *Son of Porthos*, which was not his work. There were volumes of Scott in an early Waverley edition, two columns to a page and difficult to read. There were Defoe, Fielding and Thackeray, Harrison Ainsworth and James Grant, Charles Lever, Stevenson, Henty, W. H. G. Kingston and Stanley Weyman. There were large volumes of the *Illustrated London News* covering each year of the Boer War, full of graphic and absurd work by talented war artists. There were some volumes of Napier's *History of the War in the Peninsula* which I soon abandoned, numbed by the dry record of repetitive bloodshed and heroism. There were innumerable volumes on Victoria's little wars, and also several annuals of the *Boy's Own Paper* and *Chums*, which had unconsciously prepared young men's minds for the willing surrender of their lives in the first two years of the Great War. In this bouillabaisse of entertainment and information, enriching my fifteenth and sixteenth years, there were also more recondite books like Melville's *Typee* and volume one of the first edition of Ruskin's *Stones of Venice*, which opened gaps in my slender knowledge rather than closed them. If this extraordinary collection of books and magazines survived another decade, which it could have done, it was undoubtedly lost when a German bomb demolished the northern end of the Hall.

I returned each book to the room when it was finished or abandoned. Some, however, I kept beside my bed for as long as my parents allowed. My father frequently complained that I always had my 'head in a book', and although in later years, my mother told me, he regretted this criticism, within the context of our lives it was perhaps justified. One of the books I retained was Richard Jefferies' *Bevis*, which I have not read since. It disturbed me, sadly, and eventually led me to the early novels of his admirer Henry Williamson. This was a long and possibly excessive attachment in my late adolescence, for Williamson's work was a passionate threnody for the loss of his generation in the Great War.

My youth and early manhood were overshadowed and sometimes obsessed by the thought of war – wars past and the war to come. The memory of the Great War dominated the two decades that followed it, darkening thought and hope even when it was ignored, although it did not become an entertainment cult like its successor, an unending source of comic-book folk-lore. There was also a deep uncertainty, nagging my mind. What I knew of that obscene struggle – vividly illustrated in the *Photographic History* and in the stunning agony of soldiers' prose and verse – was so terrible that I believed it could have been endured by exceptional men only. The omnipresent survivors of its horror and betrayal – a gassed and yellow-skinned uncle gently coughing over his watch-repairing, blue-coated and maimed figures seen across the green parks of military hospitals in the Home Counties, kerbside buskers with greasy ribbons and tarnished medals – all these must be superior men from a now broken mould. When my father dressed himself in his navy-blue Sunday suit, pinned on his decorations and went to stand with others at the Cenotaph, he was separated from me by a deep gulf of time, character and experience, or so it seemed. On the eleventh hour of the eleventh day of the eleventh month at that minor public school to which a scholarship took me, we stood in silence with the rest of the nation and then listened to a reading of the long roll of pupils killed, died or missing. My emotional reaction to a past and future war consequently manifested itself in some execrable verse and the self-pitying prose of a daily journal. Graver than this unhealthy introspection were dark dreams from which I awoke abruptly, shouting strange words and names, a terror ended by cold wakefulness and the white figure of a disturbed parent in the doorway.

I can still believe that my father's generation was extraordinary, but mine has shared much with it, as our fortunate children have not with us. We did not have the sturdy confidence of our fathers, nor their spiritual strength and blessed naivety, and for the most part our apocalyptic experience of war when it came was less terrible. But we too were ordinary human beings obliged to accept an extraordinary burden upon spirit and body. Perhaps that was what the one-armed Lancashire Fusilier believed as he walked along our motionless ranks at Kinmel Park.

When war became inevitable after Munich, and in the belief that it would repeat the slaughter of the Great War, I could see no reason to hope that I would survive it. I faced this with an absurd equanimity, I think, and 3 September 1939 was an odd day of calm resignation after the brief alarm of the first and false air-raid alert. My wife and I walked in Kensington Gardens under the early autumn leaves with the usual idlers of a Sunday afternoon in London, and we spent the evening with a younger and noisier group outside the Victoria and Albert Museum, filling sandbags on the site where Bernard Shaw and others had hoped to build a National Theatre.

My part in the war was modest, often ineffectual and, apart from occasional periods during bombing raids and the anti-aircraft defence of Britain, it was without danger and fear until its last year. Remembrance of it comes in response to a word, a mood, the casual recall of a forgotten name, and the reading of disturbing letters and diary notes. The last weeks of that final year, the invasion and surrender of Germany, were cathartic. The troop in which I served was by its nature engaged in action at night but sought its employment during the day, and although we seemed to have no need of it we must have slept, for I remember times of great exhaustion and shattered emotions. In our tactical role – conceived by Montgomery, it was said, and certainly praised by him in his report of the campaign – we were literally torch-bearers for infantry, armour and engineers. We moved almost daily after our dawn stand-to, travelling in chaotic convoy along the division's forward area, the Troop Commander calling at brigade or battalion headquarters like a commercial traveller, offering our artificial moonlight for any proposed activity that night, from a fighting patrol to an assault in strength. We were not always welcome, and sometimes when we off-loaded our projectors in the line, the units we had come to serve would move hastily away from the source of our insane illumination.

Exposing our diffused beams on low clouds above the timbered darkness of the Hochwald in the first week of March, we were often deployed too late for proper entrenchment, and our sites near Gennep were troubled by searching mortars, the thudding explosions about us curiously muted by the soft earth. We lay beneath the three-tonner as the fire of heavy machine-guns from across the River Niers cut through the lower branches of the trees and scattered twigs like snow-flakes in the white glare of our ninety-centimetre. We felt naked and foolish and often frightened in the great bowl of light we created. We saw nothing beyond it. Canadian infantrymen passing along its perimeter were colourless figures in a moving frieze, white faces turned below helmets hummocked with field-dressings. Their rifles were sometimes reversed and protected from the night rain beneath their ground-sheets, just as Cumberland's men, marching that morning from Nairn, covered the pans of their muskets with the skirts of their red coats. Some cursed us for the treacherous light they thought we made. Others shouted in bitter good-humour, mocking an officious air-raid warden, 'Put that light out, you bastards!' Some walked on without looking at us, responding to our call of good luck by lifting two fingers in fraternal derision.

March 7. Moved to the other side of the Hochwald into the last green valley before the Rhine. This is full of artillery, 25-pounders, 5.5's, 4.2's, 3.7's, Bofors and rocket guns, and in the misty dusk to-night they stab the shadows with flame. A German counter-battery pounds a small hill in the valley down which a road runs, thick with traffic. We came that way and had an uncomfortable time under fire. From here we can watch the shells bursting – white, black and amethystine clouds down the valley. Our heads ache with the noise, and now the stuttering of a dozen Vickers.

German trenches, houses, still have white flags fluttering from them. German soldiers lie doubled in their holes. Death came in horrible ways. It is most horrible when it takes away a man's face.

One half of the detachment is digging slit-trenches. The other half is laughing at them.

I sometimes forget how much we laughed. Laughter is a reassuring friend to a soldier's faltering spirits. Boredom and danger are best endured with mockery. There is no wit, only occasional brutish humour in the contemporary records of Culloden that I know, but I cannot believe that in each platoon of the advancing battalions there was not one keen mind and one sharp tongue to mock the silliness of a soldier's life. Grief and despair in defeat, the growth of suffocating legends, do make it difficult to believe the same might be said of the waiting clans, but it must have been true of them also.

Towards dusk on some of those confused days between the Maas and the Hochwald I rode in the back of the radio-truck with Frank, the wireless operator. He was a northerner, with a mordant sense of humour and an unwavering conviction that all organized society was controlled by deranged men whose minds had been unhinged by an incompetence so profound that it could easily pass for wisdom. The paradox, he said, was arrived at during his formative years in the service of local government. During one night of appalling and bloody errors, Troop HQ never reached the site where it should have deployed. It was caught in a convoy of mixed vehicles and walking men, feeling their demoralized way towards the front under occasional fire, through dark trees and along a broken road that was recognizable only by the white tapes that kept us from the mines. Rolling a cigarette with contemplative precision, his face momentarily illuminated by a shielded match, Frank decided that the proper way to respond to the noise and growing fear was to realize that it was only another field-exercise, at home in the hills where the Battery had trained, because that too, he said, had always been a shambles. We sat together elaborating this notion until the convoy was abruptly halted, its leading vehicles blown away by mines or mortar-fire. In the brief but unnatural silence that followed, Frank stood on the tailboard, grasped the frame of the canopy and shouted into the reddened darkness ahead, his voice outraged but still mocking in its W/T jargon. 'Sunray to Charlie Three. Sunray to Charlie Three. Correction. This is not an exercise. I say again for Christ's sake this is not an exercise!' Peacetime betrayed his free mind into mundane employment from which he seemed to have no wish to escape. He was a talented cartoonist and continued to send me sketches that became increasingly acerbic in comment. A cycling accident, I think, robbed him of a leg and later, not long before he died, he sent me a postcard upon which was a single sentence, stretching out a hand across the years. 'Don't bother to stop the world, I'll get off while it's going.'

The troop had entered Germany three days before that night in the Hochwald, at twelve minutes past noon on a Sunday, moving northward from the pontoon bridge at Gennep to join the Canadians. It was raining heavily and the German trenches across the Maas were full of water, the dead floating face down. At night the convoy was a shining serpent, twisting through the Reichswald where the Siegfried line was passed unrecognized, except for a triumphant string of Canadian Army underpants, pegged out in the rain. We came to the front before Kleve. Our beams gave moonlight for the artillery observers during the last bombardment of the town, and we watched their changing, rain-glistened colour above the flames and smoke. Three hundred bombers, it was said, and eleven hundred guns were being used to destroy the defences of Kleve, and when we entered the dust-cloud of its ruins we were halted by a German counter-battery, reducing what remained. At stand-down we slept, to be awoken as often before by the silence when the bombardment on both sides of the front was ended. Jimmy the cook brought us gun-fire at noon, and I drank the dixie of richly sweetened tea without tasting it.*

I did not know then that the Jacobite lieutenant-general, Lord George Murray, had lived in exile here at Kleve, denying himself the company of his children because he did not wish to jeopardize their future. He was a skilful soldier, and might have avoided the disaster of Culloden had his advice not been rejected by the head-strong Prince. In his pleasant but lonely house near Kleve he called himself Monsieur de Vallignie to avoid attention. To those in Scotland who might visit him – 'there is from Amsterdam to Cleves a coach twice a week' – he could write of the Rebellion with generosity as well as bitterness.

I wish you all happiness and contentment in the Land of Cakes, where I assure you my heart is; and though the pleasure of being there be debarred me, yet I promise you it gives me much satisfaction to know that some of my fellow-countrymen, who were engaged with us, have escaped the jaws of the voracious wolves; though I am

---

* *gun-fire*: strong, sweet tea drunk at reveille. The name and custom comes from British India, where native servants brought it to the soldiers' beds as the firing of a signal gun began a new day.

apt to believe it was more owing to their oversight than mercy. Be that as it will, I wish from the bottom of my heart more were in the same situation, and that I myself were the only sufferer, which would make me bear my own private loss without a grudge.

The house in which he spent much of his permanent exile may have lasted until this century, and survived the ground and air attack upon Kleve. If it did, I have no doubt it was thoroughly looted by the British, the Canadians or the Poles. On the edge of this once placid town I was able to be alone for the first time in so many months. It was dusk, and the air was moist from the day's rain. There were birds chattering, finches I think. I stood on the rim of a shallow lane and looked eastward over the valley of the Rhine to the sporadic fall of artillery shells across the river at Wesel, and southward to the distant glow of many fires in the Ruhr. The lane had been occupied by a mortar platoon and its signature was everywhere – empty tubes that had contained its bombs, yellowed canvas tapes, a bloody field-dressing, compo-ration tins and crushed cigarette packets, the scrap of a Canadian newspaper, torn letter-cards and excrement. Rats were busy in this debris. I threw stones to disperse them and sat down to begin a letter home. It was finished that night in the cellar of a ruined house, the owner of which had proofed it against poison gas. The electricity for its single light-bulb came from a power station still in German hands across the Rhine.

Two nights ago I watched the flame-throwers burning their way along a ridge on the other side of the valley. The buildings burst into great orange flowers and black smoke hung above the ridge at dawn. Memory of the time since the advance began is kaleidoscopic. Roadsides littered with cartridge-cases and mortar-boxes. A crucifix wreathed in signal-wire, rising from a Calvary of shell-cases. Strange graves, mass graves in the woodlands. The first book I picked up [in Kleve] was a wedding-copy of *Mein Kampf*, in a garden rutted by tank-tracks, close to a house that had been cut in two so neatly that furniture and pictures in the half still standing were apparently unaffected. A German girl stared at me impassively from an empty window as I stripped naked and washed myself from a rain-tub, the first real wash in ten days, and my socks came away from my feet in scales. Five nights of shell-fire and the only comment I could write in a pocket diary as I lay in a slit-trench with a grunting Don R, was *I don't like this*.

Michael Hughes, that steady volunteer of Bligh's Foot, did not write so self-consciously. From the tone of his *Narrative* – his own work, I am sure, and not cobbled by a literary ghost – it is clear that he wished his family to know that he and his comrades had done their duty when facing the 'terrible boasting Highlanders'. That duty was given divine approval by the brigade chaplains shortly after dawn at Nairn. As directed by the liturgy, from which the service was read, the psalm for the morning was the Seventy-ninth.

> O God, the heathen are come into thine inheritance: thy holy temple they have defiled, and made Jerusalem a heap of stones.
>
> The dead bodies of thy servants have they given to be meat unto the fowls of the air: and the flesh of thy saints unto the beasts of the land.

It was an age of godly wars – as all wars must seem to be, that the wastage of young lives may appear justified. I do not know where the brigade chaplains stood when the battalions formed their lines, but perhaps the savage words of the psalm would have strengthened their needful courage too. 'O let the vengeance of thy servants' blood that is shed be openly shewed upon the heathen in our sight.' Michael Hughes, Alexander Taylor of the Royal Scots, Enoch Bradshaw of Cobham's Horse, and other private men of Cumberland's army, had no doubt that the slaughter in which they were engaged was savage but necessary. In the second line, Hughes watched his front where the Royal Scots Fusiliers shuddered, steadied and then held the greater part of Clan Chattan's charge. Though it was dreadful, he said, to see the broadswords circling in the air after each stroke, it was equally so to watch the Fusilier officers cutting and lunging, sergeants thrusting the points of their spontoons into the throats of the Highlanders, and soldiers forcing their bayonets home to the socket. But it was still more terrible 'to hear the dying groans of either party'. He remembered Major-General Huske, who commanded the second line, yelling above the beating of drums, the firing and the screaming, warning the men of Bligh's that if the front line broke they should fire and reload as soon as possible, and 'if not, to make no delay but thrust our bayonets and make sure work'. John Huske was a soldiers' general, and like Henry Hawley he was both feared and admired. According to Bishop Forbes, these two generals drew up the orders for 'the slaying of the wounded on the field of battle etc.' An ex-provost of Inverness who called upon them at this time, interrupting their work with an appeal for clemency, was promptly kicked downstairs by a knightly staff-officer. It is unlikely that many soldiers thought the orders inhuman or excessive.

> This rebel host [said Hughes] had been most deeply in debt to the public for all the rapine, murder and cruelty, and since the time was come to pay off the score, the people were all glad to clear the reckoning, and heartily determined to give them receipt in full.

He was writing of the mood before the battle, but the dreadful receipt was taken again and again during the summer months that followed. I have been trying to recall, not with any certainty, my own feelings in an occupying army at the close of the War. We were citizen soldiers and we rejoiced in the defeat of an enemy who had aroused far greater hatred than any felt by Cumberland's professionals, and with stronger justification. Perhaps some of us were more self-righteous, but our opponent was not a dynastic Pretender but a terrible, unequalled threat to humanity. As we waited to cross the last barrier before peace, the Rhine so swift and wide, we were young and light-headed, overwhelmed by what we had done and what we were seeing of the enemy in defeat and despair.

> It is the evening hour when sounds seem sharper, the glow of a petrol-fire most vivid. In the ruins of a farm-house where American paratroopers – a day, or two days ago – slaughtered fifty Germans, the red face of Jimmy the Cook shines at us from the vaulted cellar. 'Any of you scouses gotta match?'
>
> You must know by now that I am in Germany. I have watched it being destroyed. I have not seen a German village or a German house untouched by this war. I have seen German towns so furiously beaten by shell-fire that all emotion is exhausted. The trees here are symbolic, broken, stripped of new leaf and branch, lacerated by splinters. Great craters beside roofless walls, and the dusty litter of scattered furniture, clothing and paper. So much paper. Livestock is killed, cooked and eaten as its owner watches us silently. Our vehicles are piled with looted bedding to give us some rare comfort in the short hours of sleep we may have. I suppose we are drunk with the madness of being here in Germany. Its people watch us apathetically, showing no anger and no resentment. Speak to them

C Troop Headquarters before the Rhine crossing. The author is third from the left in the top row, with Corporal Alec on his left.

and they are embarrassingly polite. They are not Germans, they say, but Poles, Alsatians, anything but Nazis. They hated the Nazis. Their fathers were Communists. We are sick of such talk.

I wrote more letters home in the same mood a few weeks after the surrender on Luneberg Heath. Throughout my soldiering I had been corresponding with an old friend and mentor, Alex Furst, who worked for a news magazine in London. Some of my more recent letters were shown to his editor, who now asked me to contribute something to his paper, a 'literary re-enactment' I think he described it, describing the life and emotions of a British soldier in occupied Germany. The invitation seemed bizarre, almost obscene, and for a while I ignored it. One day on Orderly Room duty at Troop HQ near Dusseldorf, I went with a corporal, my comrade Alec, to collect the bountiful issue of wine and spirits for our small officers' and warrant officers' mess -- one captain, one lieutenant, and one troop sergeant-major. We withheld three bottles of their champagne for ourselves and drank it in the Orderly Room that night. Pleasantly drunk we both wrote letters, Alec to England and home, and I to the editor.

We live in a country that has felt the breath of life stop in its throat. It is easier to say 'There is nothing, *alles kaput!*' than make any attempt to describe the expedients, the make-shifts and the time-killers that keep life in motion here. You cannot describe Cologne or Dusseldorf, Munster, Osnabruck, Wesel or Kleve. See these cities on one of the moonlit nights that are touching them with a grim beauty. Block after block of ruins, the green tentacles of weeds climbing over the stones, dividing roadways from pavements. And in the cellars below, in crude brick cottages built within the shells of great office buildings, some of the survivors now live. The light shines up from their homes at our feet.

At curfew, sirens wail over this sepulchral city of Dusseldorf, and the quick rustle of footsteps hastening home gives way to the heavy fall of ammunition boots, the whine of Army vehicles outside the 94 Club or the shattered Opera House. At curfew, the people go to ground beneath the ruins of a society that was to last a thousand years.

We are the only reality in this nightmare, the only people who will be warm and well-fed this winter, who have transport, comfort and homes. The Germans are a shiftless mass which we curse, deride and pity. Somehow they seem far, far away from the disciplined threat that faced us in Holland. Their wish for friendship seems genuine, their abnegation pathetic. *Kamerad, you have cigarettes, coffee . . . ? Uncle, you wish camera . . . girl . . . ?*

The style of this may be excused in remembrance of the hour, the place and the wine, and its arrogance is long past. But to have been part of the liberation of Europe is still a matter of deep pride to me, and my life would have been poorer without it. Those who did not experience it cannot imagine the exhilaration, the joy and laughter, the unforgettable tear-wet faces that welcomed us, the clutching hands of children and the scent of crushed flowers about our necks. The great events of history are often recognized in hind-sight only, but there was no doubt here that we felt the momentous hand of Time upon our shoulders. I know this is a warm recollection in old age, and I must also remember our indifference to the bowed and shaven heads of those young girls, the old men and women in France, Belgium and Holland who were accused of whoring or collaboration with the Germans and were now paraded before us in a Roman triumph for Liberation. Yet the pride endures, it has not soured with age, its truth is still sweet.

As it was for us, spring brought an end to war for Hughes and his comrades. While still quartered in and about Inverness, Cumberland's soldiers spent much of their time gathering the arms and supplies abandoned by the enemy or themselves. It was a needful duty, as old as soldiering, and in this century it has been entered upon Daily Orders as Battlefield Clearance. The list of *matériel* retrieved by the redcoats was substantial, brought down from the moor by the great wagons of the Train and carried along Ness-side to the quays whence it was ferried to Admiral Byng's transports, anchored off Longman's Point at the mouth of the Beauly Firth. More than two thousand muskets were gathered, fifteen hundred cartridges, twenty-two ammunition carts and five hundredweight of musket-balls, as well as thirty pieces of ordnance, broadswords, dirks, pistols, targes and axes, powder-kegs, tents, canteens, pouches, flints, saddles and harness. The soldiers worked with a greedy vigour, for the recovery of all this brought them a share in the awards paid by the Ordnance Department – one shilling for a sword, half-a-crown for a musket, and the handsome sum of sixteen guineas for the prized flag of a clan regiment.

Fourteen or more rebel standards, bloody silk and painted cloth, were picked up from the moor or along the track of the rout. Twelve were publicly burnt in Edinburgh. The Prince's standard, or one so described, was carried to its ritual destruction by the chief hangman of the city; the rest were dragged through the mire of the streets by chimney-sweeps. Behind them walked the Sheriff of Edinburgh, with heralds, pursuivants and town constables. Two more banners were burnt on following days. When they heard of this, in-pensioners of Chelsea Hospital protested, asking why the captured colours had not been lodged with them, to hang in their dining-hall with the standards of the French regiments they had fought in their youth.

Although it was unpleasant, our battlefield clearance in Germany came as a relief from the toy-box soldiering that was intended to sustain our morale and keep our thoughts from unrealistic hopes of early demobilization. All troops of the unit were now gathered about the skirts of the Battery HQ on the Nordrhein plain. In the fields and the shattered woods around us lay the broken shells of the gliders and Dakotas that had carried the Airborne across the Rhine, and the growing wheat was scarred with black crosses of burnt earth. Briefly off-duty in the afternoon, we lay beside the lifted brailing of our tents and watched the vehicles of a Grave Unit bumping across uneven ground to another lonely objective, white wooden crosses moving uneasily in the back of a jeep. An unnatural sun turned our winter-pale skin to dark brown as we mounted guard in shirt-sleeve order, or white-washed the stones and gravelled the pathways of our tent-lines, swelling the proud heart of the Battery Commander, his blouse already decorated with the laurel leaf of his recently awarded Mentioned in Dispatches. In the lilac dusk of those long evenings, standing motionless at the Slope before the guard-tent, we were mercilessly attacked by great cockchafers which spun on whirring wings from the chestnut blossoms above, stunning themselves on our steel helmets and falling in twitching disorder at our feet. One flinch before the attack, or a small movement to crush the insect beneath an ammunition boot, brought an angry roar from the guard-sergeant behind, or a weary reproof from the Battery Commander himself, across the parched grass of the parade-ground where he was enjoying a gin and lime beneath the cooling fly of his tent.

I cannot remember precisely how I occupied my mind during those long twenty-four-hour guards which sour the memories of all soldiers, two hours on post with no muscle relaxed, and four hours on a guard-room cot in full webbing, with only a belt-buckle released for comfort. On guard duty in the first weeks of my service, below the Clwyd Hills in the summer of 1940, I suppose I thought sadly of home and mournfully of the future. I would like to say that I was able to follow William Cobbett's inspiring example, but I cannot. At the age of eighteen, newly enlisted in the 54th Regiment of Foot and beginning seven years of remarkable soldiering, he passed his hour or two on sentinel by silently reciting passages from Dr Robert Lowth's *Short Introduction to English Grammar*, which he had copied and re-copied until he 'got it by heart'. In time, I think, I was able to make my mind a blank, thus speeding the hours. I have stood my post in many places and under differing circumstances, but never so resentfully, I think, as in that canvas camp on the low land of Nordrhein. In the cruel heat, just beyond the shade of the chestnut but within range of the cockchafers, it was almost possible to recall with affection a night-guard on the

Maas in sub-zero cold – an hour or so only, no more could be endured. Past one o'clock in the morning and grateful to my tardy relief, I stumbled into the operation bunker for a mug of tea, laced with rum from the Winchester behind Frank's W/T set. I was too awake for sleep. I sat beside him and wrote home in haste and because, however trivial it may seem now, it was then important to tell someone of an uneventful sixty minutes in the rutted snow, within sight and sound of the unsleeping war.

A hand grasps you by the shoulder and you start into consciousness. You have been dreaming that you were standing by Marble Arch waiting for a 30 bus and you could see it as it turned into Oxford Street by Selfridges. Then a hand grasps your shoulder and shakes you. It is only a gentle shake but you feel as if your body were being subjected to great torture. It is agony to open your eyes. You keep them closed, hoping that nothing will happen. But the sentry is anxious to be relieved. He shakes you again and you open your eyes and look at him blankly. You push down the collar of your top-coat and pretend you do not know what he wants. Ten minutes, he says, All right, Johnnie? All right, you say, Light the lamp. Black-out, he says. But you turn up the lantern a fraction. You can see him now, the light glows warmly on his face, framed in a balaclava beneath his helmet. He bangs his hands together and looks at you anxiously. He is afraid you will go to sleep again and he lights a cigarette and pushes it between your lips.

Cold? you say. Cold enough for a walking-stick, he says. I've got an extra pair of boot-laces, you say. They'll do, he says, All right, Johnnie? All right now, and you sit up and cough to clear throat and lungs thick with foul air and smoke. The sentry is gone now. You dress quickly. That is you put on top-coat and equipment and soon you are enclosed in a tight chrysalis of overcoat, leather jerkin, webbing equipment, two pairs of woollen gloves and a balaclava. You slip out the magazine of your rifle to see if it is full and you thrust the short bayonet on to the barrel. You are ready and you move slowly into the open. The cold strikes cruelly on your eyes, your breath already frosting on the balaclava. The sentry is waiting. All right, Johnnie? O.K., you say, Anything doing? Not much, he says. There was some machine-gunning about ten minutes ago, and they slung some dirt over too. Got your extra boot-laces? Yes, very comfortable. Good-night, Slash. Good-morning, he says, Christ it's cold.

You are alone. It is cold, and you feel sick as a pig. Then you begin to walk up and down, walking faster and faster to get a reserve of warmth, sliding in the slush. The noise of the shelling comes suddenly and you swing round in alarm. It is ours, and for a few minutes or so the shells pass overhead like a hurrying train. When they explode across the river the noise seems to fill the sky with flame. It is quiet again and now you are truly awake and you stand with feet astride waiting for the gun-flashes. You see them away to the rear and you count the seconds until you hear the noise of the discharge and the fluttering whistling passage of the shells.

Then it is quiet again. Behind the front, forward of the rear, you are waiting for a response, and yet it comes unexpectedly almost. A far distant discharge in the east and the great rustling overhead like a cane passed through the air. The shells explode so far to the rear that they are scarcely heard. Oh yes? you say, as if it were a wise observation.

A machine-gun, a Bren you think, stutters along the river where the beams of the detachments are motionless in the sky. It is answered by a Spandau and then the thud of mortars. The noise of this orchestrated action dies away slowly, one machine-gun firing to the last with careful precision and ending with one single round. It is silent. You are alone. You feel as if the whole war depends upon your vigilance at this moment, but it is almost impossible to keep your eyes open, and the edge of the balaclava on your cheeks is now hard with ice. You think of daylight. Of yesterday, a week, a life ago. The town by the Maas, one road leading in to it and none leading out. They are all closed. *Road heavily mined!* Another that says *Stop! Enemy ahead*. An infantryman sits on a felled tree with a Sten across his knees, chewing gum and reading the *Daily Mirror*. The streets of the little town are full of civilians, all afraid and waiting for evacuation. A shire-horse pulls a little sports car full of furniture. You grin at the memory of it and the lift of your cheeks is a sharp pain in the cold.

A Bren-carrier comes up the road towards you and you stand before it stupidly, rifle lifted. The driver sees you in time but swears at you amiably. He wants to know where A Infantry Echelon is. On the back of the carrier is a large Winchester of rum, and in the light of your torch you see the spirit lifting and turning in response to the throb of the engine. You tell the driver where to go, or where you think he should go. Thanks, Charlie, he says and rocks away.

You are alone once more. You have not noticed that the Bren is firing again down by the river, long, irritable bursts. You no longer feel lonely. The hour, the hour and a half is almost over. You look into the operations-room. The wireless operator is making tea in a biscuit tin. Time, Frank? you say. Zero one, one fiver. In English, please Frank. Quarter past one. Want some tea? Of course. It is strong and sweet. You are glad your stag-duty is almost over, and with the mug in your hand you go to find your relief. He looks at you with hate across his blankets and coat. Ten minutes, Ginger. O.K., he says, closes his eyes and pulls up his blankets. He has sewn them into a sleeping bag and it will take him a long time to emerge. You shake him again, take a mouthful of the tea, and press the mug against his face. Ginger? He sits up. O.K. Thanks. What's doing? Nothing, you say. There's something over there. Machine-gunning. And they slung some dirt over now and then. O.K., Ginger? O.K., he says and sits up grinning. He looks like a caterpillar in all that bedding.

You go outside and wait for him in the light of the beams, watching silent gunfire far, far to the south. The relief comes at last, swearing at the cold and pulling his rifle by the sling. You're a slovenly soldier, Ginge, you say. He nods and bids you an obscene good-night.

After my third twenty-four-hour guard in less than ten days, and desperate to escape from the tedium of the Nordrhein camp, I volunteered for battlefield clearance. Or so I believe now, though it may well be that I was told to step forward, just as I later volunteered under orders to write a history of the Battery, until then the unfulfilled responsibility of a subaltern. In this my military career momentarily shadowed that of Corporal William Cobbett, whose expert literacy brought upon him the neglected duties of ignorant and incompetent officers.

The troop I joined for battlefield clearance was deployed beyond Osnabruck, as far as Celle. It is old campaigning ground for the British Army, with village names that appear in gold and blue on many regimental honours. Through a three-tonner's trailing dust I saw the word *Minden* on a leaning signpost, and although I saw no roses in the ravaged gardens I mentally nodded an acknowledgement to the Lancashire Fusilier. Unlike the miserable weather that followed Cumberland's soldiers upon such duty, we worked under hot and cloudless skies so drained of colour that my memory of those days seems now to be in monochrome, relieved only by a startling blue, scarlet or yellow where resurgent flowers fought to survive in the suffocating ruins. Our night-camp – no more than unwalled fly-sheets, a field-kitchen and a long fraternal latrine-pit – was on the outskirts of a silent village, dark at night and almost invisible in the daylight dust of military traffic. We must have been cautious with the material we handled, although I can remember no specific orders. We loaded trucks with abandoned weapons and with ammunition large and small. There was a great deal of loose explosive, black grains spilled carelessly or in desperate haste. To move this volatile waste we used non-metallic spades, wore canvas shoes or worked bare-footed, always aware that a spark could cause a terrible ignition, not an explosion but rapid and engulfing flame.

I saw this once. A man standing half-naked in the back of a truck, joking in obscene good-fellowship, was suddenly gone in a brief but monstrous fire, with no more sound than might be caused by a fierce rush of air. I did not know him, we were not in the same troop, but his death was almost a personal loss. My father's brother, whom I resembled, my mother said, was killed in this manner and upon such duty in the November silence of 1918.

I was recalled to my troop a day or so after it was sent south to a prisoner-of-war camp at Paderborn. My transport joined a convoy travelling at night, a journey of unrelieved discomfort and stunning boredom. There were long halts during which we stirred in cramped semi-consciousness, lit the nipped half of a cigarette and listened to the sound of arguing voices at the head of the convoy. Much of a soldier's life is spent in such dark vacuums of ignorance, in a snoring, murmuring slumber with the grinding of teeth and the breaking of wind, ancient oaths and the old appeal for Mother to sell the pig and buy a poor swaddy out of his misery. 'Soldier on, son . . . pig dead, soldier on . . .'

In recalling this familiar stupor, the brief stop at Belsen is now a shadowed memory. I do not know why we were halted yet again, but I remember the junior NCOs who walked down the line of the convoy, striking the side of each transport and calling tonelessly. 'Stay in the truck . . . Do not get out . . . Stay in your vehicle . . . !' We stayed, half-awake and at first indifferent to the pale light beyond the tailboard curtain. How did we know that this was Belsen? Who told us? We were held in a paralysis of mind and body, hearing nothing but our own breathing and the distant cough of a jeep engine. Those who at last pulled up the edge of the canopy, or leant beyond the tailboard to stare at dark shapes in the milky glow of distant lights, were pushed back by the patrolling corporals. A Don R went by on the roar of an opening throttle. There were more angry voices at the head of the column, but curiously muted now. Half-asleep or fully awake, we were all aware of something indescribable, unthinkable, a feeling real or imagined . . . 'Christ! What is it?' The unanswering silence was ended by a peremptory whistle and the responding roar of engines. When we realized that someone – the *Someone* leading the column – had taken us to the wrong camp, there was derisive laughter. Almost immediately it was choked by appalled shame.

At dawn, which came in bloody splendour on the low clouds beyond the eastern timber, we were again halted. We uncurled ourselves from the sweating embrace of each other's limbs. We observed the start of yet another day with a soldier's customary matins – hawking, spitting and consoling obscenities. The convoy moved, but after a few miles it stopped once more. What now? The Don R rode his motor-cycle down the line, in oiled jerkin and round helmet like a herald at a joust. The corporals came by as before, but now at the double. 'Stay in the truck . . . You are close to Paderborn . . . Stay in, you dozy bastards!' I cannot recall whether we knew then what we would find here, what our role would truly be. We believed that we were to guard a temporary camp for men of the Wehrmacht. Then again, we believed or we were told that it was not a camp for German soldiers but for Displaced Persons, the spindrift of the war, slave-labour taken from all Europe, now liberated, in need of care and bitter with hate. In the lengthening shadows of time I recall the medieval town of Paderborn as I saw it that morning, for the first and only time, a cruel view from the back of a rocking truck, pitiful ruins and red dust rising. I did not see it again, for the camp was in a woodland outside the town and we were given no off-duty passes. Nor do I remember how long I was there. This is strange, for our duty was unpleasant and unforgettable.

The men and women behind the wire were not Displaced Persons but Germans. Many of them had been administrative staff and guards at concentration camps, and some had come from Belsen. We were told that Josef Kramer, the commandant of Belsen, was imprisoned in one of the paint-blistered huts, but no one could rightly claim to have seen him. Few male prisoners came close to the wire during the day, and even in the distance most of them kept their backs to us. The women were different. Some stood at the wire for hours, in the rain or harsh sunlight, staring at us, at the sky or the distant trees. The SS women came now and then in a group and to taunt us, I think, some of their faces still defiant and arrogant, others marked by growing unease. Their black uniforms, stripped of all insignia, were too small or had been deliberately cut to emphasize their figures. All were obscenely overweight, their calves swelling in knee-high boots – or so it seems to me now.

When we were not on guard duty, plodding along the camp perimeter with rifles slung, our daylight hours were spent in sleep, our faces covered to avoid the big black flies from the camp-lines. The outer wire was ringed by a wide clearing from which all trees and brush had been removed. Our ninety-centimetres were placed at intervals along its woodland edge. At dusk the Lister generators, sited in the trees, pumped into life one by one. Carbon rods hissed and spat as the current leapt the arc and our brutal light sprang skyward, diffused beams destroying night and illuminating the camp with an awesome, shadowless glow.

Almost immediately the prisoners began to move towards the wire, calling to the trees. The noise, as it increased, was *animal*, and some of the patrolling guards retreated to the centre of the clearing, away from spittle and occasional missiles. The shouting – a peculiar howling in which anguish and impatient anger were curiously mixed – lasted a brief time only. There was then an equally unnatural silence as the prisoners stood at the wire, immobile in the white light of the beams. The shouting began again when furtive figures came out of the trees in a stumbling run towards the wire, but this time the noise was encouraging, as a crowd might cheer at a race-meeting. The visitors ran straight to the wire where they could, or dodged to avoid guards who had no wish or power to avoid them. They carried bundles in their arms, or dragged them in haste across the earth. Some of the parcels were thrown over the wire, others were opened and their contents thrust through the barbs into clutching hands – clothing, a little food, letters, books, paper, shoes, tins of carefully gathered cigarette-ends. All this the British soldiers watched as if it were a sporting event, and sometimes supported with partisan shouts. The frenetic haste and urgency were necessary, for there was a brief time only before the arrival of the Military Police, two and sometimes three jeeps turning and weaving in the clearing, avoiding the scattering Germans with a skill of which the drivers were obviously very proud. Their red cap-covers and white webbing were luminous in the light, their faces distorted by the downward thrust of visor-peaks. When they had herded the last German back into the trees we congratulated them with ironic applause, which they sensibly ignored.

One of the SS women in the camp was said to be Irma Grese, Kramer's mistress, for whom he had ordered the tattooed skins of prisoners to be made into lamp-shades, to ornament the bedroom they shared. She did not deny she was Grese when challenged by us. She ignored all attempts to talk to her and seemed to take a fierce pleasure in the abuse from some of the men who patrolled the wire. She would stand close to the rusting thorns, in a circle of her women, their jackets unbuttoned in defiant challenge. When nettled by a sentry's taunts they shouted abuse in return and sang Nazi songs. But she did not shout or sing. Once she stopped me as I passed, a sharp call, 'Tommy come here!' I turned automatically, taking a step to the wire and thereby received her broken spittle in my face.

The memory of this was in my mind on an evening two years later. In 1947 Oswald Mosley held his first press conference since his release from internment, to announce his return to political life and the formation of his Union Movement. The meeting, modest even by the standards of that time, was held in a small room in Vauxhall Bridge Road, with the whine and clang of trams below an open window. There were no seats, I think, only one chair, upon which Mosley was seated. Thus he was surrounded by reporters, some kneeling, some crouched, and others craning on their toes at the rear. In the centre of this frankly hostile audience Mosley was calm and unruffled, his smooth and slightly absurd features touched by a polite smile. The level and temper of his voice did not change as he turned his head slowly from one question to another, and the coolness of his evasive answers increased the irritation of his interrogators. He knew that most of us had recently been servicemen and his condescension in acknowledging that, his repeated phrases of respect, only increased our irritation. Although we stood above and about him, his few bodyguards or companions now pushed back against the wall, it was as if he were raised above us in contemptuous self-confidence. I have forgotten the questions we put to him, even my own, although they may be easily imagined since they were conceived in bitter memories. I do remember that at the close of this hot and sweating occasion he announced that in addition to the Movement's newspaper he intended to set up a publishing company which would produce non-political books only.

One of its subsequent titles, and perhaps the most successful, was the autobiography of a German dive-bomber.

The whole of Germany during that hot and implacable summer of 1945 was a bewildered penitentiary in which gaolers and prisoners stared at each other in exhaustion across the ruin their struggle had created. Until I left the Battery to go to a British Army Newspaper Unit in Hamburg, I sometimes let my mind sink into inertia beneath the emotional weight of time and events, and sometimes I struggled against it with the only weapons I had – the will and the wish to write. I began a second novel at this time,* in a deserted restaurant on the Rhine near Duisberg, where Battery headquarters were now established. What I wrote was fragmentary, notes and impressions, disconnected pages of dialogue or descriptions. I gave more care and placed more hope in the pieces I also wrote for *Soldier*, the BANU magazine I wished to join in Hamburg, but I do not know how many were published. I found stories where I could in the stunned countryside on both banks of the Rhine, and it was upon such aimless journeys, then rightly termed 'swanning', that I visited two other internment camps on the hot oven-plate of Nordrhein. I had neither rank nor authority. I was a private soldier, but my absence from the Battery at such times was protected by the inventive lies of my comrades and the waning competence of a Provost lance-sergeant whose mind was exclusively concentrated upon his early demobilization. I was told about the camps by a Pioneer corporal who worked among them as an interpreter. He was an Austrian Jew who had been a teacher in Vienna, I think, escaping to England after the *Anschluss* of 1938, one among many Jews and other refugees from the Axis countries who had been interned by the British when the war began and then allowed to enlist as Alien Volunteers. Until the last year of the war they were callously used for non-combatant and menial work which risked nothing but their own sanity and self-respect. At one time the kitchens and large mess-halls at Kinmel Park were staffed by these AVs, working as dish-washers, cleaners and orderlies, mature adults with academic distinctions, younger men and women whose intelligence and abilities exceeded those of the British soldiers whom they served with respect and courtesy. I remember them with affection for their enthusiasm and their spirit, and I remember

* *The Edge of Darkness*. See p. 21.

them with shame for the subsequent betrayal of the countries to which many of them returned.

The Pioneer was a sardonic man who believed that Europe at this moment was populated by devils and children, the Germans being the former and ourselves the latter, although of course, he said, the roles were sometimes reversed. He was a Zionist, I believe, marking time until he went home, not to Austria but to Israel where, no doubt, he fought the British. The first camp we visited was for Displaced Persons, mainly Eastern Europeans, and like others it was then in chaotic disorder. At night its occupants broke out in small bands looking for food, drink and clothing, some for rape and fierce revenge, and some in hope of finding the long road to their homeland. Although isolated farmhouses and small hamlets were the objective of these forays, the Germans were usually in no great physical danger provided they offered no resistance. Nonetheless, and understandably, they asked for protection against the hostility of those who had recently been their enslaved labourers.

In Hamburg later that year, in a winter-cold building on the Rothenbaum-chaussee, I attended the minor War Crimes Courts where some DPs brought complaints against their recent employers – charges of neglect, starvation, beatings, rape and occasional murder. In that large chamber, white with the light of the snow outside, the proceedings were unemotional, brief, and conducted fairly as far as I could judge. I wrote nothing about them, or nothing *Soldier* wished to publish after its coverage of the Nuremberg trials, but I went to the Court whenever I could. I watched the farmers, factory managers, housewives and local officers entering and leaving the box like automatons, only a few showing the fear or despair of guilt. Most, I believe, did not understand why they should be charged. And I remembered the hot and windless nights of summer when part of the Battery was ordered to join the pursuit of raiding DPs, light vehicles and utilities bouncing across the rough fields towards fleeing shadows, a Bren-gunner standing in the turret of a leading truck and firing a parabola of warning tracers into the dark sky. We meant no harm to the DPs, but what did they think of us, their liberators, on such a night?

The DP camp I came to with the Pioneer corporal was commanded by a major of engineers, a middle-aged man whose battle-dress blouse was richly coloured with the ribbons of that other war. He greeted me pleasantly and without any emphasis on our disparate ranks, and he talked with candour about his responsibilities and the difficulty of honouring them. The camp staff assigned to him by Allied Military Government was inept and undisciplined. He understood the anger and the impatience of the DPs, but he deplored their behaviour which, he felt, risked a response in civil disorder. He spoke of the Germans as the Boche, and he remembered the Allied occupation of the Rhineland in 1919 with nostalgic regret – a time of loyalty and honour it seemed to him now. He did not believe he could control the camp as it was presently organized, and he had thought of a solution which he explained to me with disarming condescension. Beyond Wesel, he said, he had visited a German prisoner-of-war camp and had been impressed by its morale and discipline. Did I not agree that if some of these prisoners were sent to him, under command of the Military Police, they would make resourceful and trustworthy camp-guards? My reply, I hope, was equivocal. Beyond the Major's pink and earnest face I could see the Pioneer's ironic smile. He knew, as I knew and had no doubt the Major knew, that that prisoner-of-war camp contained men of the Waffen SS.

The second camp was for Russians, and was thus my first human contact with a nation whose influence upon me had been so intense and so distracting. As this is written the Soviet Union is fragmenting, destroying itself, changing to an extent that was once inconceivable, and with results that are still beyond imagination. It has consciously discredited the false hopes it gave a world eager for humanity and justice, and the power its ideology once had over mind and conscience outside its borders has quickly withered. It is strange to realize that the only emotion this historic event seems to arouse is relief, and that I can myself accept without pain a monstrous betrayal of youthful hope. It would be easy to say now that my disillusion with and departure from the Communist Party began at this Russian camp in Nordrhein, but there was no such theatrical moment, only a slow change, a sloughing of emotional and intellectual skin over many months. And I am aware that two or three years earlier, instead of being sadly amused by what I saw, I might have found reasons to admire and justify it.

The camp was an example of the obtuse and sometimes frightened bigotry of Allied Military Government at that time. The Russians had been given an arid patch of broken earth, by the lip of a disused and shallow quarry. Very little had been done for them, indeed nothing, the Pioneer said. He added that the cynical attitude of the AMG towards displaced persons from Russia was matched by the indifference of the Soviet Union. When the Russians came – under the command of two officers of the Red Air Force – they were told to build what housing they could from what materials they might legitimately find. They received little help, apart from rations. The DPs were mostly old men and young boys. We did not know then, although I believe AMG should have known, that these wretched people would receive no joyous welcome when they returned to the Soviet Union. Their forced labour for Germany was too easily seen as collaboration.

The Pioneer had first aroused my interest in the camp by telling me that the Russians had performed a miracle there, clearing stones and building hut-lines, turning the dispirited earth into a remarkable garden, not of flowers but of brightly painted stones which they arranged in cunning grottos and flowing borders. Their huts were constructed from debris collected in the country about, and they too were colourfully painted – each one, said the Pioneer gravely, in a different shade of red. The perimeter was wired and guarded, and the Russians rarely left it except in orderly parties for essential supplies. None of them broke out at night. Their own sentries patrolled the wire, armed with German rifles which they had found in the water of the quarry, now cleaned, oiled and restored to use.

We came to the camp on a Sunday afternoon, a lazy drive down a long Rhineland road. Spangled beams of sunlight fell through the splintered trees which whispered in rhythm as we passed. There were omnipresent columns of German refugees with all manner of transport from bicycles and ox-carts to wood-burning automobiles. The men ignored us, but now and then a child or a woman stopped to watch us pass. The Pioneer acknowledged interest and indifference with a brisk Victory signal on the horn of the jeep. We came upon the camp suddenly, half a mile beyond a sharp bend. The Soviet and British flags hung at the same listless height by the entrance where a blond boy in denim fatigues stood guard, a rifle on his back and a pick-helve in his hand. He recognized the Pioneer immediately, grinned like a schoolboy and lifted the barrier-pole without a challenge.

The camp was silent but not, the Pioneer explained in mock disapproval, because it was Sunday. Even enlightened atheists needed a day of rest. When he switched off the jeep's ignition we heard the notes of a balalaika from a British fly-tent near the gate, a scarlet hammer and sickle painted on its weathered canvas. We entered the tent without ceremony, the Pioneer calling a greeting in Russian as he pushed the flap aside. Inside two young officers were lying on camp-beds, one playing the balalaika and the other similarly occupied with a German girl. They rose quickly, and the player was more careful with his instrument than his companion was with the girl. Half-naked on the floor, she began to complain petulantly until silenced by a single barked word. When the Pioneer had explained that I was a writer and wished to see the camp, the young men said nothing until they had put on their hats and khaki tunics, easing their shoulders beneath the heavy gold and scarlet straps. They saluted me stiffly, each bending his body in a short bow and slowly lifting an open hand to his head. I responded clumsily, for my side-cap was thrust beneath my shoulder-strap and a bare-headed salute was not a British custom. There was then a brisk and brief speech by the senior lieutenant in which, the Pioneer said, I was welcomed as a man of culture and heroic fighter against Fascism. This was followed by toasts in vodka, the glasses filled from the dregs of several bottles lying on the beds or the floor. The senior officer, who was perhaps no more than twenty-one, then strapped on a German pistol-belt and led us from the cool shade of the tent to the sun outside.

The hut-lines were still deserted. No one was visible except the boy on the gate, and he came rapidly to attention. The Lieutenant took the Luger from its holster, pulled back the bolt and lifted the weapon above his head, pausing briefly before he slowly discharged its magazine. Before the echo of the last shot had faded, all members of the camp were standing in line before their huts, some half-awake, some still struggling to button or belt their trousers. I marched beside the Lieutenant on a slow and increasingly unhappy tour of the lines. Now and then the Lieutenant stopped, waiting for some response from me, an approving nod, a smile. At the door of each hut he spoke briefly to the silent line of its occupants, his voice high and sharp. Whispering behind my shoulder, the Pioneer told me that I was being described as an important visitor, a valiant British soldier, a man of culture and a stalwart anti-Fascist. This information was sometimes received in stolid silence and sometimes with a soft growl of approval. The Lieutenant then inspected the hut, moving its sparse furniture and bedding with the toe of a polished boot. If he liked what he saw, he embraced each man or boy in a bear-hug, kissing him on the lips. When he was plainly dissatisfied he shouted at the hut-leader and struck him violently across the face with an open palm. Returning to the officers' tent, we were offered more vodka and asked if we had any American cigarettes.

The Pioneer corporal drove for some miles before he made any comment about our visit. He stopped the jeep at last and stared intently at my face. He then slapped my shoulder and leant upon the wheel in silent, painful laughter.

The effect of such experiences was cumulative. I did not know how deeply they disturbed me. And more – the elation, the fear, horror and boredom of the long warring months from summer until spring, the joy of peace and the conceit of triumph, were now dragging me into a dark trough. I was only dimly aware of this, but I recognized my response as anger and *hate*. Hatred of the war, the waste, the pain of inconsolable waste. Hate, too, for this land and its people who were responsible. The pressure of this sad confusion was strongest at night, urgently needing release and finally exorcizing itself.

The Germans were still an enemy immobilized by peace, kept at a distance by the monstrous ruins of their country and by the absurdly impracticable regulations against fraternization. The Battery Major, in common with other unit commanders, was stubbornly determined to impress the Germans with our authority and our presence. We were now in a little town to the north of Duisberg, a sad desert of crumbling stone, rusting metal and twisted wire. In this bleak landscape the Major's love of ceremonial was intensified. Away from the heat of the tented camp we were obliged to wear full battle-dress, as well as webbing, pack, and steel helmet when we mounted guard. Before the twenty-four hours were ended our left shoulders were raw from the weight of a rifle upon sweat-soaked cloth. Yet it was still a summer of great beauty, and standing post at dusk I watched in disbelief as that beauty emerged miraculously from the ruins, light and shade in dying harmony. But with the coming of night that nagging hate returned.

Absurd though it may seem now, we were encouraged to believe that German resistance still survived in the menacing hostility of the Hitler Youth. We were persuaded to think that the hollow-cheeked boys who loitered about our vehicles during the day – sharp-eyed below the peaks of Wehrmacht caps and offering us their mother's jewellery, their father's medals and their sister's company in return for cigarettes or coffee – that these children were abroad at night with rifles and determined to kill us. Good sense should have told us that in the shock of defeat they were more likely to admire than to shoot us.

Yet all things were believable at night, on guard in that concrete cemetery. Hate creates its own enemies and excites a need for retribution. Past midnight, long after curfew, another sentry and myself stood together in silent companionship, each with rifle slung and a cigarette in a cupped hand. Now and then, if we listened, we could hear the slip and slide of small masonry as the maimed buildings of the town eased themselves into unhappy sleep. Each locked in his own thoughts, we did not immediately hear the whispering approach of a bicycle and the anxious panting of its rider, and before we could react he had passed us in a wavering shadow. My companion appealed to the Son of God in three spitting words and stared towards the departing sound. In a similar reflex, I shouted the customary order to halt, each challenge stumbling hastily upon its predecessor. After the third, I opened and closed the bolt of my rifle, bringing the weapon to my shoulder. I heard the live round I had expelled strike the roadway, the slide of the oiled bolt replacing it. Only a few seconds passed, but they were long. I remember my *hate* and a fierce, unfamiliar readiness to fire. I had felt nothing like this in Holland, firing at shadows, real or imagined, during the night, beyond Meijel when the Corridor was cut. It was not the madness of using the Browning, taken from the wreck of a Liberator and mounted outside the butter factory at Heldern, for defence against the low-flying planes that came darkly and swiftly out of the eastern sun. I was ready to kill this man because I was there and he was responsible for all the agony the world had suffered. With this great sin on his conscience he had the arrogance to disobey me. Such was my foolish sickness.

The sound of the rifle-bolt halted him, the cycle falling away noisily as he stumbled. He limped towards us in the light of my companion's torch, a frightened, middle-aged man who gabbled unintelligibly while fumbling for his identity papers. He dropped them, but instead of picking them up he grasped my blouse and began to cry. I pushed him away and my laconic companion gathered the papers and offered them to me. When I shook my head he did not examine them but thrust them into the German's pocket. Then he said, 'Don't point your rifle at him, Slash, and for Chrissake take the round out of the spout.'

As I did this I tried to understand what the German was saying. The word *schnapps* was repeated several times. I translated as best

I could for my companion, whose only response was to lift the German's wrists to see if he had a watch worth taking. He had been playing chess with a friend, the man said, and as they drank and talked the curfew was forgotten. Again and again he apologized, touching my arm and saying *'Soldaten . . . wir sind Soldaten . . . ?'* 'Soldiers . . . we are soldiers?' My companion was bored. He repeated his blasphemy and wandered away. The German and I looked at each other in the light of my torch and across six years of war. He knew that I had been ready, had wished to kill him. *'Wir sind Soldaten . . .'* he said again, but this time as if he were forgiving me. There was nothing to say. I shook my head and waved him away.

May the Twentieth

There are hornless cattle lying on the shore of Arisaig, tawny hides on the white sand. The thin lip of an incoming tide is scarcely fifteen yards from the nearest beasts and none has yet responded to its threat or to the melancholy call of curlews in warning flight. The sky is clouded above much of the sea and the mainland, but beyond the reef of skerries at the mouth of Loch nan Ceall a long finger of sunlight touches the distant island of Eigg. It is thus lemon-yellow, luminous and seemingly alone now that the larger shape of its companion Rhum is lost in the blue shadow of a squall. Twenty years before I first saw this seaward scrap of land I created its fictional image, unaware that what I was describing had substance in reality. I have allowed this simple coincidence to assume an unnatural significance, in consequence of which I have never visited Eigg and now doubt that I ever shall. My island, the eponymous location of my first published book, took shape by night in an Army work-shop at Kinmel Park. Its description was typed on a soldering-bench where I stood rather than sat, and the smell of hot resin, bright beads of solder, can still recall those writing hours.

It was a small island and it stood alone in the sea. It was shaped like a wedge, with a hollow in the centre of the gentle slope. It was there that the bomber had crashed. The wedge sloped away to the east, towards the mainland, and on the steep side, which was almost perpendicular, there was a cliff, high and gashed with dark coves. There the sea was never calm; even at low tide it beat against the rocks and there was no shore to be seen. The spray was flung high into the air, and sometimes the sea-fowl, as they hung above the surf, looked as if they were part of the spray too. The rocks were black, and the sea, grey in its anger, washed against them until they shone like pitch that had been cut with a knife.

It is not an exact description, for Eigg has two escarpments and the greater is in the south, columnar pitchstone sixty million years old, rising eleven hundred feet and more to the pinnacle of An Sgurr. The low ground falls largely to the west and not to the east where the mainland lies. But when I see it, hull-down from Arisaig or the Mallaig ferry, it is without doubt the island of my book. That remarkable man Hugh Miller, writer and evangelist, stone-mason and geologist, visited Eigg in 1844 aboard the little yawl *Betsey*, the home of a Free Church minister and therefore known as the Sailing Manse. Miller climbed the southern brae to its ridge, and something he saw below him I also saw on the page before me. The island, he said, was 'basking in yellow sunshine; and with its one dark shadow thrown from its one mountain-elevated wall of rock, it seemed some intense, fantastical dial, with its gnomon rising tall in the mist'.

In Gaelic, Eigg means a notch or nick, and may describe the gap in the wedge where the land falls to the sea. The name I gave my island, and the book its title, was also an allegory for its theme, my belief in how the War might be resolved. This was perhaps more a political wish than informed judgement, equally unsound. The book was written on impulse, inspired by a short newspaper item. The crew of a Japanese bomber, having crashed on a Pacific island, refused to surrender. They mounted guns taken from their plane and established martial law, waiting for the arrival of a Japanese invasion force. I chose a Hebridean island and its people, the latter more simple, I now think, more poetic in imagery than reality would justify. My German survivors – a pilot, a navigator and two crewmen – are clearly characters in a moral argument, the resolution of which I placed upon the navigator, whom I called Mann. Whatever literary qualities the novella may have, I did in time discover that the axe I wished to grind had cut no real kindling. But the title of the book – *Where the Sea Breaks* – came honestly from the writing.

'I don't believe you have taken the mainland,' she said pathetically.

'We know we have.'

She looked about her. 'It's our island,' she said.

'It's a good island,' said Mann approvingly. 'If I were a boy I'd like it here. Do your children collect eggs from the nests on the cliffs?'

She looked at him curiously. 'Why do you ask that?'

'I'd like to know.'

'They're too young,' she said. 'But I did when I was young.'

'You must be brave.'

'No, but it's our island, you see.'

'It belongs to us now,' he said. 'What do you call it?'

She told him.

'I don't understand. That's not English, is it?'

'No, it's our own tongue, man. They say it's the tongue the wee folk taught us when we first came.'

'What does it mean?'

'The place where the sea breaks.'

There is mindless savagery in the history of Eigg and in the brutality of the invaders in my book. The island was once a small fragment of Clanranald's land, the wide sweep of the great MacDonald's power from the Outer Hebrides to the mainland, to Moidart, Morar, Arisaig and Ardnamurchan. The captains, so styled, of Clanranald ruled this rich swathe of the Lordship of the Isles for five centuries, three hundred of them from Castle Tioram. Standing upon rock and a tidal sand-spit at the narrows of Loch Moidart, and in the green shadow of protective hills, it was almost unassailable. Its grey and empty shell today is not a relic of siege and conquest but of a melodramatic gesture in Homeric defiance. Leaving for the Rebellion of 1715, and believing that he would not return from battle, Allan the Red of Clanranald set the castle afire so that the English could not occupy it again as they had done in his boyhood. Folk-legend says that he watched the burning on a sombre October evening, from a rock high upon the flank of Beinn Bhreac. More prosaically, before a torch was put to the timber of his castle, he and five hundred men of his clan were away southward across the Great Glen to join the Jacobite army on the Braes of Glenorchy. He was killed in battle, by a silver sixpence, it was said, fired from a gun of his own clan.

Set strategically among the Small Isles of the inner sea, the island of Eigg played its part and took its harsh punishment in the feuds and bloodshed between the Captain of Clanranald and those who disputed his right to so much land, or envied his continued possession of it. At the time of Allan MacIain, the ninth chief – 'of whom little good can be written', according to Father Charles MacDonald, the gentle nineteenth-century annalist of Moidart – the entire population of Eigg was killed in an act of senseless ferocity. It surpasses the Massacre of Glencoe in numbers and horror, but since it had no justification beyond an urge for violent revenge, it is now scarcely remembered.

Towards the close of the sixteenth century a galley manned by men of Clan MacLeod was driven on to the singing-sands of Eigg's little bay. They were welcomed as hospitable custom required, but when they abused some of the island women they were bound hand and foot and set adrift in their boat. Instead of perishing on the open sea far beyond the Hebrides, they were carried by wind and tide to their own shores on Skye. Their chief decided upon a swift reprisal. His resolve, according to legend, was strengthened by the shameful treatment of his sister by her husband Clanranald. Highland mythology is often improved by such embroidery. A large force of MacLeods was dispatched to Eigg, and as soon as their silken banner and long galleys were sighted the islanders retreated to a cave below the southern escarpment, its entrance hidden by a waterfall. Here they might have escaped discovery had not one of them – and there is always such a one – emerged too soon. Following him to the cave, the MacLeods closed its mouth with dampened fire. The thick smoke, blown inward by a western wind, suffocated all – men, women and children.

This was but the second act of the tragedy as told. In the third, a body of revengeful men from Clanranald's people on Uist came to Skye in their longships, running the keels ashore on Ardmore Bay to the north of MacLeod's keep at Dunvegan. On a bare plateau above the sea, the people of the township were at Sabbath prayer in Trumpan Church when the MacDonalds barred its door and fired its sod roof. The raiders stayed too long in enjoyment of their revenge, for when they returned to the shore, war-galleys from Dunvegan were already there. The following struggle was bloody and merciless. The MacDonalds were driven back to a dry-stone wall against which they stood and fought until all were dead, a battle still remembered in a renowned pibroch. The wall was turned upon their bodies, and grass and heather were left to cover the stones. The lasting mound is there still, above the dark shore and facing westward to the wind. Storms from the Atlantic, it is said, sometimes expose a bone, the remains of a skull.

But no Highland story such as this is precisely true, of course. In another version, sometimes heard on Skye, the suffocation of the islanders was the MacLeods' revenge for Clan Donald's raid upon Ardmore, the burning of Trumpan church and its worshippers.

The natural sepulchre is below the columnar ridge on the southern heel of Eigg, not far from the crofting houses of Glamisdale. In his *Description of the Western Islands*, published in 1716, the Skye-man Martin Martin wrote of a large cave below the escarpment 'capable of containing several hundreds of people', which may have been an oblique and considerate reference to its contents. Towards the end of that century, when the wild Highlands and Isles first attracted peaceful visitors, a landing upon Eigg was an exciting and macabre experience. Until then its population, restored long since by Clanranald's tacksmen, had discouraged strangers and resolutely forbidden Protestants to attend burials in the graveyard of Saint Donan's chapel. Exploring Eigg became more popular when access to it was made easier by the tall-funnelled, low-hulled paddle-steamers that came bravely out of the sea-lochs into the hostile waters of the Minch. From the beginning, visitors were eager for grisly souvenirs. In 1814 Walter Scott came ashore from the Lighthouse Yacht with his friend, the engineer Robert Stevenson. The entrance to the cave, Scott wrote to James Ballantyne, was no more than three feet in height, but inside the ceiling rose to eighteen. The whole cavern was 255 feet in length and perhaps as great in breadth. Remembering that visit three decades later, Stevenson said that the stony floor was strewn with bones which 'by this time are no doubt much more reduced by the steam boat visitors'. The bones were all black or chocolate-coloured, from the smoke he thought.

Like Scott, Stevenson believed there could be no harm in 'taking away a bone or two', and said so to the captain of the yacht. The sailor, characteristically a superstitious man with precedents of disaster to quote, was appalled by the suggestion. 'God help me,' he said, 'I hope not!' And he watched his crew carefully, preventing them from bringing any fragment and resulting misfortune aboard his ship. He was unable to control Scott, however. 'I brought off, in spite of the prejudices of our sailors,' Ballantyne was told, 'a skull, which seems that of a young woman!' To the best of my recollection, from occasional visits to Abbotsford, this is not to be seen among the arms and armour, the shields, books, manuscripts and other historical artefacts that reflect the numbing nature of Scott's theatrical romanticism.

Thirty years later another visitor, the zoologist James Wilson, joined a boat-party which foraged deep into the cave and found . . .

. . . a considerable number [of bones] at the far narrow end, to which it may be supposed the wretched creatures had retreated . . . We found the scalp of a little child at the back of a large stone, and between the stone and the cavern side, as if it had been making a vain attempt to creep outward from the smoke . . .

Wilson was no worse than others who grubbed for souvenirs in this dark and sorrowful pit, but he had a fine disdain for the people of Eigg and a poor sense of humour to accompany its ignorance. They were 'extremely tenacious of their ancestral glories', he said, and ridiculed this notion with a jolly Latin pun. During the potato harvest the island's pigs were herded into the cave to keep them from mischief among the crop . . .

. . . and a fine mumbling work they will make of it, while grumphing to each other – *de mortuis nil nisi bones*. Now as the people eat the pigs and the pigs the people's predecessors, it follows logically that the present natives are a race of cannibals of the very worst description.

Such loveless humour may illustrate the nineteenth century's general contempt for the Highlander's way of life, and a consequent lack of concern for victims of the Clearances.

The Isle of Eigg sent its young men to the mainland in 1745, and they were among Clanranald's warrior rent-roll at Culloden. The recently published list of this MacDonald regiment* gives a chilling indication of how great was the price paid by the small island community to the chief, its father. How many were gathered, and how many were killed at Culloden, is unknown, but twenty-four are on record as captives, and of these three died in prison or on the Thames-side hulks. One gave King's Evidence and was released. Another did the same but was transported nonetheless. The agony of the island did not end with this. The invasion and brutality which I imagined for my island in *Where the Sea Breaks* had a curious if small similarity with events on Eigg.

When Mann went inside he found a little room with a low ceiling that darkened the place. The room was full of furniture, and in one

---

* *Muster Roll of Prince Charles Edward Stuart's Army*, ed. A. Livingstone, C. W. Aikman & B. Stuart Hart, Aberdeen University Press, 1984. See also *Prisoners of the 'Forty-five*, ed. Sir Bruce Gordon & J. G. Arnot, Scottish History Soc., 1928.

corner there was a radio set, an old-fashioned thing with many knobs and wires. The lieutenant stood by the table with feet astride. The body of a young man was slowly sliding from a chair beside the radio set. When it reached the floor it rolled over and Mann saw its face. The heavy bullet, in emerging, had torn away the frontal bone of the skull.

'There was no need to have done that,' said Mann.

The pilot swung round, his pistol was raised. *'What do you mean?'* His voice was shriller than usual, and his eyes bright.

"That is only a receiving set,' said Mann. 'It could transmit nothing. I imagine he was repairing it.'

The pilot raised his chin and eased the collar of his tunic about his throat. 'If the man was a technician, he might have proved dangerous.'

Towards the end of June 1746, H.M. Sloop *Furnace* dropped anchor off the Isle of Eigg. Its commander, John Fergusson, was a great pursuer and persecutor of Jacobite fugitives, and was commended by his superiors as an honest, gallant fellow. 'May there be a bodkin in his eye,' said the Clan Donald bard, John MacCodrum, 'to the back of his head.' Fergusson sent a hundred seamen and soldiers ashore where they terrorized the inhabitants, according to one of Bishop Forbes's informants, 'slaughtered all their cattle, pillaged all their houses ere they left and ravished a girl or two.' This behaviour was secondary to Fergusson's principal objective, which was to find one John MacDonald, a doctor, brother of the laird of Kinlochmoidart, and lately an officer in the Clanranald Regiment. He was found without difficulty, was stripped of all his clothing including shoes and stockings, and then chained below decks on the warship.* Forbes was told this six years later by another captain of Clanranald's, a kinsman of its chief who described the doctor's capture as the beginning of 'the poor people's additional misfortune'.

There was a devilish paper found about him, containing a list of all the Eigg folk that were in the Princes service. Then that catalogue

* The account given to Forbes says the doctor was taken aboard and 'barrisdall'd in a dark dungeon'. This was an instrument frequently used by Fergusson, a rack which, it was said, no man could endure for more than an hour. Ironically, it was invented (for the interrogation of thieves) by MacDonald of Barisdale, a Jacobite of dubious loyalties.

was read [to the assembled islanders] in the name of giving them protection, which ilk one answered cheerfully and was drawn out into another rank, so that there were no fewer than 38 snatched aboard the man of war, were brought to London, from thence transported to Jamaica, where the few that lived continue as slaves yet. Many of them dyed and starved ere they arrove at the Thames.

There are now few inhabitants of Eigg and none, perhaps, can be a descendant of Clanranald's people. These were finally cleared early in the last century, and sheep were set to graze among the ruins of their homes. But there remains an echo of their names and of others similarly transported from the Highlands and the Isles. Forty years ago, when the first great wave of immigrants came to Britain from the Caribbean, it was my assignment with other newspapermen to cover the arrival of their boat-train at Victoria. The names given by those who happily answered my questions were often Highland. These may have been acquired by marriage or union between white slave and black slave, by casual choice or by the adoption of a slave-owner's name, as was the custom among the freed slaves of North America. But I like to think that some memory of Clanranald's people, and of all those Highlanders transported in a long century of rebellions, came home within the spirit of these singing, hopeful West Indians.

Early in my life I was easily entrapped by the sound of Highland names. By my last school year in West London I was already in love with a country I had yet to see, and inspired by a history I had yet to understand. My Jewish friend, Walter Flack, shared my interest, if only as an alternative to post-examination boredom. We gave ourselves Highland names, adding them to our own and writing them in full on exercise books and in impudence upon school and house notice-boards. Walter was articled to a surveyor in the year I was employed as a rent-collecting clerk. He served in the ranks throughout the war and when he later became a millionaire, through property development, it pleased him to give the chair of his company to a man who was not only Highland but also a field-marshal, Auchinleck, one-time commander in the Middle East, where Walter had been a tank-sergeant. As schoolboys we each had a retentive memory for verse, and we filled our minds with stanzas from Scott, Aytoun and others, lines we chose for their cadence, rhythm and the wildness of the names they recalled. One snatch alone remains with me.

Clan Chattan is broken, the Seaforth bends low,
The sun of Clanranald is sinking in labour.
Glencoe and Clan Donnachaidh where are you now?
And where is bold Keppoch, the Laird of Lochaber?

Neither the sun nor the son of Clanranald sank in labour, but in debt, gambling and profligate self-interest. Ranald George Mac-Donald, the twentieth chief, was educated at Eton. He became a Regency buck who preferred life in London or Brighton to Arisaig or the Isles, although he was for a time the commander (*in absentia*) of a Hebridean regiment of militia. The debts he inherited were increased by his own, and he failed to resolve them by successive marriages to one American and two English women. He at last met his financial obligations and his personal desires by selling almost all his land in less than three decades, retaining only an ironic hold on Tioram's dour ruin. He lived for another thirty-five years beyond the last sale, a Londoner still, and he is buried in Brompton Cemetery. As a boy in Philbeach Gardens I sometimes wandered among the stones of this graveyard, marvelling at names and inscriptions. I regret that I cannot remember the sarcophagus or headstone of Clanranald's most calamitous chief.

Between 1813 and 1838 he disposed of twelve major estates for which he received almost £215,000. Eigg was bought for £14,500 by Hugh Macpherson, a physician in his early life but lately a Professor of Greek at the University of Aberdeen and the sub-Principal of that establishment. The son of a minister in Golspie, on his mother's side he came from a West Highland family. Indeed, in the beginning all twelve properties were sold to Highlanders, Clanranald's kinsmen or neighbours. They were gentry for whom Walter Scott had little good to say, although he charitably admitted that it was vain to abuse them for 'the inevitable consequence of a great change of things'. But abuse them he sometimes did. Highland gentlemen, he told Maria Edgeworth in 1830,

> . . . are fond of *spaghlin** as they call it, a sort of showy vanity – they are desirous to keep abreast of the English in expence and maintain their own privileges of chieftainship besides. They must therefore turn their farms into sheepwalks where the black cattle

---

* Gaelic *spaglainn*, defined as 'fools' pride, conceit, bombast, ostentation'. *A Pronouncing and Etymological Dictionary of the Gaelic Language*, Acair and Aberdeen University Press, 1979.

supported scores and hundreds of men, hence high rents (which have proved of late fallacious) and emigration of its people.

In the same letter and context Scott tried to be fair to the wastrel Clanranald, who had given his piper 'to one of the Princes of Blood' and now had one deer-hound only to maintain his dignity as a chief. 'I was sorry,' said Scott, 'for he was good natured with all his faults and follies, yet the spendthrift humour which is after all utter selfishness does not deserve much pity.'

Arisaig and Moidart are the sweetest of the Rough Bounds. Copses of seaward birch step down the white sands to meet the gentle summer tides of sheltered bays. Stunted rowan and oak rise from cracks in rocks split by primeval heat and ice. There are moist-eyed seals on off-shore banks, yellow flags in the dark peat-water of roadside tarns, sea-fowl like scattered paper above the waves, and the up-tipped wings of hovering predators on the high braes. Ranald George sold Moidart for no more than £9000 in 1827, to a Clan Donald cousin who sold it again to southern incomers. Whoever owned the land now, cousin or stranger, sheep and the sporting gun became the eventual possessors, and the people were gone. In 1852 almost one half of the remaining population of Moidart went to Australia, many against their will, said Father Charles MacDonald. A naval captain from Durham bought the estate of Shona, a serene and hospitable island, an emerald in the serpent mouth of Moidart. He willingly helped most of its people, and others from the south shore of the loch, 'to flit and remove themselves', as it was described in the harsh poetry of the writs of eviction. They were not under great pressure to go, said Father MacDonald, and 'seemed glad to avail themselves of the opportunity of trying their fortunes' in Australia. And glad they may have been, for there was no future for them now on the captain's sporting isle.

Clanranald's land in Arisaig, where every green inlet and rock-bound glen seems to be waiting for the return of lost voices, was first sold in 1826 for £49,500. It slipped sideways from the gambling fingers of Ranald George. The public story was that he sold it to his second wife, Anne, a rich American widow who, despite her marriage to Clanranald, continued to be known as Lady Ashburton. Scott said that MacDonald 'used her but indifferently and parted with her', and indeed the sale of the estate may have eased the separation for one of them. Throughout the rest of the century, up to and beyond the day when the raddled corpse of Ranald George was lifted to Brompton Cemetery, the sad and beautiful hills of Arisaig passed from hand to uncaring hand, and with each change the population was decreased. When Lady Ashburton died in 1848 she left the property to Lord Cranstoun, a Lowland Scot and a relative. After following the popular policy of Improvement and Clearance, albeit in a desultory fashion, he sold the estate to Hugh Mackay, laird of Bighouse in Sutherland. From him it passed to an Englishman, Francis Dunkinfield Palmer Astley of Felton and Dunkinfield, who had other estates to match the weight of such a name in Cheshire, Lancashire and Yorkshire, as well as a Highland lodge near Fort William. He and his descendants held Arisaig well into the twentieth century, and the memory of the last to occupy the big house hangs like a whisper on the air above Loch nan Uamh. James Mitchell, that honest engineer and road-maker, did not like Astley, or his methods of dealing with the land and its people, and his strictures on the incoming English squire could be applied to a dozen or more Highland proprietors at that time.

> This gentleman had no Highland sympathies or feeling for the native inhabitants. He removed the [MacDonald] family of Borrodale from their ancient residence, and having razed Arisaig House to the ground on account of its damp situation, he built a new mansion at Borrodale. He deprived the people of their old crofts and employed them in cutting down the woods, and when that work was over they had to search for habitation and employment elsewhere.

That new mansion still exists, above the wooded flow of Borrodale Burn and overlooking the islands and the deep water of Loch nan Uamh, where the Errant Prince landed in 1745 and where he departed after his year of disaster. The building stands in a tailored garden among theatrical trees, Victorian in pretension, ennobled by old stone and warmed within by good panelling. It is an hotel now, but those with knowledge of its past may imagine the ghosts that could linger at its stair-head or move soundlessly along its quiet corridors. Francis Astley's heir, an only son, died early, and the whole of Arisaig passed to Gertrude, the eldest daughter, a woman of tenacity and intelligence. Her husband, Captain Arthur Nicholson of London, is lost in her formidable shadow, and did not seem to gain much in substance or stature when he was given a knighthood.

All these incoming families, changing the land and reducing the Gaelic population – or at best trying to transform it into an English peasantry – soon became interlinked by marriage, establishing optimistic and self-rewarding dynasties.* Nicholson was a great-nephew of Octavius Smith, who acquired much of the wild peninsula of Morvern, once the land of the Macleans and the victim of pitiless persecution and burning after the 'Forty-five. Smith too was from London, the eighth child of a wholesale grocer who was also a philanthropist, emancipator and the first Unitarian to hold a parliamentary seat. Wealthy by inheritance, no doubt, Octavius became richer still from his distillery on Thames Bank, Pimlico, where he lived in a house hard by. In the Highlands he became an Improver and a renowned patriarch, with a brood of relatives gathered about him for the ritual photographs on sheep-cropped lawns, their faces darkened by sun-hats and parasols. In the vein of a Greek tragedy, Smith's life was cursed by a wayward son who, at the age of fifteen, married a woman of thirty-three. He later left her to live with a mistress whom he subsequently married. Reconciled to his father, he inherited much of Smith's fortune and increased its value to almost £2,000,000. In 1929, when the estate passed from the hands of his inheritors, family papers that might have given a rich account of Octavius and his clan were deliberately destroyed by fire. The subject awaits a novelist who is inspired by it, and who has the ability to tell the saga in half a million words.

The youngest daughter of Octavius married the youngest son of Patrick Sellar, the object of enduring hatred and bitter Gaelic verse. A successful landlord in the south of Morvern, Sellar was once a factor on the Sutherland estates of the Marquess of Stafford, and he lives in folk-memory as the cruel evictor of Strathnaver. I have written much about him that is harsh and critical, but we agree in our recognition of a similarity between the Gael and the North American Indian. I do not, however, share the contempt of his conclusions. Both, he said, were 'shut of from the stream' of European enlightenment.

---

* A fascinating account of some of them is to be found in *Morvern Transformed*, by Philip Gaskell, C.U.P., 1968. Gaskell says that most of the new proprietors wanted profit from their new land, but Octavius Smith bought his 'for its glamour'. He also describes him as 'a wealthy and original member of the English intellectual aristocracy' which, in the context of Highland history, may not be the compliment it seems.

Both live in turf cabins in common with the brutes; both are singular for patience, cunning and address. Both are virtuous where least in contact with men in a civilised state, and both are fast sinking under the baneful effects of ardent spirits.

There is small reason to believe that any new proprietor, including the 'English intellectual aristocrat' Octavius Smith, would have argued strongly against the proposition that the decline of the Gaelic people was largely their own fault. Between such enlightened land-owners and an increasingly deprived native people there was consequently a great gulf, unbridged by any real familiarity. The view from either side was at best of shadowy figures about whom little was truly known. The residual Gaelic inhabitants of Arisaig found it difficult to define or describe Captain Nicholson when they gave evidence to the Napier Commission in 1883, but they knew what the coming of his wife's family had meant to their homeland. Two of the witnesses were Colin MacDonald and his friend Ranald Mac-Donald, both crofters from Bunacaimh on the twisting coastal road northward from Loch nan Ceall to Mallaig. Before they were questioned, Aeneas MacDonell, the tenant of Camusdarroch further up the coast, asked the Commissioners to give them protection 'from the proprietor and factor and ground officer, and all other people in authority who may harass them for speaking the truth'. This assurance the Commissioners requested and were given by the factor of the Astley/Nicholson estate.

The crofters talked freely of the changes they had seen or knew of since Morar and Arisaig passed from Clanranald's hands. They spoke of neglected land and emptied houses left to decay, of indifferent promises and unfulfilled pledges given by 'intolerable' factors. They spoke of crofts without leases and thus no security, of notices to quit that were 'incontestable', and of a people departing 'in shiploads, put away without consent'. With an irony that could not have escaped the Commissioners – who were almost all Highlanders themselves – Colin and Ranald declared that there had been a better life under the old proprietors, of whom two had been insane. As for the present . . .

Are the people of South Morar, generally speaking, the class that you represent, very poor in their circumstances? – *Very poor*.

Then the sale of the estate has not been an advantage to the people. It has stopped all work? – *It has stopped all work*.

Is the present proprietor of South Morar a Highlander? – *Perhaps
he is for all I know. His name is Nicholson, he may be a Skye man:
I believe he is.*

Why do you call him the proprietor? – *Because he is our proprietor.
He married Miss Astley, and that is the way we call him the proprietor.*

Another witness from the same stretch of the coast, John MacEachran, aged seventy, brought a petition signed by twelve crofters
of his district. Its particular bitterness, as he emphasized under
questioning, was aroused by the manner in which the Astleys had
cleared, and placed under deer, land from which Clanranald 'when
he was going to war [had raised] about 400 or 500 people'.

Seeing that our forefathers have been here from time immemorial,
we consider we have as much right to live in comfort here as the
proprietor has to be superior over us. As to emigration – what land
has a greater right to sustain us than the land for which our forefathers suffered and bled? Why should we emigrate? There is plenty
of waste land around us; for what is an extensive deer forest in the
heart of the most fertile part of our land but waste land?

There is a resemblance here – but not Patrick Sellar's ignoble comparison – between MacEachran's emotional appeal and the words
of Ten Bears. He was a Comanche spokesman, confronting white
men who were determined to remove the Indians from the open
plains and confine them within reservations. I used part of his
impassioned address as a foreword to my novel *The Buffalo Soldiers*. The writing of this book, more gratifying than others, was
inspired by a terrible irony. Much of the 'pacification' of the Plains
Indians was carried out by two regiments of United States Cavalry,
the 9th and 10th. They were black, freed slaves enlisted at the close
of the Civil War. Since most American officers were unwilling to
serve in such units, some commissions were given to sergeants from
white regiments, and many of these were Irish. Thus men who
were once slaves, commanded by junior officers who were the sons
of evicted immigrants or had themselves been dispossessed, were
now used to subdue, remove and confine a free people. 'There are
things which you have said to me which I do not like,' said Ten
Bears.

You said that you wanted to put us upon a reservation, to build us houses and make us medicine lodges. I do not want them. I was born where the wind blew free and there was nothing to break the light of the sun. I was born where there were no enclosures and every thing drew a free breath. I want to die there and not within walls. So why do you ask us to leave the rivers, and the sun, and the wind, and live in houses? Do not ask us to give up the buffalo for the sheep. The young men have heard talk of this, and it has made them sad and angry. The whites have the country which we loved, and we only wish to wander on the prairie until we die. Any good thing you say to me shall not be forgotten . . .

I am recalled by Eigg by the voices of the MacDonalds, of Mac-Eachran and his companions. Or rather, I am reminded of their thin coastal land, the way the road now twists along it, with the railway in friendly competition. Although I have said that I did not see the Island of the Notch before I wrote my novel, I believe now that this may not be strictly true. I must have seen it, but felt no conscious awareness that could become a memory. I must have seen it five and a half decades ago during my first visit to the Highlands, south-eastward from the quay-side at Mallaig or from a carriage window where the railway line comes out of a narrow glen and runs for a mile along the shore from Glasnacardoch to the station. But I had no memory of it in the summer of 1942 when I wrote *Where the Sea Breaks*.

In that year, having escaped, I thought, from Kinmel Park and its constraint, I was returned to it by the bloody-minded nature of military posting, or by some higher authority that wished to keep me where I had already been an intolerable nuisance and might therefore be watched with foreknowledge and caution. I was now a radar mechanic, at that time an extraordinary military man whose real or assumed understanding of the mysteries of radio-location set him outside normal discipline and employment. Drawn from the ranks of all regiments and corps, by virtue of our prior knowledge of electronics or the education to acquire it quickly, we were an exclusive body engaged in what was thought to be secret work, and thus we enjoyed an unbelievable liberty for one brief summer. We were excused all guards, fatigues, dress requirements and other duties that plague a soldier's daily existence. Such was the oc-casional hazard of our work with high voltage and alarming amper-age, we were allowed to ignore all passing officers when working, lest an obligatory salute or a leap to attention endangered us and the equipment. Similarly, when occupied with live components of murderous temperament, we were permitted to keep one hand in a pocket if we wished, a primitive earthing that might save us and the set from incineration. We suspected that these absurd privileges – which were withdrawn as time pulled us back into the ordered insanity of normal Army life – had been insisted upon by our own officers. At this early stage they had been commissioned in haste, snatched from university or industry, thrust into rank and khaki with no knowledge of what either meant or demanded. Unable to give orders with any confidence or authority, unnerved by the weary experience behind our steady stare, they sought their own liberty by opening some of the doors that enclosed us.

We understood, and were grateful. Like William Cobbett, soldiering at the end of the eighteenth century, we taught them how to give an order, what to say and where to stand when the critical eye of a Gunner sergeant-major was upon us all. But they were not commissioned oafs, the privileged and ignorant gentlemen whom Cobbett despised as he stood on parade with a corporal's worsted shoulder-knot on his red coat. Our workshop officers did not provoke contempt such as his, but I can appreciate a common irony.

> There was I [he wrote] in the ranks amongst other men while those who were commanding me to move my hands or my feet thus and thus, were in fact uttering words which I had taught them.

Encouraged by the conditional freedom of our little enclave, and by the tolerance of the camp commandant, we became more ambitious in our activities away from the bench or the projectors. We took the largely neglected pamphlets issued by the Army Bureau of Current Affairs – which aroused a limp interest only in a beneficent post-war Britain – and used them as a platform for more polemical and politically biased debates and lectures. With money tolerantly granted us by the Regimental Institute we acquired Chinese and Russian film documentaries of astonishing naivety and screened them in a hut without much effect on rival programmes at the Garrison Theatre. We welcomed visiting lecturers to talk about these films. I remember but one, an earnest Chinese Nationalist from Liverpool. He came at short notice, and was perhaps

intended to be somewhere else that evening. I wrote the announcement in consequent haste.

Come to the NEWS ROOM, Lower Naafi
CHINA
A TALK: by Dr C. Z. CHEN
A FILM: 'China Fights on'
If you liked the film 'China Strikes Back' which we screened
recently, you will enjoy this magnificent sequel
6.45 p.m.

More successfully, we organized concerts of classical music in the
recreation room of the NAAFI or the small green hut where Captain
Fereday, the non-conformist chaplain, held his friendly Sunday
services. The more skilful among us applied our ingenuity to the
creation of a primitive form of stereophonic sound for use in
the recreation room. From its open windows on a still evening
the sonorous majesty of Sibelius or Beethoven flowed over the
camp towards the Clwyd Hills. We also 'broadcast' plays from the
church-hut – Wilde, Shaw, Priestley and others – the words
and sound-effects carried by cable from the microphone to
some of the barrack-rooms. The women's parts were taken by girls
we recruited from the Alien Volunteers, their middle-European
accents giving a throat-catching charm to the very English roles
they were playing.

But the war was still far, far away. Whenever possible I continued
to volunteer for any service that would release me from intolerable
inaction in North Wales. I had escaped it once, and now that I
had been returned to Kinmel Park there seemed to be an official
determination that this mistake would not be made again. No application I made was forwarded beyond the regimental office, upon
the assumption, perhaps, that no soldier who had been returned to
his unit at his own request from an officer-training school, who
had appeared before a Court of Enquiry on a charge of conduct
prejudicial including sedition, and who was known to be distribut-
ing copies of the *Daily Worker* and encouraging sympathy for Com-
munism, no such soldier should be granted a transfer, even one
that might conveniently remove him beyond further embarrassment
to the Army, or indeed beyond life itself.

I used the wasted time well, I hope, and in that effort I was able
to keep some of my sanity. I wrote a great deal, much of which I
discarded, but some short stories were taken by the little magazines.

I also edited and wrote much of a wall-newspaper we published for the camp and its neighbour, a training-regiment of the Field Artillery. Our publication, *The Beam*, was a length of board, mounted on an easel in the recreation room, upon which were pinned articles, cartoons, verse, criticism, complaints and suggestions. Its editorial staff was mostly recruited from talented, anarchic radar mechanics, and from a few Gunners and NCOs of the Artillery. In time we encouraged others in the camp, recruits in training, to contribute what they wished. The paper was a successor to one of the kind I had established at Kinmel when my initial training was over and I was a junior NCO and instructor. I believe that was the first wall-newspaper in the British Army, and like others later it was inspired by Soviet models. In retrospect, official tolerance was remarkable, particularly at Kinmel Park with its dark history of mutiny after the Great War. I now think we exaggerated the influence and importance of the newspaper, and I know that the tether upon which our enthusiasm was held was much tighter than we liked to believe. We were occasionally reminded of this when the Regimental Sergeant-Major, having read each item slowly and intently, carefully removed those he thought were in breach of Good Order and Military Discipline. He then warned us against the dangers into which ignorance and immaturity could certainly lead us. We were simple enough to welcome this interference, and to congratulate each other on provoking it. The pleasure of such activities relaxed taut emotions and eased frustration, but for my part there was always an uncomfortable shame in the knowledge that the months of war were passing without my proper involvement.

The writing of *Where the Sea Breaks* was an escape from this depression, of course, but the work was compulsive from that inconsequent moment when its opening sentences came to me, remaining unchanged and releasing the story from my mind. We had contrived another small privilege and secured a further freedom from the strait-jacket of that great camp. Most of the training projectors, upon which the radar units were mounted, were sited upon the high ground to the south of the perimeter. We argued that our maintenance and repair of the equipment would be more efficient if it were begun at dawn, before reveille and without the hampering presence of recruits in training. The proposal was sound, but our main objective was to have much of the following day to ourselves. It was a good summer, the mornings bright with sunshine, and the young grass of the hillside glistening with dew. We finished the work quickly and then sat on the projectors in silent contemplation, watching the distant shimmer of the sea and waiting for the sounding of reveille. Below us at last, on the main street of the camp, we saw Badgie the trumpeter leaving the guard-room, one bright instrument on his back and a bugle swinging at his thigh, both held to shoulder-strap and blouse by the red and yellow coils of a lanyard. At the crossroads he halted with a small hop and a stamp, turning through ninety degrees and bringing the bugle to his lips in a sparkling flourish. Upon its first cheerful note we slipped down from the projectors and left the field. Sometimes we gathered mushrooms and took them to the empty cook-house where a tired catering orderly – in return for a liberal share – fried them with bread and bacon for our breakfast. It was sitting there, with six good friends at a scrubbed table, tobacco smoke curling lazily in the long bars of greasy sunlight, that the beginning of the book came to me. I wrote it down quickly on the back of a maintenance-sheet.

The wounded bomber came in low over the island and crashed on the hill. Every night the islanders had heard the raiders going over to the mainland, and after dusk the sky was busy with the purposeful traffic of aircraft. This activity was the prelude to invasion, so it was said.

To continue writing with as little interference as possible I withdrew from dawn work on the top fields and volunteered for the unpopular duty of night orderly. I was sometimes alone as I wrote and sometimes joined by others before Lights Out, for we had made the workshop a clubhouse too. When it became common knowledge that I was writing a book, undoubtedly a scurrilous attack on Army life, I was visited by Regimental Sergeant-Major Mulvanney. He was a Liverpool Irishman, a time-serving soldier of the Royal Artillery. His skin was leathery-brown from many years under an Indian sun, and his expressionless eyes were the palest blue. Remembering the trouble I had been during my first service at Kinmel, and in dark suspicion of my present comrades, he was convinced, I am sure, that the radar workshop was the centre of disaffection and 'Bolshie-plotting', or at best a rest-room for skiving and slovenly soldiers.

He came late when I was alone for once, his arrival unheard in the sound of a twanging piano in the nearby NAAFI. The Orderly-Sergeant was with him, red-sashed and regimentally stiff, but I had known him as a Gunner, and behind the RSM's back he stared at me with one eyelid momentarily lowered in warning or reassurance. I stood to attention as required, beside the bench and my typewriter. The RSM said nothing, but moved the pages of my manuscript with his cane before picking one up and reading it slowly from the first line to the last. He then put it down, paused and gathered all the sheets into an orderly pile, square with the edge of the bench. The neatness pleased him, as if he had somehow corrected my lack of military style. He sucked air between his teeth and along the furrow of his tongue. And then, 'Difficult this sort of thing, is it?' 'Sometimes, sir, yes it is.' 'Got your officer's permission for this, have you?' 'Yes, sir.' 'And the CO's? Got that, have you?' 'So my OC tells me, yes, sir.' 'Right, carry on, then. And watch the black-out.'

Much of the book was written in the workshop, but sometimes I carried typewriter and paper three miles over the hills to the Elwy Valley. We went there often on Saturdays or Sundays, by sunken lanes rich with the scent of meadow-sweet, no sound but the broken step of our ammunition boots, bird-song and the hum of insects. Thus we fled from the Army into the Dolben Arms. This tiny inn was still there last summer, or the summer before, above a white-arched bridge at the throat of the valley, and not greatly changed in half a century. In 1942 it was an ale-house kept by a dear, fat woman whom we called Ma. It was always untidy, always littered with cats, children, bobbing hens and the dishes from which they fed. It had one bar only that any of us would remember now, smelling strongly of soap-washed stone and rich beer. When she could, Ma fed us as if we were princes, with white bread, eggs and good Welsh bacon. Sometimes I wrote in an upstairs room where ceiling and floor slanted towards each other, and daylight came weakly through a dirty window jammed by years of dust. I sat on a box, with paper and typewriter on a sagging bed, its springs thrumming to the urgency of my fingers. I preferred to work below in the bar, where my friends argued and joked as they did when I wrote in the workshop. This was the only *public* writing I have ever done, apart from work in a news-room, which is a different form of writing altogether and takes strength from the companionship of collective achievement.

The Dolben Arms had few customers that I can clearly remember, but one has been unforgettable. Alec was a poacher. Coming down to the bridge in the morning sun we sometimes saw him up-stream, a furtive shadow taking all the cover it could on the bank. If he ignored our shouts we knew that the pocket of his coat was heavy, and that the fish he had gaffed would be on cold stone in Ma's larder before noon, awaiting an evening buyer from Denbigh or Rhyl. He was a little man of indeterminate age, with a hunched back that was surprisingly straight when he stretched himself in an animal yawn. He was bald, I think, but then I do not believe I ever saw him without his cap, its cardboard peak crumbling through a gap in the cloth. There was a bloom of white stubble on his cheek, and his sharp eyes sparked above a thin nose, as if a keen intelligence enjoyed hiding behind his simplicity. He was always dirty, sun-dark skin and harmless grime. And ruffianly, I suppose. Winter and summer he was wrapped in the whole of his wardrobe – two raincoats, an old jacket, a sweater, collarless shirt, trousers too small and boots too large. Nowhere was there a holding button, only blanket-pins and string. 'Buttons,' he said, 'come off, man. See?'

He lived in the fields, or in the woods, constantly changing his hide after discovery by The Insurance or The Employment or The Police. He went rarely to St Asaph or Denbigh, and said the people there must be in a very bad way. 'All so dreadfully unhappy-looking they are. See?' He usually sat in his own corner with a black ale to be drunk slowly. He listened intently to our conversation, nodding where necessary, his laughter pursuing ours. He played darts sometimes, but was quickly bored when he beat us all. Talk of the war distressed him. He believed that we were still fighting the Kaiser, and he could easily weep at the thought. 'War's a *dioul*, soldier, isn't it? I know, see? I was at Eepers. In the trenches, man, we were all there.' We, in this case, were his long-dead comrades of the Royal Welsh Fusiliers, and he could name some of them and how they died. And how the grey enemy had died, too. 'The snipers was hanging from trees like lambs, they were. Aye, war's a *dioul*, isn't it, man?' Although he was certain that his war had never ended, that we were now engaged in it, he could remember how he had entered Germany as a conqueror. 'I was in Munster, man, and Berlin. We marched all over the country, over it all. I wanted to see the Kaiser, but he had gone away, see.'

When one of our number left, posted to another camp, to North Africa or the East, we celebrated his departure at the Dolben. Content at other times to accept hospitality without return, on these occasions Alec insisted on buying the departing friend a drink, searching his clothing for the pennies. His sorrow for one who, he believed, must shortly be dead on the wire was deep and tearful, but his valediction at the evening's close was encouraging. 'You give my regards to the Kaiser, will you, boy? He's a *dioul*, but an *aristocrap*, mind you.'

The novel was quickly written, I think, although those days passed slowly and the hours were long. It was almost finished when it inspired a question so profound that I have yet to find its answer. There was a young Gunner of eighteen attached to the workshop, a recruit who wished to be trained as a wireless mechanic. For reasons unknown or since forgotten he was sent to the workshop where he may have acquired some knowledge of electronics as he swept the floor, cleaned our tools, polished our brass and ran our errands to the NAAFI. He watched my writing from a distance at first and then, because others had done the same, he came close enough to read what I was typing. He pointed at the page. 'How do you know what these people said?' 'I don't know, it's fiction, a novel, I'm making it up.' 'That's right, Corp, but how do you *know* what they've got to say?'

The novel was taken by Fredric Warburg. He was the second publisher to whom it was sent, the first having rejected it, unread I think, within a week. I went on short-leave to London and listened in disbelief to Warburg's urbane and only gently patronizing enthusiasm. I was given the report of his partner, Roger Senhouse, written in a minuscule hand with bemusing references to Stevenson, Conrad and Erskine Childers. I was not ready to have my writing taken seriously by strangers, and I could not be at ease in this cool green office, on a Georgian street sloping down from the Strand to the river. It was a hot day, my boots were heavy, my battle-dress blouse wet with sweat. When I left, soon to be a writer with a *published* book, my rising euphoria was checked by an air-raid alert. This too was absurd. There was no hostility above, only barrage balloons floating straight-stemmed in an empty sky. I realized that I was lonely for the warmth of my friends at Kinmel. We celebrated the acceptance of the book at the Dolben, sitting outside in the cool of the evening. We left the valley arm in supporting arm, and it was long past twenty-three fifty-nine when we entered the camp by a hole in the top-field hedge, avoiding the guard-sergeant and his late-night roll.

It was two years before the novel was published, and at the time I was on my way from the beach at Arromanches, in search of a unit that would take me on its strength. I did not know until much later that the book was almost destroyed before its birth. A flying-bomb struck the office in Essex Street, damaging most of the copies ready for distribution. Nor did I know then that this house, or the one into which the publishers moved, was where Charles Edward Stuart made a bold and unexpected appearance in London four years after Culloden, under the alias of 'Mr Douglas'. He came without warning into the drawing-room of Lady Primrose, the energetic hostess of what remained of an English Jacobite movement. What he wanted, why he came – to be persuaded that another rising was possible, or to destroy that sickening hope for ever – are unanswerable questions, but the visit, unlike the legends of others later, was real enough. My discovery of the story, and my connection with the street, is an example of the serendipity that is one of the quiet pleasures of my life.

The navigator Mann in *Where the Sea Breaks* finally turns upon the lieutenant, in sympathy with the islanders. His words at this point are declamatory and with wider experience they could have been better written.

> 'You say we're lost without you. But it isn't so, without us *you're* lost. So long as we let you, you will live, and go on doing the things you've been doing for years. Just so long as we let you.'

I was 'talking out of the book', as one reviewer observed, reminding me that German Fascism would not change its mind, would not collapse as the German people turned against it. The writer was Jack Lindsay, and his Marxist magazine had published some of my stories. He believed, he told me later, that men of conscience like Mann had long since been lost in Dachau or Auschwitz; they were not awaiting an Allied invasion, preparing for a revolt like the Prussian rising against Napoleon. 'Real resistance to fascism,' he wrote, 'is a bloodier and more entangled thing and above all a thing of organisation.'

I did not read this, or indeed any review, until the war was over and I was given leave. The publication of my first book was not a celebrated event; it was no event at all. I do not remember the date, precisely where I was or what I was doing, except that it was the same as the day before and the day following, and none the better for that. It was almost forgotten until some time later when my mail was dropped to me in the slit-trench I had dug between the sleepers of the abandoned station at Mook. It was raining, I recall, and I read the letter beneath a hooded ground-sheet, to the sound of desultory small-arms fire in the timber before Groesbeek. The letter was from Captain Fereday, the padre at Kinmel. Uninhibited by the prejudices of Anglican chaplains, he had given sympathy and support to our newspaper, our debates and our politicking. He had been left in no doubt about our aggressive agnosticism, but had tolerated it with courteous tact. I think he was pleased to disarm me by praising the book in the context of his faith.

In my mind it is one of the best religious tracts for the times I have read. I was impressed by the way you portrayed the old Presbyterian faith, or should I write soul, overcoming the Nazi mentality. I think I might yet preach from your book on the subject and use your picture of the islanders strengthening themselves with the old faith by singing the Paraphrases, as an illustration.

If there were men like Mann in the defeated Germany of 1945 I did not meet them, which says no more, perhaps, than that my association with the people was limited. There was, of course, the middle-aged man who was often to be found near our cook-house on the Nordrhein plain, doing any chore in return for food or cigarettes. He wore a red and black brassard and an eagle badge from which the pendant swastika had been cut. It was his own creation of authority, no doubt, but it was not challenged and he was occasionally used as an interpreter. It was assumed in the ranks that he was a deserter from the Wehrmacht, from its corps of old men and boys hastily conscripted in the last days of the War. He told me that he had been a factory worker, a member of the German underground, and a Communist since 1933, but he would give no details. As time passed there were other drifting figures making similar claims in the steam of the cook-house. Of all the Germans I knew I remember three only in clear light and distinct form – Burckhardt, Schroeder and Mr Helmuth. None, I think, was my navigator.

I went to Hamburg in the autumn, to become a sergeant-reporter with No. 1 British Army Newspaper Unit, and was there throughout a hard, bitter and relentless winter. The centre of the city, between the Alster lake and the Elbe, was largely a desolate ruin. On the hills of its lunatic landscape a scree of bricks, stones and dust was always in motion. This was the effect of wind and rain, but to an appalled mind it seemed that the dead beneath were struggling to escape. Sometimes, when a surviving wall collapsed under intolerable strain, a cloud of nauseous dust rolled slowly along the street. At night, as if to recall the horror that had created this desert, curfew was sounded by an air-raid siren, after which the only human movement was a Provost jeep on patrol, its white bumper and menacing lights rising and falling over the rubble.

Every morning we were reminded that we, the victors, were responsible for this awesome destruction. Although the charge was made in a tone of daring impudence, we were aware of an impotent anger behind the levity. When we arrived at our office on Grosse-bleichen-strasse one of the German women employed as clerks always rose with a smile and a customary greeting, 'Good morning, barbarians!' There was also a phrase which occurred eventually in almost every conversation with the Germans, indicating a signal change in their lives. All experience had happened before or after 'the Holocaust', the brief but eternal moment when the world changed. For nine days and nine nights in the summer of 1943 the city was remorselessly bombed by the British and American air forces. A million people were made homeless, we were told, and 85,000 were killed. Estimates since have reduced that figure, but the horror is not diminished. Most precisely, the Holocaust described the 'fire-storms' that followed the fall of phosphorous bombs. Winds of great strength, aroused by the explosions and the heat, drove high rivers of flame along the streets, incinerating all. The smell of fire, of damp and charred wood, returned on days of rain, even two years later, and it is my most persistent memory of Hamburg. The Germans we knew talked of that summer with a curious, unemotional detachment, because it now seemed unbeliev-able, or because they were unsure of what our response might be. They told us that many people, running from the fire-storms, some with clothes burning, threw themselves into the Alster and were drowned. It was true, no doubt. Three or four times in the spring, when the ice broke, we saw some proof from the back of our truck, from the step of a Dammtor tram or the Lombard Bridge as we walked across in an afternoon sun – a body, no more than a bundle of rotting clothes, rising suddenly to the surface of the grey water and bobbing there.

We produced our magazine *Soldier* in a ruined print-house on Grossebleichen-strasse but were quartered in Binder-strasse to the north, beyond Loigny Platz in a district that had perhaps suffered least from Allied raids. The house was large, built as a comfortable family home in the last century. It occupied a corner with Schlüter-strasse, opposite a telephone exchange. This was bravely manned by a corporal of the Royal Engineers and a polyglot flock of young girls, released slave-labour from Western and Eastern Europe. At the end of the street there had once been a synagogue, according to an old map I found in the office, but no one I spoke to could or would remember it. The house also overlooked the green square of Ansucht Garten in which every tree of any size had long since been cut for fuel. Not many of the city's trees survived the last black winter of war and the first of peace. Old men and women now gathered meagre twigs in the parks, and children stood on the stumps of once magnificent lindens, bargaining for cigarettes and coffee.

There were three storeys to the greystone house and we – ser-geants and sergeant-reporters – lived on the first floor. Below us were the unit's drivers, mechanics and clerks. We never went to the floor above. We left it to Mama Le Moult and to those she sheltered. Our vehicles filled the small front garden, wheels and petrol tanks locked at night against black-market thieves. They were mostly skilful amateurs, but there were dangerous professionals among them, and the market sometimes seemed to be the only power in the city apart from ourselves. A newly formed police force, in uniforms of inoffensive green, carried no weapons except for the pistols worn by their British officers. One of these was an emotional Ulsterman who commanded his hesitant section from the front, brandishing a revolver on night-time raids and shouting Orange slogans. Disliking the English nature of the Officers' Club by the Rathaus, he came sometimes to stay with us, and after he had drunk enough he would practise with rifle and bayonet on the walls and furniture. When restrained he was good company. To increase our monthly allotment of wines and spirits, any overnight guest was immediately added to the numbers of our establishment by our quartermaster, once the manager of a bookstall at Victoria Station. The Ulsterman's driver, who often came with him, had been a war cameraman with the Wehrmacht on the Russian front. He said nothing, or nothing that I can remember, but he drank a great deal in solemn silence. Both men were killed on the Bremen road, by a mine it was said, or by the dealers they were pursuing.

The apartment was never comfortably warm, although we dis-persed a number of electric fires throughout its rooms. They frequently blew the fuses and burnt the wires, which I was expected to repair. My small collection of cable and fuse-wire was soon exhausted, and since I had no wish to approach a base-workshop – where my local-acting-unpaid rank of sergeant would certainly have been questioned – I maintained the fuse-box with safety-pins from Mama Le Moult's sewing-box. She was a widow in middle age, and the house or apartment on Binder-strasse had been hers before the British came. She should have been evicted by the billeting officer and perhaps was at first, but the advance party of BANU, arriving from Brussels that summer, had reinstated her. She ran the apartment as our housekeeper, and when she drank the gin we pressed upon her she was sometimes overcome, smiling through tears for her good fortune among such suffering. She cooked, cleaned, repaired and washed, arriving almost immediately from her kitchen in response to a shout of 'Mama!' At any moment she could appear in the doorway of our living-room, a gentle moon-face with tightly stretched hair, and a high voice asking in the only English she seemed to know, 'Will you tea . . . ? Will you breakfast . . . ? Will you soup . . . ?' Her gratitude was disturbing, for there was fear behind it, not of what we, the victors, could do, but of what we might have done. We undoubtedly exploited her, but we were not cruel, I think, not discourteous or unkind, only unthinking. When demobilization took me away in the spring of the following year, the truck was beyond Loigny Platz before I realized that among many farewells I had forgotten her. On the power of my spurious stripes I ordered the vehicle back. She was still standing on the steps of the house, more lost than waiting. Now she embraced me, pressed a wet cheek against mine and said, 'Wiedersehen, Sergeant John . . . Leb'wohl, Sergeant John' . . .

She had a room or two at the top of the house where she supported others upon our liberal rations – a girl, an old woman, and the young man simple in mind who had spent much of the war in hiding to avoid military service. We gave him cigarettes, which undoubtedly made him rich on the street exchange, and he repaid us with music on his violin or Mama's piano. He had no skill with either instrument, and he wept as he played 'Lili Marlene'. When there were German guests in the mess they wept also. It was a time of vulnerable nostalgia and the song was now the anthem of a bewildered country. British soldiers from North Africa and Italy had brought it like a trophy to Normandy, where the Second Army too had surrendered to its maudlin, haunting melody. It can still disturb my emotions. The woman who made it famous, a radio voice singing to the German Army, came once as an entertainer to a party in Binder-strasse. Here she sang it for the first time since the War, I think, and we paid her with coffee. Still uneasy about her past and future, she sang badly and blamed this upon the sad young man at the piano.

Burckhardt was a journalist and had attached himself to BANU before I arrived in Hamburg. He rarely came to Binder-strasse, preferring to meet us in the office of *Soldier*, perhaps because he had been long denied any access to the noise, the smell and the tension of a print-shop. The damaged building had once produced *Signal*, a photogravure magazine for the Wehrmacht, and some of its machinery had survived to be of use to us. A falling bomb had cut a large slice from roof to basement, leaving most of the floors open to the air. Some attempt was made to board up the gaps, but elsewhere a false step meant a fall into an inner pit of twisted metal and ice-covered masonry. On the worst days of winter great icicles hung from the wounded stone and iron, and the misted view from above was like looking into an Arctic inferno. The type-setting room was unboarded, and an enduring picture in my mind is of snow spiralling on the up-wind from the pit. It was drawn into the floor where it fell gently upon the hunched shoulders, the scarves, coats, caps and woollen mittens of the printers. They were mostly middle-aged men, and because they did not want Occupation Marks they too were paid in kind, in cigarettes, tea, coffee or other barterable commodities. Having no English, they set type letter by letter and made fewer mistakes than I have known in Britain. They said little about the past, nothing of Hitler and the War, but some spoke calmly of the days before 1933 when they had all been Social Democrats or Communists, or so they said. The life they had hoped for then had been betrayed, by what or by whom they would not say. All had clean *Fragebogen*, the questionnaires designed by Military Government to determine a past guilty or innocent of Nazi association. If there had been membership of the National Socialist Party, the date of joining was required, before or after 1937. In that year membership was made obligatory for workers in many industries, including printing and publishing, and that compulsion was acknowledged by Allied Military Government. Those, like Burckhardt, who had refused to join the Party or Goebbels' print unions had not worked in their trade or profession for eight years.

On our floor in Grossebleichen-strasse we were perhaps too

sceptical of the *Fragebogen*, although we had some knowledge of their occasional absurdity. Below us, on the first or second floor, German publishers were producing Hamburg's first newspapers since the end of the War, a daily and a weekly. Members of the editorial staff, in the Continental fashion, had doctorates of philosophy, literature and the like, and were thus objects of our ill-considered scorn. They came precisely on time to work, each wearing a dark Homburg, a long coat of leather or cloth, and carrying an ubiquitous black briefcase. If we passed them on the stairs, we greeted them civilly and were answered with a nod and polite '*Morgen!*' There was no wish on either side for professional companionship. In contrast to the raucous, military noise from *Soldier*'s floor, there was little sound from them but muted telephone bells and the decorous tapping of a typewriter. On their first day of publication, the street below our windows was suddenly alive with jeeps, and there were more on Bleichen bridge with a Hillman staff-car. They were manned by blue-cap military police, some of whom came up the stairs and into the Germans' editorial office. When they left, shortly afterwards, they took a number of the doctors with them, the majority of the editorial staff, or so it seemed. At this later hour, we were told, their hitherto ignored *Fragebogen* had revealed their Nazi affiliations before 1937.

Burckhardt, who witnessed this with us, said he had known about these men, but would give no explanation as to why he had not informed on them. He may not have cared, or lacked the energy for such a decision, although his newspaper career had been destroyed by Goebbels. He was a strange, gaunt man with restless, apologetic eyes. His body was afflicted with a continuous trembling, so slight as to be almost imperceptible until he lifted a cup or lit a cigarette. He liked to hear us talk of life in journalism before the war. He brought us small items of news which were of no use to us, but we paid him in kind and promised to pass them on to the British Press Corps in Hamburg. Burckhardt knew, I think, that his little scraps of paper were useless, but they served his self-respect. In truth, he visited us for warmth, for comfort, conversation, and for the food and cigarettes we gave him.

He brought his son one day, a boy of ten or twelve who would not speak to us or smile. He sat by the wall, tightly holding the bars of chocolate we gave him. The gift was well meant but perhaps cruel, for we knew he would not be allowed to eat any of it, and he stubbornly resisted our efforts to make him. The chocolate was his proud contribution to the family's store for barter. Burckhardt told us that he shared the boy's interest in philately and that at one time they had a joint collection. When approaching British armour was first heard in Hamburg the boy destroyed his complete issue of Nazi stamps since 1933 because, said Burckhardt, he believed their discovery would bring trouble to his father. A fool among us, myself perhaps, said the stamps could have been worth a great deal had they been kept. With a distant smile, Burckhardt asked us not to disillusion the boy, but he meant that he was proud of what his son had done.

In time we discovered the reason for Burckhardt's sad, shaking affliction. Throughout the Holocaust he had stationed himself on the roof of his house, or some other high building. There, night and day, he watched the sustained and terrible fall of bombs, the rippling explosions and the fearful fire-storms. This was not stupid curiosity; he was following his old trade as a newspaperman. Crouched by what shelter there was, but always within sight of the bombing, he made careful, detailed notes of the raids and their effect. He was, of course, at great physical risk, and more from discovery by the Nazi authorities. When the War was over, and the first members of the Royal Air Force came to Hamburg, he passed this information to the most senior officer who was willing to see him. What use was made of it I cannot say, but it seemed just and proper at the time to encourage his belief that it was eventually read by the Commander-in-Chief of Bomber Command.

As the weather hardened, Burckhardt came less frequently to the print-shop. There were mornings when we ourselves were reluctant to leave our beds or the billet. A year had weakened the fortitude with which some of us had faced the harshest of Dutch winters. The north wind, pressing across the frozen Alster from the Baltic and the Luneberg plain, was like a glacial wall. Every morning, as the truck took us across Loigny Platz, we saw snow-covered figures huddled on the pavement below the Dammtor railway bridge. We had no doubt that some were dead. If the weather was oppressively cruel that day, restricting all but essential activity, their bodies were still there in the evening, their positions unchanged. As our truck turned into the unlit canyon of Binder-strasse, its yellow headlights made sharp crystals of the moving, freezing air. Only the telephone exchange blazed with lamps. Here and there a dark figure stumbled over the frozen snow, disappearing like the White Rabbit into its subterranean home.

And there was Christmas Day. In the morning I worked at the print-shop, finishing another story I was writing on the lesser War Crimes trials in the Rothenbaum-chaussee. The accused was a farmer's widow, I think, who was said to have beaten a young Jugo-Slav to death. I wrote in the cold passion I must have thought suitable to the subject and to justice generally. As I remember, it was not published in *Soldier*; very little of our serious work was. Our masters in Eaton Square now required us to produce encouraging, brightly illustrated stories that would reassure the young National Service men who were replacing us in this graveyard of Armageddon. I recall no single word I wrote, but I remember the approaching sound of pipes, at first cruelly distorted by the squeal of turning tram-cars at the Dammtor, and then loud and challenging. By leaning from the window I could see the line of pipers strutting along the Jungfernstieg, marionette figures against the white and blue ice of the Binnen Alster. They were followed by a slow convoy of open trucks, moving with caution over the pitted street. In each vehicle were Highland soldiers, recognizable as such by their slanting Balmoral caps. They sat facing each other with rifles between their knees and packs on their backs. All were young men grown old and going home, or boys coming out.

Our Christmas dinner in Binder-strasse began at two o'clock in the afternoon and continued in one form or another until well beyond midnight. It is preserved for ever in a clouded photograph, half-remembered faces leaning forward over the littered table to be in shot. Not long after it was taken we heard the sound of children's voices singing 'Stille Nacht' in the street below. Through the misted glass we saw ten or twelve small figures, girls, boys or both, hunched together on the yellow snow. They saw us, and one or two added grace notes to the carol. 'Tommy, have you cigarettes . . . chocolate . . . coffee . . . ?' Warm and sentimental from drink taken, and I hope with goodwill, we went down and gave them oranges and tangerines, rich sunbursts of colour which none had seen before or could now remember. We gave them sweets and bread and coffee, and pushed Occupation Marks into their pockets. Burckhardt's son was among them. I recognized his eyes and pinched face in a wrapping of wool. For the first time, he smiled at us.

It was easy to remember Christmas past. Then the troop gave a party for the Dutch children whose parents had remained in the village after the line moved through it and forward to the river. It would be good, we thought, to have decorations of green and red paper. At morning stand-to we asked leave to find it, and waited for the Troop Sergeant-Major to agree, stamping our feet, banging our hands and blowing frosted air. It was Sunday, and we watched a little crocodile of children on its way to the village church, six hundred yards along the road. We stopped them, running from the parade on the TSM's nod, our arms held wide and gathering the children into a shrill, giggling circle. We did this every Sunday. Despite our warnings they were always sent at this hour and if not halted would arrive in the village when a self-propelled 88 fired its morning salute from across the Maas. Today some of the children escaped us, scampering on with laughing shouts. We heard the arrival and watched the fall of the shells, three or four columns of dirty smoke rising about the spire of the church. One of the children was killed, a girl. When we drove through the village, four soldiers in a truck looking for Christmas paper, we saw a silent group standing about her body.

There were people in outlying houses, and in winter-tired farms, who were ready to fill our arms with orange paper, but none had red and green. We drove beyond the signs that warned against further advance, along a road that was not yet taped for mines. I remember a vague surprise, close to amusement, when I looked down at the ditch in passing and saw three young men of the Resistance lying there beside a machine-gun. They wore unscarred helmets like pudding-bowls, and each man had an orange band on his sleeve. Our eyes held each other's stare in a brief moment of mutual incredulity. The village we came to was Grubbenvorst, I think, a single street gently arching towards a distant gleam that must have been the Maas. The houses were deserted, but down the middle of the street was a long line of abandoned loot – cheeses, hams, wine, bread, preserved fruit, bottled snails and potatoes. Who had left them in such haste was soon clear. From across the Maas came a familiar sound, the fluttering approach and explosive arrival of mortar-shells, so well described as *stonking* in the footsoldier's onomatopoeia. We left hurriedly with what we could grasp of the abandoned food. On our drive back, beyond the Resistance men who waved this time, we met the first advancing patrol of the 15th Scottish, slow-plodding in single file along each side of the road. As we passed, I saw the yelling, open mouth of an outraged NCO.

But we had no green and red paper, and with little hope now we made our last call, at a building not far from the troop's head-quarters in the butter factory. Although the house was quiet, we could see that it had been prepared for a child's celebration of Saint Nicholas' Eve, a week before. Our polite, unsmiling hosts gave us Hollands in small, thick glasses, a dish of biscuits and the dried peel of fruit. When we explained what we wanted, the husband left the room. On his return he filled our arms with green and red paper and a few toys, new and unused. Outside in the gathering snow we waited for Chappie, the Don R, to rejoin us. Having given a graphic indication to the Dutchman that he wished to relieve himself, he had left the room. Now, when he came out to the truck, his face was red. He walked about the vehicle, swearing savagely and kicking its wheels in violent anger. He had blundered into the wrong room, where lay the small girl killed by a shell that morning.

There was a remembrance of this in Binder-strasse, but it was brief, I think. The day was noisy, the celebration endless. Some of us made telephone calls home, the lines carrying them by erratic routes across north-west Europe until the Channel was crossed. The engineer corporal in the exchange had made this possible for us alone. Now, in return, we invited him and his staff of chattering girls to join us, and further use of the telephone in Hamburg became impossible. As we opened the windows towards midnight, to admit cooler and cleaner air, we could hear a buzzing from the gaunt building on Schlüter-strasse, like the swarming anger of wasps. We sang all the songs we knew. We taught the young man Karlheinz to play 'Long ago and far away' and we sang it many times, each with his own reason. We sang 'Lili Marlene' and heard voices singing it with us, across the street among the tree-stumps of the Ansucht Garten.

The Germans we knew came and went during the evening. Some came and stayed. Schroeder was one of these. He always seemed to materialize rather than arrive, and nobody could remember how and when he had attached himself to us, only that we now expected him and found his presence sometimes necessary. He was tall, with a long face and wings of white hair. He was always neatly dressed, a blue suit immaculately pressed and an impossibly white shirt. What we needed, he could find should the Army be unable to supply it. I think every unit in Germany at that time had its Schroeder in one form or another. He was indifferent to abuse or insult, smiling deferentially as if denying a compliment. He addressed us all as *Mister* Sergeant, in what he believed to be impeccable English. In fact his accent was American, its idiom a decade and more out of date and learnt from old films. He accepted cigarettes as a circus animal might take sugar, in payment for tricks performed. Sometimes he put mine in a cigar-case already full. As if I had not further enriched his wallet of Hamburg's essential currency, he would smile and say, 'That's mighty swell of you, Mister Sergeant. I'll take this home to Mrs Schroeder. She'll be right glad to get it. She likes . . . what do you guys call it . . . a fag?' This Christmas evening, standing on the periphery of a noisy, whirling crowd, he nodded his head gently in time with the music. He seemed content to be ignored, but when spoken to he was confusingly patronizing and obsequious in response. 'Well, Mister Sergeant, are you having a fine time? Isn't this a swell evening? I always reckon it's good for folks to enjoy themselves. You know, during the Great War we had plenty of dances, but this time, what do you know, that guy Hitler wouldn't let the boys have their dances.'

On the day of my demobilization he was in the hallway at Binderstrasse, standing to attention, his face grave in acknowledgement of a sad occasion. When the driver of the truck came to the door to ask if I wanted to leave the Army or not, Schroeder lifted his hand in cautious reproval and appeared not to hear the obscene abuse he got in reply. None of us realized at that moment that he was organizing my departure, telling one to stand here and another there, and keeping Mama Le Moult and other Germans to the rear. He also pressed an envelope upon me, which at first I refused and then thrust into my pocket. I did not open the envelope until I had been in a cold and crowded train for six hours, with Tournai still eighteen hours away. The heating had failed yet again, the air was blue with smoke and thick with foul breath. As I thrust my hands deep into the pockets of my great-coat I felt the envelope once more and now read it. For the first time, as if acknowledging my coming civilian status, Schroeder addressed me formally.

Dear Mr Prebbl. The time may come when England is willing to do business again with Germany. In that case there may be a good British House wanting a reliable and effective representative to take care of their interest in Germany.

If you should hear of any such vacancy I should be very much obliged if you would recommend me. Having lost everything through the war, this would mean a new start on life for me and you may rest assured that I will absolutely give only the very best of service. Thanking you in advance for everything you might be able to do for me, I am, Sincerely Yours . . .

Schroeder was not uncommon, I suppose, and he reminded me of Mr Helmuth, the manager of the Lorelei restaurant and beer-garden on the Rhine to the south of Duisberg. Here the Battery established its headquarters after our departure from the Nordrhein plain. A decade or more later I wrote a short story, *Mr Helmuth stays on*, which began with a sincere if somewhat dogmatic assertion.

Whenever I think of it I know that it was Mr Helmuth who won the War. I remember him best as he was on the last day we saw him . . .

The alcove of the bar was a charcoal smear in which the outline of Mr Helmuth's body was only a deepening of the general shadow. His round face, palely lit from within, was balanced on a neat bow-tie of scarlet silk and the triangle of his white shirt. This distinct geo-metrical assembly seemed to be floating above the glistening taps and idle glasses on the counter. Yet it had a nervous animation, for across Mr Helmuth's face there flitted a curious play of fretted light that gave his thin mouth and the scar on his right cheek an expression of unusual emotion.

The Lorelei had been built for Party leaders and businessmen of the town, a rendezvous for celebrations and pleasant summer evenings. It was white-walled and squat, and where it faced the street it appeared to be windowless, reminding me of those surface air-raid shelters which had survived the relentless bombardment of the Ruhr. Its name was painted in black Gothic characters above the entrance. There was a wide esplanade at the rear, facing the river in which was moored the listing, rusting, scuttled shell of a paddle-steamer, also called *Lorelei*. Mr Helmuth's father had been the manager, and when he was killed in an air-raid his son returned from the Russian front, with an Iron Cross and a scarred face, to be his successor.

The building was empty when an advance party under the quartermaster came to clear it of rubbish, to patch its roof and prepare it for Battery HQ. Mr Helmuth appeared on the first or second day, offering help and guidance. There was something about his correct and precise English which clearly offended the quarter-master's notion of how a conquered people should speak, and he briefly told the German to go to hell. Mr Helmuth clicked his heels in polite acknowledgement, upon which, as if she had been awaiting this cue, Mrs Helmuth came from the doorway to the kitchens.

She was tall and slim, crowned with hair that gleamed brazenly. Her face was heart-shaped with a hard and immodest beauty. The slender stem of her body followed the curve of her hips and was balanced on one knee. In her arms was a sheaf of flowers, like a torch of red and gold. She spoke English with a faint and slurred accent, and we watched the Quartermaster's face flushing as he listened. She had cut the flowers for the restaurant tables, she said . . . The QM pursed his lips meditatively. As he turned away he looked back over his shoulder and said, almost unwillingly, that if they both came the next morning there might be something they could do.

They came every day. Mr Helmuth re-assembled the waiters and the kitchen staff, and his wife brought table-cloths to replace those we were using as sheets, an unimaginable luxury. Mr Helmuth found paper and distemper for the walls, labourers willing to work for the cigarettes and coffee given to him for distribution. Maintaining self-respect, the QM sometimes bullied the German, always referring to him as 'the Wog manager', but he was much more polite to Mrs Helmuth. Upon her request, Mr Helmuth was permitted to use his office again, to open a locked safe into which he put a great many papers. Here in this small room Mr Helmuth and his wife were soon entertaining the QM with a glass of schnapps and a plate of hard, sweet biscuits. As we lay on our beds during those beautiful, sun-soaked evenings, we could hear the QM's throbbing guffaw and Mrs Helmuth's tinkling laugh.

When the main party arrived, the CO came through the door in service dress, his leather cane in a gloved hand. Mr and Mrs Helmuth were waiting a few paces behind the QM, and her arms were again full of flowers. The CO looked at them with suspicion. 'Who are these bloody people, Q? No civilians in Army quarters, you know that.' The QM breathed heavily and explained their previous connection with the Lorelei, quickly adding a word about the help they had given him. Mr Helmuth's heels came together in a gentle click, his head bent. 'Get them out,' said the CO, 'the old days are over.'

Mrs Helmuth stepped towards the CO and handed him the flowers. She was wearing fine silk stockings and her skirt, caught up by the flowers, was raised slightly above one knee. She smiled and said huskily, 'Would the Herr Kommandant like me to put these flowers in his room before we go?' The CO looked at her carefully, not at her body but at her face, just as he did when defaulters were brought before him. Then he said, 'Very good of you, ma'am. Thank you.'

Mr Helmuth stayed on. He and his wife lived on the north side of Herman Goering Platz and they came early in the morning – at first on foot and later by one of the unit's jeeps – she to arrange flowers in the mess-hall and the officers' quarters, and he to superintend the German staff. After breakfast he read the English newspapers which we discarded. He cut items from them and pasted them in a book. Most were about the Nuremberg trials.

He became omnipresent and thus unnoticed, always ready to be of service and thus soon indispensable. He was obsequious without distaste and obedient even to soldiers who baited him. In addition to writing a history of the Battery at this time, I was also using the opportunity, the typewriter and paper allowed me, to write something of my novel. Mr Helmuth would come behind me, soft-footed, to read what I was writing. 'That is very good,' he said more than once. And again, 'You write extremely well. Have you perhaps a degree in literature?' When I swore at his presence we were overheard by the Adjutant, and I was reported to the CO for reprimand. There was a vase of flowers on the Battery Commander's desk, beyond which he looked at me with unhappy eyes. 'Are you going to make a balls of things here too, Prebble?' 'No, sir.' 'Good. Then treat these people with respect. Dismiss.'

Mrs Helmuth was soon a regular guest at the parties which the officers held in the ball-room, valedictions to those going home for demobilization. They always ended noisily when the younger subalterns drove the Don Rs' machines in throttling thunder about the ball-room and out into the street. I was on guard at the end of one party, standing to attention at the Slope as the Battery Commander wished. Although it was long past curfew, a jeep was waiting to take the Helmuths home to Herman Goering Platz, its driver maintaining a mumbling, cursing commentary on the noise within. Mrs Helmuth came out at last, accompanied by two or three officers, one of whom was shouting, 'No, no . . . one more dance, Frau Helmuth! One more, please . . . !' Humming the conga, he put his hands upon her hips and stamped his feet encouragingly.

Behind them, Mr Helmuth was as correct and as impassive as always. His wife laughed and led the serpentine dance, her hands clutched to her breasts, which seemed to be even more generous than usual. At the jeep, the subaltern released her hips and grasped one of her arms to help her into the vehicle. By this unintentional violence her hands were pulled from the front of her dress. Cascading from her breast, like a conjuror's trick, came a wave of cigarettes and loose toilet-paper. In an astonished silence, the Germans eased themselves into the jeep. As he drove away, the driver grinned happily.

Mr Helmuth's control over the German staff was cold, firm and unquestioned, but the kitchen girls, secure in the rough friendship of the Battery cooks, were openly hostile to Mrs Helmuth.

One spat at her beautiful feet. In sudden rage Mrs Helmuth raised a hand to strike, but the girl struck first, across Mrs Helmuth's lovely mouth with a dish-rag. Mr Helmuth calmly reported the matter to the CO who leant across the desk and said he would have no damned Nazi tactics in his unit. Mrs Helmuth was away for four days, suffering from shock, and when she returned she brought an armful of flowers for the CO's table. He told the cooks to keep the girls in hand.

Mr Helmuth suggested that there might be more understanding between the British and the Germans if one could learn the other's language. With the CO's permission, he undertook the lessons himself.

While the sun drenched the dusty air of his little office and fell in bars across his face, he taught us simple, everyday phrases which, he said, with a smile that was only faintly insolent, we might sometimes need. *Will you walk with me my dear? No, I am married. It is a pity you are married. Yes indeed, but perhaps you have a cigarette? Also chocolate?*

Almost without our knowledge Mr Helmuth had recovered the management, the organization and the ownership of the Lorelei, and he told us that his re-instatement had been confirmed by the Military Government of the district. Yet it was plain that he was becoming increasingly uneasy. He would stand for long periods on the esplanade staring at the Rhine, his hands clasped behind his back. He no longer smiled at us, and no longer asked for our newspapers when we had finished them. He knew, before we did, that the unit was moving. When the order was posted, the German staff rejoiced, confident that the Helmuths would now be removed. But we were all mistaken.

Before we left, the officers of a new unit arrived. Our last truck was at the door with the CO's jeep behind it, the engines turning and drowning the sound of all conversation. Below the tailboard small boys jumped and scuffled for our cigarette-ends.

We moved first, away from the stationary jeep, but were halted at the cross-roads to allow a bullock-cart to pass. The CO shook hands with the major of the incoming unit. We saw him turn and point his stick at Mr Helmuth who was standing at the entrance to the Lorelei. The German clicked his heels and bowed slightly from the waist, but the new major shook his head. We waited for Mrs Helmuth to appear and she came in animal loveliness from the darkness of the Lorelei. The flowers in her arms were wonderful. Someone in the back of the truck whistled sardonically, and the CO turned his red and angry face toward us.

The bullock-cart was gone and we moved on. Before we slowly turned the corner we saw Mrs Helmuth throw back her head and laugh. The new major tucked his cane beneath his arm, thrust his hand into the flowers to find hers and nodded his head.

The novel I began in the Lorelei was called *The Edge of Darkness*. I worked upon it spasmodically in Hamburg and completed it in England, writing in the early morning before my journalist's day. Some time after its publication Fredric Warburg invited me to a reception for Thomas Mann. It was not an intimate occasion but the last opportunity, perhaps, for England to see the great German author. The reception was held in the River Room of the Savoy Hotel, the summer sun of late afternoon broken by the shade of discreet blinds. I stood in line with others to meet and possibly talk with Mann, whose almost motionless head and shoulders I could see above the bobbing figures of others. When I arrived at his chair, where his daughter also sat to translate, his handshake was weak but acknowledging. Warburg told him that I had been a soldier in Hamburg and that I had written about it in a novel. Mann looked at me without any deep interest, and with eyes which in that light at least seemed an extraordinary blue. In a tired voice he asked if

I remembered a certain street, by the Alster he thought. I said I did not, and added that if it were of importance to him I hoped it had not been destroyed. There was no reaction and his eyes did not follow me as I was passed on.

February the Thirteenth

It is fiercely cold by the Meeting of the Waters. In this hall of mountains a narrow corridor rises steeply southward to the escarpment of Bidean nam Bian. It ends in a high bowl, a giant's porringer with an evocative name – *Coire Gabhail*, the Thieves' Hollow, more precisely Corrie of Plunder.* Here in clouded security, one thousand feet above the floor of the glen, the MacDonalds are said to have hidden the cattle they lifted from Breadalbane, Argyll and all the airts, and sometimes took shelter themselves when their forays provoked a savage reprisal. I cannot see the corrie this morning. The dusty white of wind-blown snow comes down the cliff of Beinn Fhada to dance spirited reels on the black roadway and mask the frown of every rock-face. I have known more considerate weather in Glencoe and felt the warmth of a generous sun, but today it has pleased an editor in Glasgow to have me photographed here by the Meeting of the Waters, hatless and unable to endure the cold for more than five minutes. It was on this day, in such wind and snow three centuries ago, that two companies of the Earl of Argyll's Regiment of Foot rose before dawn to kill their hosts, whose hospitality and trust they had enjoyed for twelve days. This upon orders from the King and from his Secretary of State for Scotland, with an assurance that it would be 'a proper vindication of the public justice to extirpate that sept of thieves', the Mac-Donalds of Glencoe.

I was scarcely out of my schooldays and had seen nothing of Scotland when I first thought of writing the story of the Massacre, in the form of a novel. With chilling self-confidence, I believed it would improve upon its inspiration – John Buchan's imaginative and recently published account. I knew little of the history of the

* But *gabhail* has other meanings beyond that chosen by legend. It can be a farm, the course of a ship, wood for firing, the way a man carries himself, flames, fermenting, and more.

Highlands and was the willing captive of preposterous myth and crass Victorian romance. I had also surrendered to the beguiling novels of D. K. Broster and mistook her Anglicized characters and sanitized Gaelic society for a truth more elusive and less easily stomached. I abandoned the project when the stark narratives of the *Lyon* revealed my ignorance, but there are those who would argue that I am still in thrall, that my books have the emotional style of a novelist, a journalist or a screen-writer. Since I have been all three, there can be no dispassionate debate on the proposition. If I regret that my small shadow on recorded history has provoked so strong a light of academic disapproval, I can also accept with respect an occasional expression of appalled admiration.

Indignation is also the prime mover in the work of John Prebble, a writer of considerable literary skills whose imaginative reconstructions of dramatic episodes in Highland history have been influential in sustaining a generalized scorn of the enemies of the old Highland culture – the Lowlanders, the English, the Anglo-Saxons, industrialism, avarice, landlords and capitalism. Written in a strikingly cinematic style, cumulatively impressionistic in method, Prebble's histories are literary and allusive. Their main force is always individual personality and dramatic episodes. While Prebble eschews systematic analysis and the impedimenta of scholarship, his writing is nevertheless often informed by a sound knowledge of important and frequently neglected sources. His work, taken as a whole, has the force and sweep of a saga.*

The hold that Glencoe has upon me is constant, and I do not share a common belief that its appearance is always hostile and mournful. One violent dawn in a long history is responsible for that melancholy view. Under its influence Macaulay said that the valley's name meant Glen of Weeping – 'the very Valley of the Shadow of Death' – which is not the only mistake in his version of the Massacre. Another fanciful translation is Glen of Dogs and this is more pleasing, for the legends of the Feinn say that the great Fingal hunted

* Eric Richards, *A History of the Highland Clearances*, Vol. 2, pp. 143–4 (London, 1985). Professor Richards continues at length and is progressively less flattering, but he is among the kindest of my critics, and perhaps I wish I had been able to read his book thirty years ago when I was writing my own and when, to my knowledge, no academic was taking an interest in the Clearances, systematic or cinematic.

here with his yellow hounds. In records of the fourteenth, fifteenth, sixteenth and seventeenth centuries the word appears as *cumhann* and *caol*, each for narrows or a narrow glen, and *chomair* for a meeting of the waters, meaning Loch Leven perhaps, or the black and white throat of this gorge. The glen is now largely uninhabited, its stony braesides given to sheep and remorseless erosion, its bottom-land often fallow and green, but ancient visitors praised it for its bounty and beauty. 'A garden enclosed,' said one, three hundred years ago, 'very profitable, fertile, plenteous of corn, milk, butter, cheese, and an abundance of fish.' It was not so idyllic, perhaps, and no doubt that traveller visited it in a good year. In leaner times its people suffered hunger and hardship. Their survival occasionally depended upon the meat and meal gathered in their forays upon old enemies or former friends. Such excursions, by all small and hungry clans, were usually conducted with cautious stealth and the wise avoidance of conflict, but sometimes killing came close to slaughter. Cloaked with honour, it appears noble in the heady language of the bards. Early in my account of mutinies in Highland regiments I tried to record this apparent savagery with the understanding I lacked when the flight of Miss Broster's heron still influenced my imagination.

Need made robbery a necessity, skill at arms an instrument of that need, and warfare the ultimate in masculine achievement. The more robust of Gaelic verse throbs with the love of weaponry, blue-bladed swords like lightning-flames, three-grooved swords in well-sinewed hands, bright-sparking pistols and dark brown muskets, silver-studded shields and the crescent sweep of axes. The bards who used such imagery were often warriors themselves and had seen what their weapons could do to unresisting flesh, but their enthusiasm was spurred rather than curbed by the experience. Poets who sang of the musk-like fragrance of their beloved's breath, the swansdown of her breasts, were also passionately delighted by the thought of necks cut like thistle-stems, arms hewn from white bodies, and skulls cleft to the back-bone marrow. Their clean-limbed young men are ever dauntless and gay, stepping lightly upon the heather with plaids belted, bonnets cocked and eyes bright. Even where it is stylistic and repetitious the verse is always vibrant, pulsing with admiration, and its strange alchemy worked upon the bewildered Highlandmen long after grape-shot had proved more deadly than the lightning-flame, and the purse of the *ceann-cinnidh** more persuasive than his ancient obligations as the father of the family.

Six hundred years ago, by romantic tradition, Angus Og Mac-Donald, Lord of the Isles, gave Glencoe to his bastard son Iain Og Fraoch, Young John of the Heather. By other traditions, more hostile if less obscure, the descendants of Heather John and his people – legendary poets and warriors, braggarts, bowmen, cunning raiders and hunters with swift hounds – were always a predatory threat to the stability of the kingdom. References to them appear briefly in Privy Council records from the Middle Ages to the seventeenth century, short and impatient sentences, sour with frustrated bile. One chief after another, his son or cousin, is described as 'an oppressor for many years, a fugitive and outlaw' or 'a common and notorious thief', and the whole clan sometimes condemned as 'thieves, sorners and broken men'.† Brought before the justices at Inveraray, a Glencoe offender who was not high enough in station to escape with a fine could expect to have his back scourged and his tongue bored with a hot iron, and consider himself fortunate not to be hanged on Doom Hill. The MacDonalds of Glencoe sometimes behaved as if they were compelled to justify the worst that could be said of them. In February 1603, paid by or in alliance with the MacGregors, they took arms against the Colquhouns of Luss and the burgesses of Dumbarton and fell upon the fertile land of Lennox. After a victorious slaughter of men and horses in the battle of Glen Fruin, one Allan Og MacIntuach from Glencoe was given charge of forty prisoners. Eager to join his kinsmen in the loot and burning of Loch Lomondside, he freed himself from his captives by stabbing them one by one. The Privy Councillors angrily ordered his arrest, but it was six years before he was taken and sent to the gallows with their thankful valediction. 'In the whole course of his by-past life he had exercised himself in theft, murder, reif‡ and oppression, and he is most unworthy to be suffered any longer to breathe the air of this country.'

During his lifetime, it was said that the chief of Glencoe who died in the massacre of 1692 was party to the murder of some of his own people. In the absence of any evidence beyond hearsay I

* *ceann-cinnidh*: a chief, literally head of a family, of his kindred, his children.
† sorner: a sponger, a beggar, an idle fellow. In this context, perhaps, one who takes food by force.
‡ reif: reiving, plundering.

believed the charge to be another extravagant invention, but in 1964, in the Argyll archives below Inveraray Castle, I found a paper that gives it substance. Written in the crabbed hand of Archibald Campbell, the luckless ninth Earl of Argyll, it is plainly a memorandum made during an interrogation or on information received. It names six cousins of the chief, men from the family of Achtriachtan who 'killed after dinner in cold blood and stabbed and cut to pieces' two MacDonalds of the glen, having first fired their house. The paper has no date but was written in the spring of 1674, I think, when MacIain was imprisoned and examined in the Tolbooth of Inveraray, the second of two Glencoe chiefs to be held in gaol during that century. He broke out and escaped by means unstated, and was safe in his home at Invercoe when the Privy Council raged against those Highland lords who were responsible to the crown for the behaviour of the western clans, and in particular of men like MacIain the twelfth chief of Glencoe . . .

> . . . since he and John M'Donald in Auchtriatin [Achtriachtan in Glencoe], with diverse of their peoples, have committed several murders and depredations whereby the country in these parts is likely to be casten loose and exposed to the rapine and violence of these persons.

Although relations between the Glencoe people and their neighbours, particularly the Campbells, were not continuously hostile, it is easy to believe they were cursed and outcast. As the Angel of the Lord said at the birth of Abraham's natural son, Ishmael, so might it have been said of a Glencoe MacDonald – 'He will be a wild man; his hand will be against every man, and every man's hand against him; and he shall dwell in the presence of all his brethren.' In a century inspired, directed and sometimes betrayed by the Old Testament, there was always divine authority to be cited for the destruction of those who were anathemas to Church or State, and whom none would mourn (the Glencoe people were arguably Catholics, and were therefore double-damned). Since weightier matters of government were to be served by the Massacre of Glencoe, *moral* justification could be claimed in the context of a general fear and hatred of its victims. This, it seems, was the thinking of John Dalrymple, Secretary of State for Scotland, writing his murderous orders by candle-light in Kensington Palace. For he would be as tender of blood as any man, he said, were not the reputation of the government in question. Therefore, in dealing with that damnable sept, use fire and sword . . . and, above all, 'Be secret and sudden . . . be quick . . .'

The glen has a beauty that always catches my heart. Never has it appeared to me twice in the same colour or light, whether I come by the iron bridge at Ballachulish or westward over Rannoch to the Great Herdsman, beyond whose indigo shadow the valley can glisten with ever-changing sunlight. I came here first on foot, almost sixty years ago. Its broad highway was then newly built, the banked earth along its edges red-black and studded with stones like a rank of shields. It was too new, too heedless an intrusion, and I followed the old road. This was still in good condition and used by young foot-travellers like myself, by carriers, shepherds, pedal-cyclists and an occasional bull-nosed Morris. Old and now abandoned for the most part, some of it stubbornly survives, recognizable on the brae-side by a break in a contour or a pause in the drifting scree, by the dark eye of a culvert half-hidden in deer-grass, and by the leaping flight of leathered motor-cyclists, delighting in its dangers and hastening its final erosion. Along the water of Achtriachtan it marches with or is covered by the modern road, but at the loch-end it branches northward about the green hump of Signal Rock, skirts the base of Sgor nam Fionnaidh and comes to Invercoe through gentle trees. Not long since on this road, near Leacantuim and by a copse of thorns, there was a small roadside cairn of grey stones. Below it lay an Argyll soldier, it was said, killed by the MacDonalds during the Massacre. In recent years I have been unable to find it, and a memory so defeated begins to doubt if it were ever there.

Although the old highway is sometimes referred to as one of General Wade's military roads, it was built towards the end of the eighteenth century, almost fifty years after his death. It was improved by Thomas Telford, who wished to make life easier for the drovers from Skye and the Outer Isles who came through Glencoe on their way to the great market tryst at Falkirk. They gathered with other herdsmen at Altnafeadh on the edge of Rannoch Moor. Here the Devil's Staircase – once a cattle-trail and then a military road of spectacular achievement – twists down to the eastern gateway of the glen. Alan Breck and David Balfour escaped this way unseen – or so Stevenson imagined, although the highway was built in the year of their flight, and there were a thousand soldiers in the road-gangs between Bridge of Orchy and Altnafeadh. In fact, not fiction, Lieutenant-Colonel James Hamilton, a dark figure in the Glencoe story, brought four hundred men over the Staircase from the north, leaving Kinlochleven after dawn and climbing through snow to block the glen in the east and thus prevent any escape from the Massacre. Captain Campbell of Glenlyon had done the work before they arrived at eleven o'clock, but they killed an old man who stumbled from his burning house at the loch-end.

Before it was a military road, the path over the Staircase was a raiding-trail for the Lochaber clans, leading to Rannoch Moor and the rich lands of Breadalbane beyond. The memory of such violent days was still alive at the beginning of the nineteenth century and timid travellers, passing Rannoch's black lochans and the white skeletons of long-dead trees, frightened themselves with thoughts of robbers and footpads. In 1803 Dorothy Wordsworth said it was 'a great thoroughfare of thieves', but was more upset by the rough meal she and her brother were offered at the Kingshouse Inn. Two and a half miles eastward from Altnafeadh, this isolated building, like others of the same name in the Highlands, was first established as a military lodging for patrols and for the road-makers. It was later used by travellers, carters, pedlars and the drovers who caroused here after mustering their night-black herds on the lower braes between Lagangarbh and the mouth of Glen Etive. It was 'as dirty as a house after a sale on a rainy day', said Miss Wordsworth, with no eggs to eat, no potatoes, bread or milk, and the shoulder of mutton served was almost meatless. She and her brother shared the inn with seven or eight drovers who sat in a circle about a peat fire, each with a dog at his side and a wooden bowl of porridge on his knee.

When working on my book in 1964 I lodged more agreeably at Kingshouse, in a room that was part of the old building, its window looking upon the Great Herdsman and the oil-black road threading towards the glen. I did not know then that Charles Dickens spent a night here in the early summer of 1841, with Kate his wife, his friend the sculptor Angus Fletcher, and his coachman William Topping. He was a young man, not yet thirty but already re-nowned, and he came on his Highland jaunt from Edinburgh, where he had been lionized for twelve days. The party arrived at Kingshouse in low spirits. They had travelled more than fifty miles that day, the last ten of which, from the Black Mount, had taken two and a half hours. Although it was June there was snow on the high peaks. The cold was intense, the wind piercing and the rain sometimes very violent. Even whisky, said Dickens, had failed to keep the travellers warm, a regret to which I respond with the deepest empathy. The road from the south had taken them through an appalling landscape – steep passes, high precipices, huge masses of rock and moor like the graveyard of giants, he thought. And Glencoe itself, seen now from his window or later the following day, was 'perfectly terrible, the pass is an awful place'. At Kingshouse, however, the landlord of what the author called 'a lone public' treated him as his reputation deserved, even here in 'the bleakest and most desolate part of Scotland'. Almost frozen when they arrived at three in the afternoon . . .

> . . . we got a fire directly, and in twenty minutes they served us up some kippered salmon, broiled; a broiled fowl; hot mutton ham and poached eggs; pancakes; oatcakes; wheaten bread; butter; bottled porter; hot water, lump sugar, and whisky; of which we made a very hearty meal.

However they fared at Kingshouse, few of those early travellers could write of Glencoe without the remembrance of discomfort, distaste and sometimes horror. A number were calmly unimpressed but said so as if they were in fact resisting a compulsion to admire. Aboard the yacht *Fairy*, hove-to on Loch Leven by the Mac-Donalds' burial isle, the Prince Consort studied the mouth of the glen without feeling any obligation to go ashore. 'It was fine,' wrote the Queen, 'but not quite so much as he expected.' Samuel Coleridge, ready for the realization of an artist's Gothic drawing, admitted that he was rather disappointed, and overloaded this judgement with another more ugly. 'There was no superincumbency of Crag, the Crags not so bare or precipitous, as I had expected.' Thomas Telford's opinion was of course practical, not aesthetic. He was troubled by the condition of the road, and the landfalls that often closed it. He put the blame on increasing numbers of sheep on the braes, remorselessly cropping the natural binding and dislodging the scree. The uneasy escarpment of Aonach Eagach today still scatters the modern road with drifts of stones like crumbling lava, grey and unfriendly. At Telford's shoulder his friend Robert Southey was lyrical, however, so enraptured by the 'serene beauty' he saw that he almost wished he could believe in that most engaging literary hoax, the spurious verse of the legendary Gaelic poet, Ossian.

In 1798 Mrs Sarah Murray, resolute as ever, abandoned her well-sprung coach, its tired horses, her coachman and her maid at

Kingshouse and took a peat-cart into and out of the glen, sitting on a cross-board or walking beside the sheltie for a bone-jarring journey of eighteen miles. Exhausted by this, and half-choked by the smoke of the inn, she fell asleep under a rain-dripping roof and in 'a sty . . . a square room of about eight feet, with one window and a chimney in it, and a small bedstead nailed in the angle behind the door'. Her maid slept elsewhere upon two chairs, and the coachman Allan with his horses, no doubt. The hardships of travel neither deterred nor wholly disgusted Mrs Murray and were grandly compensated by such sights as Glencoe, to which she surrendered in breath-taking similes.

> Tower-like crags . . . of a very black and dark green hue, consequently very gloomy. Adjoining this extraordinary weeping mass is a continued range, of a mile in descent, of other crags equally perpendicular and high; in most of which appear caves and arched passages, with pillars, like the communication from one aisle to another, high up in the sides of Gothic cathedrals; also small Gothic-like windows and doors. The whole mass, to an eye below; appears like an immense and inaccessible fine ruin, mouldered, defaced, and become uneven by a vast lapse of time.

At the Meeting of the Waters she met a small chaise and a mounted party, the chief of Clan Macnab and his family on their way to Kingshouse and greatly amused by the sight of a female traveller on the cross-board of a peat-cart. She ignored their humour and congratulated herself on having secured one of the best 'pig-holes' at the inn. She was determined to return there before The Macnab ousted her from the room, which indeed he did attempt.

I do not believe that Stevenson ever entered Glencoe, although he placed his fugitives there. Alan Breck and David Balfour first hid in a mountain cleft high on the Pap of Glencoe, Sgur na Ciche, which Stevenson called Corrynakiegh. From here they made their way to Rannoch, whether by the glen or by Loch Levenside and over the Devil's Staircase is not clear. What could have been a remarkable journey, and a descriptive account of compelling power, is dealt with in one sentence. 'More than eleven hours of incessant hard travelling brought us early in the morning to the end of a range of mountains.' Ahead of them 'lay a piece of low, broken desert land', the Moor of Rannoch. Stevenson's favourite book was written far south of the Border, in a Bournemouth villa called

Sea-View which he quickly re-named Skerryvore.* When he came to the end of the five days his fugitives spent at Corrynakiegh, he may have regretted a boyhood decision that robbed him of first-hand knowledge of the country now ahead of them. In August 1864, at the age of fourteen and travelling with his uncle and father on the lighthouse yacht *Pharos*, he wrote to his mother explaining how an evening's enjoyment of a shipboard band in Oban Bay had disrupted his plans for the following day.

> Next morning I slept on, or I should have gone to Glencoe. As it was blazing hot, so I hired a boat, pulled all afternoon along the coast and had a delicious bathe on the beautiful white sands.

In my weeks at Kingshouse I twice walked there and back from the Meeting of the Waters to Invercoe, and made other shorter excursions. In an excess of hubris, I congratulated myself with the lie that I had not done better thirty years before, although, in fact, I then walked to the glen along the northern edge of the moor from Rannoch station, and slept one night amid the ruin of MacIain's summer house in Gleann-leac-na-muidhe. I had no clear objective other than to become as much a part of the glen as I could. I often sat high upon the brae, as high as heart and lungs would carry me, letting my eye direct my mind, and sometimes merging what I knew of the glen's history with its beauty below, before and above me.

There is little carrion to be seen on the broad motorway through Glencoe, or so it seems to me – a mangled hare or a hooded crow which arose too late from this bloody meal and now enriches its companions' feast. Although it is said to be colonizing the West Highlands beyond Benderloch, I do not think I have seen a magpie in the glen, but fancy alone may support that belief, for the Campbells adopted this strutting, chuckling predator as their familiar messenger. Sometimes in the fall, away from the rush of brown water at the gorge, you can hear the deep roar of stags as they come down to the territory of the hinds on the slopes of the Black Mount or the Black Corries. Within earshot of this lonesome primitive sound, you wonder why the Gaels called the red deer 'fairy cattle'

---

* Skerries are small islands, seaward rocks. Skerryvore – *large* islet – is ten miles to the south-west of the Isle of Tiree. Its famous lighthouse was built by Alan Stevenson, the uncle of R.L.S., and first lighted in 1844. The writer thought it was the noblest of all deep-sea lights.

Four generations spanning 150 years. The eldest, born in 1808, sits with his arm about the shoulders of a young child, my father John William, who died in 1959.

ABOVE: *The Rising Sun at Barnet in the late nineteenth century. The figure on the left in the doorway is probably my great-grandfather James Clark, miller and innkeeper, whom my mother remembered as 'a tubby Dickensian man in heavy boots'.*

ABOVE: *My maternal grandfather Henry Wood who was 'late home, and often drunk, but never noisy or quarrelsome'.*

LEFT: *My father was a seaman and a sailmaker, and by the custom of the times was obliged to be a tailor as well. He cut and sewed the white duck suit in which he was married, posing proudly with my mother (who made her own wedding-gown), his naval straw hat dipped forward.*

RIGHT AND BELOW: *My uncle William Wood, socialist, pacifist and trade unionist, who conscientiously refused to fight but served as a stretcher-bearer in Flanders. He emigrated to Canada at seventeen, worked for the railroad and later drove its mile-long freights across the prairie.*

BELOW: *Sutherland in the early 1940s, not greatly changed from how I remember it – the wooden houses painted white or green, with red-shingled roofs which glowed in the fire of a prairie sunset. They stood in straight, well-crossed lines on streets that were no more than rutted lanes or trenches of summer dust.*

ABOVE: *Self-mockery in the sergeants' mess, Hamburg, 1945. Left to right: John Rankine, the author, Desmond O'Neill (the only British Army film-cameraman to land on D-Day) and Ray Head, all reporters.*

BELOW: *Christmas dinner at Binderstrasse, 1945, preserved in a clouded photograph, half-remembered faces leaning forward to be included. Not long after we heard the sound of children's voices singing* Stille Nacht.

and believed they were milked by the little people. In spring there are clusters of primroses on the damp banks of the Coe at Clachaig and under the birch of the old road, appearing suddenly like nose-gays abandoned during the night. Among them, in the sun of early May, are velvet-blue violets which Highland girls soaked in goat's milk to make lotion for their cheeks. At Signal Rock in late spring white blossom rests upon the rowans like a snowfall in late spring, and the ditches are quickly filled with a sinister green mist of young nettles, the source of a strong yellow dye and still gathered as an early vegetable. Of course, the life of the people was not this idler's dream. It was sometimes violent, brutal and remorseless, and is now beyond true recall. On the wet earth and in the stony shadows of the glen there grows a tenacious moss, once used to staunch the people's savage wounds, if not to solace their grief.

In her nostalgic recollection of her ancestors' homeland Miss Campbell did not speak of Glencoe, but there was an oblique reference of which she was probably unaware. Second in her gallery of our Dominion's great men – although well behind James Wolfe the Conqueror of Canada – was Donald Smith the Founder of the West, styled first Baron Strathcona and Mount Royal, of Glencoe in the County of Argyll and Mount Royal in the Province of Quebec. He received this ringing title in 1897, with a remainder three years later to enable his female heirs to succeed, his only child being a daughter. There was not a boy or a girl in my red-brick prairie school who had not heard of Lord Strathcona, or the young troopers of the regiment he raised for wars in South Africa and Europe. A browning photograph of his grizzled head hung in the school's entrance hall. At Christmas, another like it looked down at us from a frame of tinsel and poinsettias in the Saskatoon department store owned by the Hudson's Bay Company, of which he had been a wily Governor, and for which his father-in-law had worked as a trading-post factor. The black earth upon which we lay and dreamed, straw in mouth on summer-hot days, the homesteading sections of Sutherland and Saskatoon, the clapboard bank-hut on Main Street where our fathers' railroad cheques were cashed, the wide wheat-farms south to Regina and north towards Prince Albert, and the sky-climbing business lots in the river city, all had some of their origin in Strathcona's fertile brain. Coming to Saskatchewan when it was only one of the Western Territories beyond Rainy Lake and the Turtle Hills, he was a dynamo powering its exploitation.

He worked on one committee after another that promoted development and immigration, including the board of the Scottish and Canadian Land Settlement Association. Raised in 1884 with a capital of £500,000, it was one of half a dozen colonizing ventures that attracted Scottish hearts and Scottish purses at this time. Its directorate included a splendid Hebridean chief with a hawk's beak and flowing Dundreary whiskers – Norman, 25th MacLeod of MacLeod, his good intentions somewhat soured by the fierce hostility of the crofters' reform movement on Skye. There was also a Clackmannan peer of bifurcated lineage, the Earl of Mar and Kellie, a Lowland laird or two, directors of steamship and railway lines, and one minister of the Church of Scotland.

The 'deserving people' from Britain, whom the Association hoped would eagerly settle a New Jerusalem upon the prairie, came forward in small numbers only at first. Disembarking in North America, they travelled from Upper Canada by paddle-boat, ox-wagon and Red River cart. Later, as their numbers increased, they were carried to the Great Lone Land of the territories by the advancing steam-power of the Canadian Pacific Railroad, now laying a track from coast to coast with a grant of $25,000,000 from the government. Donald Smith was of course influentially involved in this great scheme, being the cousin, adviser and colleague of the railroad's president, George Stephen, a Scot from Speyside and, like Smith, proudly attached by descent to Clan Grant. When my uncle Will emigrated to Canada, a young man no older than Smith had been, his first real employment was with the CPR, and he later fired his first engine on tracks laid by the pioneer gangs. Little more than twenty years before, Smith had ridden on the same rails at the miraculous speed of thirty miles an hour, to drive the last spike of the line – and bend it by a clumsy stroke. This was at Eagle Pass on the Selkirk range of the Rockies, in November snow and at a spot which the cousins named Craigellachie, recalling the slogan of their clan and its gathering-rock above the Spey. The solemnity of the occasion was then exploded by triumphant pistol-shots, fire-crackers, wailing steam-whistles, ululating war-whoops and the clanging of locomotive bells. In the engine-house at Sutherland, when I was a boy, there were men who had served the CPR for more than thirty years. They surely remembered this and other occasions of success or despair, for I know now that three decades past can be the day before yesterday. But when I watched them coming from the great door of the engine-house, lifting their faces to the sky as they stretched and yawned, wiping sweat from their arms before sitting down in the shade with their lunch-pails, I never connected their lives with what I was told about Lord Strathcona, I never asked them about the past. And that I regret.

Even now the word Strathcona is more Canadian than Scots to my ear; it does not evoke mountain and loch, the deep blue of storm-clouds pierced by slanting rods of sunlight. I think of a cooling wind teasing the short-grass flats, tall stems of Indian corn or yellow wheat stretching to the horizon, the fluttering ascent of a meadow lark before my bare feet, the smell of weenies spitting and burning on a wood-fire by the river. And perhaps this is most proper, for I do not believe Strathcona was used in Scotland before Donald Smith became the laird of Glencoe in 1894. He was not yet a peer when he bought the estate from the son or the trustees of Mrs Ellen Burns MacDonald. She was the natural daughter of the last acknowledged chief of Glencoe, Ewen MacDonald, a physician in the East India Company. Not long before his death in 1840 he is thought to have married the mother of his daughter. The Gaelic people of the glen were mostly gone before his death, replaced by the Cheviot and a handful of Border shepherds. Thomas Garnett, philosopher and physician, travelling this way at the turn of the century and making notes for his *Tour of the Highlands*, had approved of the prosperity which wool and mutton appeared to bring, but he was troubled by the fact that the creation of one sheep-farm meant the unemployment and dispersal of ten, twelve or sixteen families. 'The warriors of the mountains,' he said, 'had been metamorphosed into sheep.' Ninety years later even sheep were no longer important. When the Glencoe estate was sold to Smith it was described as 'one of the finest grouse and deer preserves in the Highlands'. And what is that, as John MacEachran asked the Napier Commissioners in Arisaig, what is that but waste land?

The purchase of Glencoe, and the ennoblement which shortly followed, further obscure Smith's early life before he emigrated to Canada. He was born in 1818, by one account the son of a small shop-keeper at Forres on the Moray Firth. His commonplace surname was perhaps a necessary anglicization, adopted at a time when many Highlanders wished to hide their immediate past. The family came from the district about Knockando, on a serpentine twist of the Spey and not far from Craigellachie. Here the surname was Gow, from the Gaelic *gobha*, a blacksmith, but in Donald Smith's maternal ancestry there was also descent from members of Clan Grant and from Stuarts who spelt their name thus in the Marian form. Earnest biographers after Smith's death said that his great-grandfather had fought for Charles Edward in the last Jacobite Rebellion, but I doubt if Donald Smith gave much thought to this until his old age, when it may have pleased him to remember his distant boyhood. Since then, as Governor of the Hudson's Bay Company, he had been both God and Mammon on the western plains and lakes, the Peacemaker in negotiations with hostile Indians or French-Canadian rebels. He had been a member of the Dominion and Provincial legislatures, and a representative of the Executive Council for the Northwest Territories, the president of the Bank of Montreal, chancellor of two universities, honorary colonel of three Canadian-Scottish regiments, and a High Commissioner in London. Finally, he had received a large clutch of honorary degrees and doctorates, and the freedom of five cities and towns, including his Morayshire birthplace. His career, his success and powerful influence over common and uncommon men, and his part in the settlement of the West, are sometimes cited by those who would argue that the pain of eviction, clearance and emigration was repaid by the richness of Scottish talent which flowered throughout the world as a result. Perhaps so, although I wonder if this would have consoled the bitterness of departing exiles as they watched the night shadows closing the mouth of Loch Broom or darkening the hills of Knoidart. But I have no doubt that the evictors, much troubled in conscience as we are told some were, would be pleased to know that their good has been for the common good after all.

Among the smaller honours given to a remarkable man, albeit one remembered by his frontier companions as a cunning buccaneer, was the deputy-lieutenancy of Argyll. It went well with his new estate within that county, and the fine house he built on the brae of Sgurr na Ciche, where seventeen chiefs of Clan Iain Abrach once had their home. In the high days before his death, this presumptuous mansion employed a great staff, more than twenty gardeners alone, and from its beginning it was lit by electricity and warmed by central heating. It is now a home for the aged.

One small matter may have marred Smith's final years as a Highland laird. It is sometimes said in the glen that he wished to be entitled Baron Glencoe, but was dissuaded by those who argued that it might be thought insensitive. He chose Strathcona instead, and that of course is Glencoe in another form. The name is resilient enough to have survived his small conceit. There is a village called Glencoe on Cape Breton Island in the Canadian Maritimes, another on the south coast of Prince Edward Island, and an African town in Natal. And others, no doubt, throughout the global diaspora of the Gael, indicating a nostalgic affection unknown to Macaulay as he developed his misleading evocation of the Glen of Weeping. 'In truth that pass is the most dreary and melancholy of all the Scottish passes . . . and even on those rare days when the sun is bright, and when there is no cloud in the sky, the impression made by the landscape is sad and awful.'

When I was taught Canadian history under the sharp direction of Miss Campbell's knuckles I was not told that there were many in our young province of Saskatchewan who had no reason to respect the memory of Donald Smith, to be grateful for the land companies or admire the courage of the early immigrants. Nor was I enlightened by the strangers who joined us in our schoolroom for one summer, two boys with olive faces and straight black hair, sent from the Duck Lake Reservation as part of some soon-abandoned experiment. If we – white, European and unthinking – spoke to them at all, I cannot remember, and so I learnt nothing from them as they, perhaps, learnt little from us.

In the early years of settlement, the land companies presented the western plains as free soil, a wilderness rich in promise and awaiting transformation by stout arms and the Prairie Queen plough. But there were at least two thousand Métis in the Territory of Saskatchewan alone, the 'mixed-bloods', a catholic people born of French, Indian, and sometimes British* ancestry. They had lived on the prairie for a century and more, farming the open grassland or trapping the sparsely wooded coulées and river-banks. Their settlements and villages were now ignored by the companies' surveyors, whose chains and section-posts crossed house, stable, barn and field as if they were not there. The Saskatchewan Métis lived in cautious amity and occasional blood-relationship with the Plains Cree, who were far greater in numbers. These proudly independent Indians were horsemen and hunters. Their land was the wide fork of the big river, and they had given it and thereby the territory a name, *ki-sis-kah-chi-wan*, water that runs swiftly.

* The British were mostly Scots, trappers and servants of the Hudson's Bay Company.

Although angered by land-stealing treaties, and fearful of attempts to enclose them still further, they were usually at peace with the white man until their uprising in the last desperate year of their freedom. Before 1800 they had rarely seen a European, and one of the first they met was a Highland Scot, on the Elbow of the South Saskatchewan not many miles from where I searched for arrowheads in the dry roots of prairie grass. He was John MacDonald, self-styled 'of Garth', a trapper and trader in the service of the North West Company, a deadly if over-enthusiastic pistoleer with a firm conviction that the first member of Clan Donald had been coeval with Noah, and had survived the Flood aboard his own craft on Loch Lomond. The Crees who challenged his canoe-party on the Elbow had blackened their faces for war, but he reasoned with them and made them tolerant of his trading-company, if not its friends.

Eighty years later another Highlander, Donald Smith, played his shadowy role as adviser and negotiator when the Plains Cree, victorious in battle but now facing more redcoats and a Gatling gun owned and manned by a young American from the Connecticut National Guard, finally surrendered what was left of their nomadic liberty. They made this humiliating submission on the banks of the North Saskatchewan at Battleford, in the last week of May when the wide water is still nut-brown from the rush of spring thaws, the grass an astonishing green and studded with prairie-flowers. The British general, Frederick Middleton, conducted the peace-talk from a kitchen chair, in the open and surrounded by his field-officers. His hair and moustache were white and military, his coat frogged and his forage-cap square upon his head. The Indian elders sat on the earth in a semi-circle before him, their leader Poundmaker in advance, a tall and handsome man. He wore a single feather in his hair, slanting to the right, and a spotted sweat-cloth about his forehead. He had argued for talk and bargaining with the whites until the bitter hunger of the Crees, and the increasing encroachment of their reserves, persuaded him to join the Métis in their rebellion. He was now charged with high treason. Because the Indians had no words for so foreign a concept, the interpreter chose an example of rude disrespect from their own culture, and thus, in European eyes, made a childish fool of a dignified man. 'You are accused of throwing sticks at the Queen and trying to knock her bonnet off.' For this he was sent to jail in the police barracks at Regina, until recently known as Pile o' Bones. Although the efforts of sympathizers secured his release a year later, his spirit and body were already broken and he soon died of tuberculosis.

I do not think I learnt much of this from Miss Campbell. I suspect that what she did tell us about the Louis Riel Rebellion, the Métis and Cree uprising of 1885, was the old imperial lie that I would later read in the books I discovered below Saint Cuthbert's Church Hall, in G. A. Henty, in W. H. G. Kingston, in old volumes of the *Boy's Own Paper* and *Chums* – a simple but savage native people, rejecting the guidance of a superior Christian civilization, commit barbaric atrocities and by resisting enlightenment cause the deaths of brave men who only wished them well. It was perhaps a lesson poorly received in that drowsy classroom, in the buzz of a trapped fly at the window, the smell and the *taste* of coloured chalk, and Miss Campbell's earnest voice tense with admiration, not for Poundmaker coughing blood in a civilizing jail, but for such men as Donald Smith, Lord Strathcona, who had brought sanity and prosperity to the plains.

The Canadian West was still a young country when I was a boy, and its mind did not dwell long on the immediate past. Yet the spring campaign against Poundmaker and Big Bear of the Crees, against Louis Riel and Gabriel Dumont, the political and military leaders of the Métis, had passed over the ground where our little township would be built within twenty years. By the Nutana river-bridge, on the outskirts of our city neighbour Saskatoon, there were undoubtedly traces of the defences hastily dug when it was known that a thousand Cree warriors had left their villages in the Eagle Hills. And along the canyon of Saskatoon's Main Street, where a nickel street-car ride took me to the Bijou picture-house, shanty huts not long gone had been used as dressing-stations for the wounded from Cut Knife Creek and Batoche.

I am aware that a boy's imagination might not have made improving use of the knowledge, but I wish I had known then that the old prairie-trail which became Main Street, Sutherland, had been ridden by Inspector Francis Dickens and his detachment of mounted constables during the Riel Rebellion. Red-haired and red-bearded, partly deaf and a stammerer, he was forty-one and in the last year of his life. He had been unadmired and perhaps unloved by his father. Charles Dickens had no faith in him, no confidence that he would *achieve*, and like other men who have themselves achieved he perhaps saw his children's failure as his own. In his youth, Francis asked his father for £15, a horse and a gun, that he might go abroad and farm. Refusing the request, Dickens argued that his son would be robbed of the money, thrown from the horse, and blow out his brains with the gun. Escaping from the journalist's stool upon which his father placed him, Francis Dickens finally went abroad, first to the Bengal Police, and then halfway about the globe to the North West Mounted.

Before the outbreak of the Riel Rebellion he was sent northward to the Cree country with twenty constables. He crossed the south fork of the Saskatchewan at Saskatoon, then little more than a scattering of sod and timber shacks, and rode to the north fork and the garrison of Fort Pitt beyond the Eagle Hills. This was both a police station and a trading-post, with its own Highland piper and a stout pier for the voyagers' canoes and the big flat-bottomed boats of the Hudson's Bay Company. It was soon a refuge for alarmed settlers, driven in by the news that the Crees under Big Bear had pillaged a settlement at Frog Lake and killed eight white men, including a priest at the altar. The Indians soon arrived about Fort Pitt with a band of armed Métis, cutting all escape or access except by the eastward stream of the river. With little food and ammunition, a defence of the fort was impossible, and Dickens drove his constables and the fugitives into the building of a large scow by which they might go downriver. Ice was still moving when the leaky vessel was finished, lurching floes grinding against each other or rising like up-thrust spears from a swirl of black water and earth-brown foam. Travelling for a week, crouching beneath occasional rifle-fire from the banks and expecting the scow to founder at every cruel twist of the river, the party of sixty men and women finally reached the tall trees and raw timber walls of the fort at Battleford. It was truly *an achievement* for Inspector Dickens, and might have seemed so to his father, if belatedly, and had the novelist been alive.

Poundmaker took the Crees to their villages on Cut Knife Creek. There Colonel Otter's command came to destroy them, but was itself outfought in a seven-hour battle and put to flight. At this time the astonished citizens of Saskatoon were watching the march of a larger punitive force, almost six thousand men under General Frederick Middleton, going north by foot, horse, wagon and – for a few calamitous days – by an unwieldy stern-wheeler on the river. The army found the Métis at their town of Batoche, nine hundred riflemen entrenched about it, their women and children in caves on the river-bank. Commanded by Gabriel Dumont, a fierce plains-fighter and a better soldier than the Queen's general, they withstood attack and bombardment for four days while their spiritual and political leader, Louis Riel, shocked by the violence of war, prayed over his silver crucifix. Then the Canadian Volunteers disobeyed their General's orders, stormed the ruined town and took it from the Métis. Middleton counted the price of the war. Seventy white men were dead and thirty wounded. The Métis had lost thirty-five killed and eleven wounded. The General gave no figures for the Indian casualties at Cut Knife Creek or elsewhere, and none are reliable apart from the eleven who were later hanged 'for murder'. It was among the smallest of Queen Victoria's Little Wars, but the last rebellion against the crown in Canada (there had been two major revolts before it) had cost the government more than $5,000,000.

Gabriel Dumont escaped across the border to Montana, but on the day following the battle at Batoche, and after sending a written message saying 'I don't like war', Louis Riel walked into Middleton's camp and surrendered. The General thought his prisoner was a mild man, and although his eyes were at first frightened, the expression gradually disappeared when the soldier said, 'How do you do, Mr Riel? Pray be seated.' Middleton told his superiors that the rebel leader was 'sane enough in general everyday subjects', which of course meant that he could stand trial for his life. He did, and after several agonizing reprieves he finally approached the scaffold with a crucifix pressed to his lips. He was hanged outside Regina jail. In that same week, Donald Smith drove the last spike at Eagle Pass, marking the railroad's conquest of the West and giving immigrant settlers unrestrained access to the plains. The Canadian Pacific Railroad had made the defeat of the rebellion inevitable by the rapid transport of troops from the east and west. Now one of its box-cars carried the body of Louis Riel down the track to St Boniface, a mission in Manitoba where he had been born forty-one years before. His people, the Métis, already dispersing, had once accepted with grace the name *Bois-Brulés* – men the colour of singed wood – and had steadfastly maintained they were a race and a *nation*. One of Canada's greatest statesmen, John Alexander MacDonald, an immigrant boy from Glasgow who became the architect and first prime minister of the new Dominion, called them 'those miserable half-breeds'. Such dismissive contempt has a long history, but it is odd to hear it voiced by a man of his name, against which another king's minister once ordered extirpation as 'a just example of vengeance'.

Part of the rodeo held on the outskirts of Saskatoon one summer was a re-enactment of the battle at Cut Knife Creek and 'the capture of the rebel Louis Riel'. The principal characters were performed by amateur actors, I believe. Riders from the Albertan ranch-lands impersonated the settlers and Volunteers, and a detachment of North West Mounted represented Colonel Otter's force. Indians from the Duck Lake and other reserves played themselves, many of them old enough to remember the real battle and the truth of it. Sitting under a cloudless sky, on a bleached bench and sharing sugared popcorn with my friends, I flinched at the explosion of blank cartridges and cheered loudly when the Indians turned their backs on their history and ran from the shining horses and the red tunics of the North West Mounted. This deluding pageant also included 'The Man Who Captured Louis Riel', his portrait reproduced and his spurious exploit reported in the *Saskatoon Star*. He had a show-tent of his own, I think, and told his story to all who would pay a dime or a quarter to hear it. More vividly, I remember the grand parade down Main Street on the opening day. I remember the dancing war-bonnets of the Cree and the painted symbols on the flanks of their ponies, as real as the pictures on a Timothy Eaton calendar. I hear again the clacking of a thousand hooves on the hard surface of Main Street, and see iron shoes sparking on the street-car lines. There were cowmen from Alberta in curled stetsons and sheepskin chaps, bare-legged and booted cowgirls in fringed leather, professional rodeo performers with silver buckles and silver spurs sweeping off their hats and bowing from the saddle like Colonel Tim McCoy on the screen at the Bijou picture-house. Following the riders were tableaux on unboarded farm-wagons – old traders of the Fur Companies buying pelts from blanketed Indians, General Middleton on an unsteady wooden horse accepting the surrender of Poundmaker, and of course Lord Strathcona, his stove-pipe hat and white spade-beard threatening to blow away as he successfully drove the last spike at Eagle Pass. For no reason that I clearly understand, I recall the mountain-cat by the pay-gate to the rodeo, a yellow-fanged, prick-eared beast caged in a small box and biting the bars. When the arena benches were silent, awaiting the next event, the animal's anguished snarl rose above the nasal calls of the popcorn and hot-dog sellers.

I am sure that John Sounding Sky was one of the old men in theatrical war-bonnets who rode with the Cree down Main Street, and later ran from the redcoats in the arena. He had shared

Poundmaker's victory and humiliation during the Rebellion, and since then had lived on the reservation with his wife Spotted Calf. They once had a son who had so powerful a voice in his infancy that his grandfather, the war-chief One Arrow, named him *Mitchi-manito-wayo*, Voice of the Great Spirit. When the police needed to make a record of it, they called him Almighty Voice. A few years after the Riel Rebellion the boy expressed his rejection of the life now imposed on his people by driving a steer from the cattle herd sent to feed One Arrow's band. He pursued it and killed it on the prairie as the Indians had once hunted buffalo. This misdemeanour led to his arrest, his escape in the belief that he was to be hanged, the killing of a constable sent to capture him, and the death of a sergeant later. The force assembled to apprehend or kill him was impressive. Forty constables with a nine-pounder gun, accompanied not altogether happily by two hundred armed settlers, surrounded a little coulée where Almighty Voice, his cousin Topean and a friend had dug defensive pits and were prepared to die. More police, more settlers and another gun came on following days. When a foolish rush was made upon the coulée, the Indians killed Corporal Hockin, Constable Kerr and Postmaster Grundy. Now the field-guns began to fire and continued their bombardment for another day, killing one of the Indians. In a pause, Spotted Calf was brought forward to persuade her son to surrender. But she reminded him of the courage of his father and his grandfather, and he told her that it had not abandoned him. Sitting close to the coulée that night, she sang his death-song with him, and at seven in the morning the field-guns began again. At one o'clock, when there had been no return fire for some time, the Europeans entered the trees and found the dead boys beside the dry holes they had dug in search of water. I wrote the story of this, of course, almost in apology for not knowing it when I was a boy, when Almighty Voice's people performed that humiliating charade for our amusement on Rodeo Day.

All the police and the civilians now came crowding into the trees, jostling one another about the pit and looking down. The women of One Arrow's village keened at the edge of the bluff, waiting for the moment when they would be allowed to take away the bodies of the young men . . . Near the spot where there had been fighting on Friday evening, some characters were found carved in the bark at the foot of a tree. A Métis squatted down to study them and, when

asked, he said that they were by way of being an honourable epitaph.
Here died three warriors.

'Meaning Almighty Voice and the other two.'

'No,' said the Métis, 'Almighty Voice carved it for Corporal Hockin, and Kerr, and Grundy.'

The defeat and suppression of the Plains Cree were inevitable after the extermination of the buffalo, and by a grotesque irony the early growth of Saskatoon was rooted in that mind-numbing event. Written history concentrates less upon this than it does upon the Temperance Colony established there on the heights above a summer ford. It was to be an asylum, its founder said, for those 'who wish to flee from the presence of their tyrant tempter'. There were enough of these ardent fugitives for the government of the day to recognize their joint stock company and grant them 214,000 acres along the South Saskatchewan, enough for twenty-one good sections and the site of a modest city. The first eighty families came by flat-boat, downriver from Medicine Hat, or overland by wagon and cart from Brandon and Regina. They arrived in the summer of 1884, and within a year they were digging rifle-pits for defence against the Métis and the Cree. The temperance virtues of the community did not, of course, wholly withstand contamination by later immigrants, but something of their influence lasted for decades in law and practice. In recollection, it was rare that I saw a drink taken in Sutherland or a household bottle darker than clear water.

In the first year of the colony its leaders and people worked industriously, and with a certainty that sprang, no doubt, from their self-confident faith in total abstinence and non-denominational prayer. They built temporary homes of sod and timber, and planned houses of worship for all sects in clapboard reproductions of an English village church. They established the framework of local government, opened a post office, hired a teacher and began the building of a school. The Louis Riel Rebellion, which might have destroyed their fledgling settlement, brought it unexpected opportunities as a base and market for General Middleton's army. They also knew that the railroad would shortly be completed from coast to coast, and that their town would thereby become an administrative and distributory centre for later immigration. Finally there was immediate profit to be got from a terrible detritus of the past half-century. They saw it from the doors of their homes, white as hoar frost in some places, it was said, and stretching to the horizon.

The first crop of the first season, and perhaps the most rewarding harvest of their lives, was the collection of bones – buffalo bones.

The virtual extinction of the American buffalo was not a natural calamity but one of the greatest and most obscene slaughters of beasts ever committed by uncaring man. Unlike the killing of whales and other species in this age, no voice spoke strongly against it, and no power acted with anything but approval. The only influential opinion was that this immense and animate barrier to western expansion should be removed. Five great herds once grazed the plains between the Rio Grande and the northern timber of Saskatchewan. A traveller in 1834, who watched part of one herd for a day and saw no end to it, believed it to be ten miles long and eight in breadth. Early in the nineteenth century there were thought to be sixty-five or seventy million animals in all the herds. Fifty years later, by an equally rough estimate, there were little more than a thousand. The killing was enthusiastic and ruthless. In one year alone, there were five thousand hunters on the plains, wearing greasy buckskin, reeking of animal fat and blood, and armed with repeating-rifles and Sharps .50 buffalo-guns. The larger gun, long-barrelled and accurate, was fired from a rest, behind which the hunter lay and made his 'stand', picking his target and firing, loading and firing again into a herd which was up-wind of him and sensed no danger, even when a stricken animal grunted down in a brief cloud of dust. This monstrous abattoir was encouraged by territorial and federal governments, accepting the Army's view that it was cheaper to starve the Indian than fight him in a long and exhausting campaign. Lieutenant-General Philip Sheridan – the Civil War victor of Cedar Creek and Five Forks and now a relentless commander in the West – was asked by a group of uneasy Texans if the buffalo-hunters should be restrained. He said, 'Let them kill and skin until the buffalo is exterminated, as it is the only way to bring lasting peace and allow civilization to advance.' ('It would be a proper vindication of justice,' said the King's Secretary of State, 'to extirpate that sept of thieves.')

At the beginning of the 1870s, almost four million buffalo were killed in two years, and of these only 150,000 perhaps were taken by the Indians. Though they sometimes killed improvidently in their hunts, they were bitterly outraged by the white man's ferocious killing, for having taken the hide he appeared to have no compelling need of the animal's flesh or bones. The Indians controlled their hunting by a strict discipline, requiring agreement upon need, time and place. The rules were firmly enforced. The Cheyenne whipped a persistent offender, the Kiowas shot his horse, the Crows beat him and sometimes broke his arms or burnt his lodge. The Plains Cree destroyed all his possessions but allowed him to receive gifts later in compensation. The material and spiritual culture of the Indians depended upon the buffalo. It enriched their mythology, dominated their graphic art and inspired their religious rites. Its head-skin and horns were worn with reverence by their medicine-men. The Comanche treated a buffalo skull as an idol, placing it at the entrance to their ceremonial sweat-lodges, and using it on the plains as a signpost, to guide a living herd towards their village. And when the smoke of a communal pipe was gravely blown to the sun and to the earth in acknowledgement of the Great Spirit, a final puff was directed at a nearby buffalo skull. Long after the animal itself was gone, the buffalo-dance was performed with intense feeling and in the confident belief that the beast would thereby return with its life-maintaining support and unifying spirituality. The belief should not be patronized, for in the beginning the People had called upon the buffalo and it came to them from a hole in the ground beneath an old man's tipi, thundering forth and covering the earth from sky to sky.

The use made of the buffalo by the Plains Indians, their material dependency upon it, is awesome. A Bulletin of the Bureau of American Ethnology* listed one hundred articles which the Blackfoot made from the animal, apart from taking the abundant strength of its meat. It gave them robes, caps, shirts, leggings, moccasins, mittens, belts and breech-clouts. It covered the poles of their lodges, the linings, floors and beds. It supplied the material for shields, arrow-heads and sheaths, all domestic articles from fleshing-tools to spoons, cups and water-buckets. Its dung provided fuel, its sinews became thread, and its phallus when boiled produced a valuable glue. Thirty of the entries in the list are for riding and transport, from frame-saddles to martingales and blankets, lariats, picket-ropes, travois skins and leather horse-shoes. An Indian child's brief time with playthings was supplied with sleds for winter and footballs in summer. And at the close of his life the buffalo gave him a winding-sheet from its matted shoulders, masks from its hide, and an altar from its skull. No other society in the modern

* *The Horse in Blackfoot Indian Culture*, John C. Ewers, Bureau of American Ethnology Bulletin 159, Smithsonian Institution, Washington, 1955.

world, perhaps, has been so diverse in its use of and so dependent upon one animal, and none so vulnerable thereby. General Sheridan cannot be faulted on tactical appreciation.

In his slaughter of the buffalo, the white man was a vulgarian. He took the tongue and haunch-cuts sometimes; the rest of the meat he left to putrefy, to feed wolves, coyotes and buzzards, the bones to bleach and whiten the earth. The buffalo-hunters were eventually joined by sportsmen from the east and Europe, attracted by killing at minimal risk. They came to the West by the new railroads, and sometimes their train was surrounded by buffalo, becalmed like a ship in the black sea of a moving herd. The sporting travellers fired upon the animals from the windows of their coach, from the observation platform of the last car and the cow-catcher of the engine. On the Nebraska plains in January 1872, Sheridan was host to one aristocratic hunter, the Grand Duke Alexis of Russia. The party left its comfortable train at North Platte Station and rode fifty miles towards the hills. It included some of the most charismatic figures of the American West – among them William 'Buffalo Bill' Cody, and, of course, George Armstrong Custer. 'The Grand Duke,' Sheridan reported to the Secretary of War, 'killed his first buffalo today in a manner which elicited the admiration of the party.' Cody alone did not contribute to the sycophantic flattery which flowed with the celebratory champagne after the hunt. He had watched the Grand Duke riding beside a lumbering bull, emptying his revolver into its massive shoulder without a kill. When he was handed Cody's favourite gun, engagingly called 'Lucretia', he did no better. With another gun passed by Cody at a brisk canter, the Russian was able to bring the animal down. After the wine, and impassioned by his success, he mounted and rode at a gallop across the snow to a distant buffalo cow. To the astonishment of all, he killed it with one shot.

As the herds decreased, so did the rich sportsmen, the hunters and the skinners. Now came the day of the wagoners, the collectors of bones for the manufacture of fertilizers and the bleaching of sugar. Free to all, the supply seemed endless. Where great stands had been made, the bones lay so thickly that from a distance they could be mistaken for small lakes of salt. In Saskatchewan the scavengers were mostly Métis, their box-wagons drawn by strong oxen. They took their loads eastward to Manitoba or south across the border to a railhead in Montana. The last known buffalo-hunt by the Cree was already ten years past when the Canadian Pacific drove its track to the fork of the big river. The Métis and the temperance farmer in his first year, any man strong enough in muscle and stomach who could rent or buy a wagon and team, brought their grim gleaning to the railroad yards at Saskatoon. The bones were piled by the track in great blocks thirty feet long and eight high, roughly the capacity of a railroad box-car. In the five years following the Louis Riel Rebellion, three thousand car-loads left Saskatoon for the east, each carrying the bones of 250 animals. The total number of skeletons, whole or fragmentary, gathered in the territory before the end of the century, was said to be two million.

When a boy, I sometimes played with my friends along the railroad at the edge of Saskatoon. Their names endure inexplicably. Doug Badger, Bill Williams, Stan Strange . . . each with bleached hair and freckled face, brown legs and naked feet below tattered overalls. The depression years were beginning, and the only busy movement on the wind-blown soil by the tracks was the rolling, bouncing dance of the tumbleweed. In the fall, if we stayed too late and heard the distant howl of a coyote, we frightened each other and raced away, shouting our fear in mockery. As we ran, our bare feet kicked up the white, grainy dust along the tracks and we neither knew nor cared what it was. 'Buffalo-dust,' said my Uncle Will, years later in the green shade of a Surrey garden. 'That was buffalo-dust.'

My family went to the prairie with the last tide of emigration after the First World War. The government was no longer giving grants to assist the passage of ex-servicemen, and my mother resented this for much of her life thereafter. Two of her brothers-in-law had 'worked in munitions' – a dismissive phrase of the time – and had been given such help when they emigrated. My mother considered this, and the rejection of my father, an insulting disregard of proper service and reward. My father was unconcerned. I think he was glad to be at sea again, if only for the voyage to the Saint Lawrence. He was never wholly at ease ashore, away from the element he both loved and feared. We were closest together when I was very young and later when he was very old, and thus I remember him with pride and affection. In my childhood he sang shanties to me and drew neat diagrams of a full-rigged ship, naming every sail, sheet and spar. He walked as sailors used to walk, taking each pace half-sideways rather than forward, to keep a balance on a moving deck. Aboard the *Montcalm*, my mother said, he was not happy below. He spent a great deal of the time on deck, not forward in the restricted space allowed the emigrants, but midships and aft, on the tolerance of the liner's crew. Benefiting from a general admiration for the Royal Navy, he obtained occasional permission for us to sit unobtrusively on a deck amidships.

If I have a real recollection of that voyage, and not one taken from my parents, it is of the ship's bows climbing above the horizon and then going down slowly into the waves between wings of foam. At night, my mother reminded me, the air was fresh, and the sky a dark blue with pin-prick stars. It was August and the southward flow of the Atlantic was sluggish with ice, the air chilling and sometimes curtained by a dank mist. The memory of a frightening disaster less than a decade before was in my mother's mind throughout the voyage, and was still strong nearly sixty years later when she wrote her autobiography.

One night Jack hopped out of his bunk and said, She's stopped, something up in front. He grabbed his coat and was off. John slept in a bunk above Jack, and Marjorie above me. And then I could hear a lot of scraping. Jack came back and said it was all right, we'd run into an ice-field. I immediately thought of the *Titanic*. I put on my dressing-gown and went up on deck. An officer told me to get down below. I used a wartime phrase, and in a very shaky voice, 'Is there anything about?'* Get down below, Madam. As I was returning I met a young Scots mother with her son, one year old, and she was terrified. Me, well my knees were knocking together, but I said, It's all right, the officer has just told me and my husband, who is an ex-Navy man, that there's nothing to worry about. So we went to our cabins, but the ship never moved till breakfast time. We were all on deck. There was a thick fog. I held Jack's arm, he had Marjorie's and I held John. I felt I could hardly breathe, ice scraping on the sides, when suddenly the fog lifted just for us to see a huge iceberg, so near I felt I could put out my hand and touch it. I said to Jack, What's going to happen? It will hit us. Jack said, Don't worry, the skipper knows the rate we are travelling. You'll see, it will pass us on our stern. Then the fog came down again, my heart was in my mouth, as the saying goes. No one spoke. There was just the chug of the engines. It seemed ages but was really only a few

* A question sometimes put to police cyclists after the maroons had sounded, warning of an imminent Zeppelin raid upon London.

minutes, I suppose. The fog began to clear and no iceberg in sight, it seemed. We all gave a bit of a sigh . . . It certainly seemed to many of us an Act of God that the fog lifted for us to see our iceberg.

I remember nothing of our arrival in the Saint Lawrence but a high green cliff brooding over the ship. Here, I would later discover in Miss Campbell's classroom, those 'brave Scotch Highlanders' had climbed to the Plains of Abraham. There is also a clouded recollection, sustained by my mother's remembrance, of a great building, of stone, iron and glass, of echoing voices and loud footsteps, long lines of men, women and children moving through a suffocating heat to tables where seated men in black suits hammered sheaves of paper with their fists. My left arm and that of my sister were bared for the display of our vaccination scars, and then my parents were told that they and their daughter were free to enter Canada, but I was not. I cannot remember the spectacular dispute which must have followed. My mother's passion for cleanliness, her class-fear of disease, and her resentment of any charge of neglect, must have exploded from her in anger and contempt. At last the immigration officer decided that only submission would rid him of this black-haired, red-cheeked woman who refused to be interrupted. After I had walked up and down before him several times, he agreed that I was not suffering from rickets and could take the cars westward with my family.

I am grateful to my mother's memories for prompting my fragmentary recollection of the four-day journey to Saskatchewan, a series of pictures fluttered quickly in stuttering animation. A dominant image is the black locomotive, taller and longer than a house, belching smoke from its snub-nosed stack, and resting like a panting lion behind the extended paw of the cow-catcher. And the clanging bell, a brass mouth opening and closing on the pull of a rope cable. Above all the warning whistle, a melancholy sound that haunts me still, as if I were again hearing it over the bending grass beyond the windows of our shack, hearing it distantly, long, long before the deep breathing of the engine. It is gone now from the plains but survives in North American folk-memory. 'Hear that lonesome whistle blow . . . !' In time my mother could think of it with sentimental nostalgia, but when first heard, as the train pulled westward out of Quebec, the irreversible nature of their exile seemed to strike her and my father. 'Goodness, son,' she would say, touching the corner of a moistened eye, 'it made Pa and me so miserable.'

We had no money for sleepers. We lived and slept as best we could in the long, brown emigrant-car, on upholstered but hard bench-seats, facing each other, our travelling-luggage built about us like the wall of a stockade. There was a wood-burning stove at the end of the car where women boiled water or heated soup. Most of our utensils and basic food were bought at Quebec, and I do recall carrying some of it to the side of the car, where a black conductor lifted me aboard with my armful of bread. This was the first time, I think, that I remember seeing a black man or taking his hand, although it was a black doctor who brought me into the world in the second year of the War, holding me up for my mother to see and pointing to my damp smear of yellow hair. 'I have a little Saxon for you,' he said.

At Quebec we had purchased a large enamel tea-pot with plates and cups of the same metal. We were told that there would be whistle-stops along the track, particularly on the prairie, where adequate food and water could be bought. Ever cautious, my mother filled a large bag with packets of Indian tea and tins of condensed milk upon which, watered down, I had been weaned, and which I enjoyed well into my youth. We had corned beef and tins of orange-red salmon, butter and cheese and great loaves of bread. The last was freshly baked when bought at Quebec, and I recall now the heat of it against my chest as the conductor lifted me to the train. We shared the car, my mother wrote, with a number of poor families. No one had been more than a finger's breadth above killing poverty in Britain, I think, and all believed that life in Canada, however hard, could only be an improvement. There were also some boys in their early teens, travelling alone, going to isolated farms on the prairie, to hard work and harsh treatment, and a few, I know, to take their lives in despair. My mother remembered them sadly.

The lad opposite us had no food. I gave him a cup of tea and some bread and butter. He said he had no money. He had been a donkey-boy in the Welsh mines, and he said he was going to his uncle who was a farmer and he was meeting him with a horse. That was farther on than we were going. Before we got off I asked a young mother if she had any food over would she give it to the lad as he had nothing. She said she would. I hope the poor boy was lucky, as we heard later that some farmers were very poor.

I was told that I spent much of that journey, day after day from Ontario and Manitoba to the Great Plains, with my face against the dirty window, looking for Indians. When I first saw them, said my mother, I was bitterly disappointed – a group of silent men in dark hats and faded jeans, standing by a buckboard near the track. The conductor came the length of three cars to tell me that they were Indians. I did not believe him. Where were the feathers, painted faces, brown and white ponies? When I did see Indians so dressed for the Saskatoon Rodeo I did not know what a mockery their theatrical costumes were. I knew nothing of the disease, alcoholism and apathy, the decaying culture and the contempt of the settlers. Even my uncle, the Socialist pacifist and generous man, sometimes spoke of them as a lesser race, unhappy savages deserving of pity.

My only clear recollection of that long journey is one that returned most vividly fifty years and more later, when I came out of Kintail in early spring. Snow was falling, a gentle shawl on the shoulders of the Five Sisters but a white darkness in the gorge at Shiel Bridge. A day begun so badly became worse when I reached the Great Glen, where the dead autumnal brown and the first colours of spring were disappearing beneath the snow. In a telephone-box at Fort William I learnt that my mother, then in her ninetieth year, had fallen and broken her hip. She was now in hospital for the first time in her life. My original intention to spend one more night in the Highlands was abandoned, and I decided to put the car on a train at Edinburgh. But the collapse of a rail tunnel had stopped all eastern traffic south. The road from Inverness was closed by snow on Drumochter, and the Glencoe road was threatened by drifts across Rannoch. But I pressed on, knowing that if I could get by the Meeting of the Waters and Kingshouse I would cross Rannoch. Coming out of the Highlands towards dusk, when sky and earth were merging in stunning beauty, I reached the Erskine Bridge and discarded an earlier decision to take a train in Glasgow. I drove on, and past midnight, as I climbed towards Shap, my car failed in clattering protest. I lowered my head on the driving-wheel in frustration, and the numbing recall of a boy's despair at the loss of a parent.

The whistle-stops on the prairie where our train had made frequent halts were often no more than a wind-pump, a few clapboard houses of sun-grey wood, and sometimes a general store with a shadowed verandah. All seemed to tremble unnaturally in the heat of the day, and at night were ghostly lit by a coal-oil lantern on the verandah, or an Aladdin lamp behind a window curtain. During these brief halts the women of the train ran to the wind-pump or the store with the largest utensil they had – kettle, saucepan, tea-pot or lard-pail. This one time, remembered that night on Shap, I watched my mother from the observation platform at the back of the last car, her skirts lifted above her small feet as she rushed to the store. At the end of the queue, she was the last to have her tea-pot filled with boiling water, which she always bought if she could. I have a clear memory of her alarmed face, turned suddenly to the train as the warning whistle blew, the wheels spun and the engine took its first coughing breath. I saw rather than heard my mother's outraged cry and watched her run towards the moving train, skirts lifted to the knee by one hand now, and water jerking from the spout of the pot. She reached the track and ran between the rails, sometimes leaping from tie to tie. She was a small woman and now seemed smaller still, and already lost. Beside me on the platform there were men, yelling encouragement to her which she could not have heard above the loud, protesting wail of the engine. Certain that I had lost her, that she had been cruelly snatched from my small life, I turned from the platform and ran along the cars, calling for my father.

Years later, when I reached the Sussex coast and the hospital, my mother did not recognize me, thinking I was her brother Will. She was still in shock, and unable to accept the indignity of a hospital ward, the loss of an independent if solitary life she had jealously preserved for twenty years since my father's death. In an effort to help her mind and her memory, I spoke of Canada and that hot noon-day when the train left her behind. She remembered me then, but she did not believe the story, thinking I was inventing it, even though she had recalled it in her exercise book not many months before.

I went with my tea-pot and as usual was the last to be served. Then I thought, how quiet it is, and turned and the train was just starting. I sprinted across. It's a wonder I made it. Two men were standing by an open door, the train was not going fast, but one man said, Be careful, jump on! I popped the tea-pot in his hand and he said, Blimey, that's hot. And that's how I knew they were Cockneys. It's a wonder I was able to jump on, as the steps were high, but those men really lifted me. They hung on to the side and put their hands under my arms. Strange, I didn't feel a bit scared. I had to walk nearly the length of the train, and folks were smiling, and so was I, but I found poor John crying.

Old age is self-deceiving, enjoying memories on selective recall. I know I was sometimes unhappy in Canada, not with my life, I think, but because of the hardships my parents were facing in theirs. They tried to hide their deprivation from their children, which meant that we were more keenly aware of it when our companions derided our clothes and our manners, our shack and the poverty it reflected, and above all the fact that we were indigent English immigrants. In the beginning we were among the exceptions to the supposed egalitarian society of the plains, little better than the distant Métis and Indians, or the *bohunks* who lived across the track, Central Europeans with comic names. My father was soon accepted by the men with whom he worked on the gangs, but my mother, who could not openly abandon her attachment to the Old Country, enjoyed the irritation it provoked among second-, third- or fourth-generation Canadians. This passed in time, and in the end I think she liked to be told that she was now 'a proper Canuck', but I could not easily forget the discomfort my loyalty to her loyalty had caused me. When I went to the birthday party for Bill Williams' sister, whose plaited hair I occasionally pulled in the classroom, we were each expected to entertain with a recitation or song. I began the only one I knew with confidence, 'God save the King!', and was led to the door in dismissal, my ear held in the sharp pinch of Mrs Williams' finger and thumb. As I turned homeward, kicking stones, I heard the sound of young voices behind me, cleansing the air with 'The Maple Leaf for ever!'

There was some dramatic irony in my father's refusal to apply for American citizenship in return for permission to work in the United States. In 1636 his collateral ancestor, Abraham Prebble, the son of a carpenter in Denton by Canterbury, emigrated to the Old Plymouth Colony in New England. There he married and settled briefly in Scituate, Connecticut. At the time of his departure the Men of Kent were once more roused by the spirit of dissent and rebellion against central authority, lay or clerical. Inspired by this 'Kentish Fire', and securing no justice or freedom of worship in England, some took their fierce independence by ship from Sandwich to the New World. Abraham's people, my people, were not gentry, although some were yeoman farmers, and the names of others have been on modest record since the beginning of the fourteenth century. I believe he was as much out of humour with the land-owning Culpepers, Oxindens, Knatchbulls and Lovelaces as he was with the episcopacy and the crown, but he went to New England three years after William Laud became Archbishop of Canterbury. Laud's hatred and contempt for the non-conformists, for their 'Dutch churches', was vigorously expressed. When asked by some to be considerate, he said, 'I will take nothing into consideration and if you conform not all the sooner, I'll take a more round course with you.'* And so he did, imprisoning three of them.

Abraham Preble, who lost a 'b' from his name on the Atlantic crossing, later became a magistrate of the Colony of Massachusetts and a Commissioner for York County. His attachment to the reformed church was reflected in the Biblical names of his children and grandchildren – Abraham, Rachel, Benjamin, Sarah, Jedidiah, Ebenezer, Joshua and Hepzibah . . . His brother Robert, my direct ancestor, was seemingly no zealot. He and his descendants remained until the close of the last century in a tight triangle of villages to the south of Canterbury, working behind a plough, herding stock, swinging a scythe, or turning hedgerows into impenetrable walls of branch and thorn. They did not prosper but they flourished, and have left me with no knowledge of them but their names.

Abraham's people prospered, in land, business and colonial politics. They became general officers in the Revolution and later highly original seamen in the Republic's new navy. One was Commodore Edward Preble, whose brig *Constitution* is still preserved in Boston Navy Yard. The young frigate captains whom he trained were known as Preble's Boys, defeating the Royal Navy in a series of spectacular single-ship actions during the War of 1812. None of this my father knew until I told him, and he was amused, I think. He had stories of his own which I heard before I had the professional skill to record them. When I had that knowledge, his memory was beginning to fail him, although he was sometimes able to put it to work. His account of his great-uncle inspired a long short story I wrote, *My Great-Aunt Appearing Day*, and at my prompting in his eighth decade he put something of what he remembered on paper.

---

* Quoted in *The Community of Kent and the Great Rebellion, 1640–1660*, Alan Everitt, Leicester University Press, 1986.

Charlie Petley came from the Chatham district, year unknown. He made Folkestone his home town. He went to sea in wind-jammers and told me that he was flogged in a Danish full-rigged ship. He served in the American Civil War with the North, went to Canada, homesteading, back to the sea again and then back to roughing it in the West. He came on one occasion to our home, in 1898 I think [when my father was seventeen] with a squaw for a wife and a pocket full of golden sovereigns. I remember him rummaging in his pockets and pulling out a gun casually. I also remember the squaw sitting over the kitchen fire, smoking a clay pipe.

Next I heard of him was that he was a ganger working on a tunnel in the Warren district [of Folkestone] for about two years. I don't know what happened to his wife. He lived by himself in a little shack in the Warren. He used to take a jaunt into town now and then, get full up, spoiling for a fight. Being very deaf, he was very touchy. On one occasion later he proposed that I should desert the Navy and go out to Canada with him. I refused, and that was that. He was short in stature, had a drooping moustache, and would fight anything in trousers. He was well over eighty when he died.

My father could not remember the name of Charlie Petley's Indian wife, but was certain that it meant Dawn. When he was 'roughing it in the West' Petley hunted buffalo, supplying US Army garrisons with hides and meat. My grandmother, upon whose mantelpiece he placed his great hand-gun, immediately drove him from the house and refused to admit him again, but my father remembered him with affection, and with admiration for the sailing-ships the old man carved and rigged. From the little he was able to tell me about the Indian, where and when Charlie Petley met her, I thought she was probably a Cheyenne woman. My father believed there must be a photograph of her somewhere, but we never found it in the boxes, drawers and envelopes which contained such familial relics. But he described it for me, his eyes closed in the concentration of remembering. When I wrote the story, I presented an image that was, I hope, accurate in part.

. . . a small, faded photograph in an oval frame. Emerging not too distinctly from a dusky cloud was a plump little woman in a black dress, covered with jet around the shoulders and throat. Her face was round and seemed to have no eyebrows, but she was smiling with a placid gentleness. Her black hair was long, parted in the middle and lying on her breasts in two plaits. She looked like a gipsy, not the Indian of my imagination. There was not even one feather in her straight, shining hair. But this was she, my great-aunt Appearing Day, a daughter of the Cheyenne, sister of the Arapaho.

I knew nothing of Charlie Petley and his wife when I was a boy in Canada. The present, not the immediate past, occupies the minds of new communities, and in those days my father rarely spoke of his youth. I was too young to understand great exhaustion at the end of a day of manual labour, and the intense pressures of simple survival. I too was pre-occupied, with the joy of growth and discovery. It is plain, no doubt, that much of my historical knowledge of the Canadian West has been acquired in later years, but memory has been a strong thread in my interest. I remember the wooden houses of Sutherland, painted white or green, with red-shingled roofs which glowed in the fire of a prairie sunset. They stood in straight, well-dressed lines on streets that were no more than rutted lanes or trenches of summer dust. I can hear my bare feet on their sidewalks, raised on stilts a yard above the earth. In some streets there were no more than one or two houses, like stranded ships, but all were ambitiously named – Seventh Street, Eighth, Ninth . . . I remember a summer heat so intense that the stare of an idle boy could truly *see* the house-paint curling, like last season's bark on a birch tree. I recall the pistol-shots on a winter's night as the clapboards of our house responded to an alarming drop in temperature. In summer the gardens, the back yards of every house were fenced by rows of sunflowers and heavily scented sweet-peas. There were ice-houses to be made in January's sun-blue days, great chambers cut into the soft snow beneath the hard crust of a drift. When the blizzard had been long and strong, a greater drift sometimes enfolded the house in its frozen embrace. If the storm-door could then be opened, a child's unbelieving fingers might trace the imprint of panel, latch and handle on a translucent wall of crystal. Winter was the occasional terror and surprising joy of an impressionable mind. It quickly followed the mischief of Hallowe'en, orange candle-light in pumpkin skulls, spun cotton-reels rattling on window-glass, open mouths dipping towards green apples on the soot-blackened water of an aluminium bath. I remember the Northern Lights, a pleated curtain of trembling colour, rustling and cracking like a distant wood-fire. I remember the runners of box-wagon sleighs, hissing through unbroken snow on a school outing. Wrapped to the eyes in blankets and scarves, mackinaws, caps and toques, we sang in calf-love and competitive friendship, shouting 'Alouette' to the stars. And when winter became too cruel for play, there was the thought of spring, arrow-flights of geese and ducks, the prairie awake with crocuses, the last foraging coyote limping away in the morning light, and once, in one memorable year, the dead wolf shot by a railroad worker near the engine-house, hanging for a day on the wall of Mr Badger's post office.

Less happy in remembrance is the glow of our burning house, five days before Christmas. The single-storey shack, bought on a crippling bank-loan of one thousand dollars, caught fire when my father was working down the track with the road-gangs, and my mother was in Saskatoon. My sister and I were at school, and my class was rehearsing its song for the seasonal concert. I was called from the chorus of 'Poor Ole Joe' to the corridor window. I could not see the shack, but the smoke of its burning, a lick of flame upon black, rose above the white gable of the Barracloughs' home. I ran all the way from the schoolhouse, across the ice of the hockey-rink, leaping broken wire and the black stalks of dead sunflowers in the back yards. At the shack, neighbours were throwing buckets of snow on the flames. I watched familiar things in unnatural motion – a towel, the pages of a book, my mother's favourite blouse, a bedroom curtain, all now black and burning and floating upward in the draught of the flames. I knew, before I heard the fire-engine coming across the prairie from Saskatoon, that I was responsible for this appalling disaster.

Like many houses in Sutherland, the shack had a privy at the end of a yard, shingle-roofed with two love-hearts cut into its bleached and splintered door, a copy of a Timothy Eaton catalogue hanging on a nail. My mother's English distaste, and her declaration that neither she nor her children would use the outhouse in thirty degrees of frost, persuaded my father to construct an ingenious soil-box in the low wood-shed at the end of the shack. This had no window, and when used was lit by a naked candle. I was the last in the house that morning, and despite all warnings had left the candle burning above a floor of wood-shavings.

The kindness of the Sutherland people following this small tragedy ended my mother's uncertainty about them. Their sympathy was immediately manifest in a Prairie Shower, a custom that may have had its origin in the old Gaelic tradition of sharing a neighbour's burden, building his dry-stone house with him, raising his roof-tree, helping to stock his barn and fill his shelves. My mother wept at the bringing of gifts – clothes, bedding, furniture, utensils, pressing offers of Christmas hospitality, of lodging until a new house was built in the spring. Two rooms of the shack had somehow been saved, although charred and smoke-sodden, and my parents decided to see the winter out in whatever shelter they gave. This choice was accepted with reluctance by our neighbours, and in steadily falling temperatures the men of my father's railroad gang shored and strengthened the fragile building. They nailed, glazed and painted, and their wives brought sealers of preserved fruits and vegetables, newly baked cakes and bread.

I remember that winter with uneasy horror. I remember it whenever I smell smoke-drenched wool or see the charred edge of wood. I remembered it in a winter that was almost as bad, the cold, cold days on the ice and the flat ground of Holland. The temperature then was so bitter that small-arms fire along the Maas sounded like breaking glass, and stand-to at first light was limited to three minutes, an hour's guard to fifteen, braced with rum and hot, sweet tea. As I stamped my feet, blew balls of frosted air through the thickness of a balaclava, I remembered that other winter, and wondered still if my parents knew who had been responsible for the fire, and why I had never had the courage to tell them.

In the following spring, the two rooms of the shack were moved down Ninth Street to the plot where my father, my uncle and their friends were to make it the core of a new house. The removal took a day. The shack was first jacked high into the air and two stout box-wagons, their walls removed, were run beneath it. A splendid team of horses – sent from Laycoe's farm, I think – pulled it slowly and gently down the street to the new plot. My mother had a natural sense of theatre, and against all warning she insisted on serving our mid-day meal in the moving house, smiling with us as we listened to the thud of great hooves, the squeal of the wheel-hubs, and the teamster's cry of encouragement. From the window I looked loftily down at my friends who walked beside us in admiring awe.

Our new home was finished before mid-summer – brown clapboard, white trim and red shingles, the rich smell of paint and pine-wood, of fresh-baked bread from a new range. The house was mounted upon piles, standing two feet or more above the earth so that a cyclone would not destroy it, merely lift it from the piles and place it somewhere else. After reading *The Wizard of Oz* I hoped in terror that one day a cyclone might whirl upon Sutherland, but all I saw, once or twice in the summer heat, was a tall and distant cone, writhing along the horizon. Before the first frost of the year, the gap between the house and the ground was walled with tarred paper and slats of wood, and then banked with earth. In summer the gap was a small boy's delight, a cool and kindly place to lurk, to store treasure, to listen to the grasshoppers, to lie with friends, chewing stems of sweet-grass, exchanging idle insults and absurd boasts.

It *was* a happy boyhood, I suppose, or the thought of it would not linger so pleasantly in my mind. My nature grew with my body, in harmony for a few years. I learnt to skate, to play ice-hockey and baseball, to brag shamelessly and wrestle in defence of my self-respect, to quarrel and quickly resume a pummelling friendship, to fall in summer love with a girl whom I now remember only as a smile from the seat of her father's buggy. At harvest-time my friends and I, brown bodies in blue-jean overalls and straw hats, gathered and stooked sheaves for a nickel an hour. Shortly after dawn we were taken by buckboard to the nearest farm, Laycoe's or Litvak's, where great steam-driven combines ate into boundless wheat-fields and blackened the sky with smoke. At mid-day we sat at a long table laden with plates of pink meat, white potatoes, green cabbage and butter-yellow cobs of corn. The itinerant farm-hands who sat with us were big, brown, noisy men speaking in all the tongues of Europe. At weekends we sometimes walked to the University Farm on the outskirts of Saskatoon where, for a few more cents, we hosed down the pigsties and stalls, drenching ourselves and lying in the fierce sun to dry. The money I earned, which my parents refused to take, was foolishly but enjoyably expended on the Hockey coconut bars we relished, on the loan of a baseball bat or a catcher's mitt, on things I have now forgotten. When some of it was carefully saved, it paid for a hard seat in the Bijou picture-house, down Main Street from the Hudson's Bay store in Saskatoon.

There were two approaches to the growing city from Sutherland. One was by street-car, a single electric tram resembling the Toonerville Trolley in the comic section of the *Saskatoon Star*. It left from the end of Main Street, opposite the Bank of Canada's hut and the Chinese laundry, and rocked over the grass to Nutana like a dinghy on a choppy sea. A cheaper and shorter route was by foot, across the prairie to the river and the railroad bridge. In my memory, this insane erection stood high above the water, a thin thread of iron and wood from bluff to bluff. It was the second on the site, the first having collapsed under the pressure of melting ice. There was a walkway across it, wooden planks and an uncertain hand-rail, but every boy old enough for the dare from his companions was expected to cross by the track, stepping or leaping from tie to tie. Although I do not recall anyone failing this test by dropping between the ties to the river, most of us must have faltered and leapt back to the walkway. It took place in the spring, when the melting river was in angry motion and honouring its Indian name, the ice-floes turning and rising in the water like wounded fish. The noise of the thaw could be heard over the prairie at night, thunder-cracks to trouble the sleep of any boy who had soon to make the walk. I feel sure that the cowardice we shared persuaded us to wait until the thaw was almost over, and the trembling of the iron was less unnerving. I would also like to be sure that I finished the crossing, but a healing darkness hides true memory.

The Bijou picture-house was a safer experience of danger and heroics. It smelt of tobacco and orange-peel, of spilt soda-pop and the crushed shells of peanuts. We sat in an unsatisfying semi-darkness during the summer when the side doors were opened to admit what breeze there was. The screen was thus in flickering conflict with long bars of sunlight, the clattering projector and competing piano sometimes drowned by the noise of engines, bells and voices beyond. The films I remember best were endless serials, all Westerns. We each had our favourite in a gallery of celluloid heroes – Tom Mix or Harry Carey, Hoot Gibson, Ken Maynard or Colonel Tim McCoy. The mystery of Ken Maynard's death clings to my memory like a burr. The last I saw of him was a familiar, white-hatted figure, erect in the saddle, motionless on the rim of a deep canyon and looking back to his pursuers. He turned from them, touched the neck of his horse in reassurance and rode off the rim to the river below. This was of course the end of an episode only, but since I did not see or did not remember any sequel, it was how Ken Maynard died – so convincingly that, many years later, when his true death was reported, I believed at first it was an error.

Away from the Bijou picture-house we sometimes recreated its excitement in play. We galloped like Maynard, shot like Carey, and bowed from the saddle like Colonel McCoy. We were too young yet to know that past and present were interwoven in our small township, and that being young and *present* we were part of both weft and warp. Once a fortnight, when the Bank of Canada hut was opened, a corporal of the North West Mounted Police came to Sutherland with the teller. Waiting rail-workers, shopping women and yelling children watched the approach of their Model T Ford, bouncing on clouds of dust by the street-car lines. The corporal wore a red coat and white lanyard, yellow-striped breeches of blue and glistening boots, the same splendid uniform he and his comrades wore for their spectacular defeat of Poundmaker in the Saskatoon Rodeo. Outraged that he should be dressed like this and yet arrive *in an automobile*, we cat-called him and he responded with mock anger. Boldly wearing a sling-shot in the holster of a hippocket, we studied the morning's business from the doorway of the hut. The corporal sat beside the teller, his red hair closely cropped, his field-hat and gauntlets on the desk beside a heavy black revolver. Because he wished to please us, perhaps, he sometimes touched the butt of the gun with his fingertips.

He came only once as the remorseless servant of the Law, getting his man. He came with a constable to arrest one laundryman for the murder of another with an axe. The Chinaman was led from the wash-house door to the Ford, manacled and with his head bowed. He was later hanged in Regina or Prince Albert. He was a gentle old man who was always kind to me. When I brought him the little washing that my mother could not do for herself, he gave me the bulbs of plants that never flowered, sweet nuts that soon became indigestible pulp in the mouth.

September the Third

Autumn's first warning appeared suddenly in the Great Glen this morning, cinnamon flares on the lower braes from Loch Ness to the Firth of Lorn. When I passed through the narrow trough of Loch Oich the day promised fair beneath a sky of broken cloud, but now on Loch Etiveside rain has moved in from the Outer Isles in the guise of mist, blinding the eye and chilling the spirit. Within the ruin of Ardchattan Priory on the north shore the ancient burial stones are black-cold and wet, and the bray of an unmilked cow in an adjoining byre deepens the melancholy of the weather. This is an historic date, or rather it is a date of historical coincidence. Twice on September the third the Almighty granted Oliver Cromwell a 'crowning mercy' in his struggle with the Scots. The phrase is his. On this day he savagely defeated their forces at Dunbar and thereby made clear his power to impose a political union in which England, he said, would live 'peaceable and quiet' beside them. One year later to the day he entrapped their futile invasion and destroyed it at Worcester, where several hundred Highlandmen, brought so far from their glens, fought on without powder and shot until they were killed. And this is the date of Cromwell's own death, on a Friday afternoon in Whitehall. His departure, it was said, had been foreshadowed by the weather at the close of August, 'a horrid tempest and whirrycane' uprooting trees and demolishing many houses in Westminster. This day is also the most important in the life of my generation, as apocalyptic as the fourth of August had been to our parents twenty-five years before. If I remember that Sunday in 1939 with any clarity of detail, autumn was also early then. As I walked in the Park, considering the inevitability of death from the sky that afternoon or in a trench a year hence, the narrow paths approaching the Serpentine were roofed with incandescent leaves.

I stopped here on Loch Etiveside by chance, suddenly curious and unaware of the discovery I would make. I knew something of the Priory's history. In 1308, on or about this day and following his wild victory in the Pass of Brander, Robert Bruce called the Parliament of Scotland here. Or so it is sometimes said. It is perhaps a wishful error grown large from the small truth that he sat in council with the barons of Argyll and the Isles, securing the inaction of some if not their allegiance. The Priory was already a century old, one of three founded by an ascetic branch of the Benedictines brought from France by the Bishop of St Andrews. In an early example of privileged education, Duncan MacDougal, the Lord of Lorn, gave them the lands of Ardchattan in return for the schooling of his son. The soil upon which the monks built their house was traditionally holy. Its name means 'the high ground of Chattain', from Cattan, the abbot of an older community. He was perhaps a Pict rather than a Scot, a friend of Columba and the brother or brother-in-law of Aidan, that warring King of Dalriada who gathered an army of Scots and Britons and destroyed the Angles of Liddesdale, filling the church of Iona with captured banners and dedicating a tenth of his booty to Christ.

The community of Ardchattan grew in size and importance as the most influential religious house in the Western Highlands. Storming along south Etiveside towards the MacDougals' stronghold of Dunstaffnage, Bruce's men could have seen the smoke of many chimneys across the water, where now there is green timber or the white, ungiving face of an occasional steading. There was a priory church, a wayhouse, hospice, school and seminary, farms, byres and cottages, fields of grain and yellow bonnets of hay. Almost a century after the community was gone, men remembered it with nostalgic awe: 'Friars, monks and nunnes were wont to dwell in the town and church in ancient tyme.' And the finest bows in the Highlands were made from the yew trees of Esragan a mile eastward from the Priory, in a green glen where the great Macaulay's grandmother lived as a child. The community was dissolved late in the Reformation, in the final year of the sixteenth century. By a compromise that seemed to satisfy all (except perhaps the Vicar of Christ), the last prior, Alexander Campbell, one of several of that name who held the office, was given the land and its buildings and thus became the first Laird of Ardchattan. Fifty years later his descendant, 'a chief Malignant in Lorn', according to the English, chose the exiled Charles II rather than the Lord Protector's offer of a quiet and peaceable life in England's bosom. And so Captain Mutloe of the occupying forces at Dunstaffnage stormed the old priory house, killed three of its defenders, and burnt what would burn of the community's fabric.

The Campbells of Barcaldine held the land of Ardchattan for two hundred years and buried their dead in the crowded ruin as late as 1880, although by then their entire estate of thirty thousand acres had been sold. The most famous of this family now lying in the south transept is Colin Campbell of Glenure, victim of the Appin Murder and the Red Fox of Stevenson's *Kidnapped*, a man ill-served in remembrance, I think. Twelve days after his death in the dark trees beyond the ferry at Ballachulish, his corpse was taken from his home to the Priory. Relays of men carried it for twenty miles down Glen Creran and its lochside, through the brown hills of Benderloch, by Glen Salach of haunting witches and redeeming saints, and past the yew trees of Esragan to Ardchattan and the Priory. And there they buried the 'noble, humble, loving and fault-less man'.* If the name of his murderer is still in doubt, the weapon is not. It was a long Spanish gun, fine for casting bullets, it was said, and it was called *An-t-Slinneanach*, the broad-shouldered.

I came here to find Glenure's grave, not from curiosity alone but because the thought of writing one more account of the Appin Murder, and perhaps solving its mystery, sometimes occupies my mind. The afternoon light was too unsympathetic, the wet stones all too much of a likeness for identification to be certain, but if I have not identified Colin Campbell's stone I have found others more poignant. By the corner of the south transept and the wall of the quire are two horizontal slabs, slipping earthward in age. They cover and commemorate MacFadyens and Macintyres who once held the tack, the lease of Achnacree, three miles to the west of the Priory. The inscriptions are not easy to read; corrosion is almost obliterating them and the vestigial incisions of the mason's chisel are made shallower still by the black rain. But when my hand wiped away some of the moss and water the unexpected words were there. I wrote them on a diary page in the lee of the wall, the ink-strokes weeping on the damp paper.

In memory of Susan McIntyre the beloved and lamented wife of Duncan McFadyen tacksman of Glen Ackrie who died 18th June 1848 aged 33 years also their sons Duncan who died in infancy and

---

* This encomium was composed by his foster-brother, Duncan Ban Macintyre, the renowned bard of Glen Etive.

Coll who died at Buffalo 10th May 1865 from wounds received in the 13th action of the 5th Michigan Infantry in the American Civil War aged 21 years.

There is no record of Coll's boyhood that I have yet discovered. His father's people may have come from Lochbuie across the firth on Mull, where the name still survives, and men of his mother's clan were renowned pipers in Glen Noe on Etiveside. The tack of Achnacree, which might have become his, went to his uncle, John McIntyre, who lies under the neighbouring stone with five of his children. McIntyre's widow, Janet McDougall, placed the stones over both graves in 1889, and from that date, it seems, MacFadyens and MacIntyres were gone from Achnacree.

I cannot explain why I am more moved by this stone memorial to young MacFadyen than I am by the thought of Robert Bruce's presence here, facing the barons of Argyll. It is a personal sadness, remembering the dead and the grieving of my generation. I strive for some intuitive knowledge of Coll's exile, the reasons that made it imperative, and more factually an understanding of the route he took from Scotland to the ending of his short life. He came by Upper Canada perhaps, through the Highland settlements on the Ottawa River and along the shore of Lake Ontario. Attracted by the beat of Union drums so close, he took the steam ferry to Detroit in the State of Michigan. This I infer from the records of the Fifth which show that he was enlisted in that city on 29 August 1862, for a term of three years.* His age was entered as twenty, although by the life-span given him on the stone at Ardchattan he was at this time only eighteen or even younger. But twenty is the age of most of the boys who were mustered with him in Company F, and it may be no more than a figure convenient to the conscience of the recruiter (who also gave Coll's name the phonetic spelling McFadden).

Within three weeks of his enlistment, he joined the regiment at Fort Wood in Virginia and was later re-mustered in Company D. As a soldier of the Army of the Potomac he fought in the most terrible battles of the eastern theatre, in the choking smoke and

* From the *Record of Service of the Michigan Volunteers in the Civil War, 1861 – 1865, Vol. Five.* I am grateful to my son Simon, residing in New York, for discovering and dispatching this and other information so promptly, thus giving more substance to the memory of Coll McFadyen than is to be found in that grieving acknowledgement on a Highland gravestone.

murderous confusion of the Old Turnpike at Chancellorsville, and the bloody rocks and gullies of the Devil's Den at Gettysburg, where the Fifth were advanced as skirmishers. He fought among the burning trees of the Wilderness, and in Ulysses Grant's flanking campaign to take the Rebel capital of Richmond. There can be no way of knowing how the young man's mind and spirit coped with the horror of Cold Harbor, where the unattended dead in blue and grey covered five acres between the armies, and men vomited uncontrollably in the stench. In the middle of June 1864, and approaching Petersburg from the east, the Union soldiers drove their opponents across the James River. This they bridged with pontoons, and advanced over them to a long and exhausting siege. It was five months before the city was taken, and on 17 June, before the investment was truly begun, Coll McFadyen was wounded, probably by the swathing fire of canister in an assault upon the Confederate earthworks. This was the eighteenth action of the Fifth Michigan, not the thirteenth, and either Janet McDougall was mistaken or time and erosion have made the two figures indistinguishable on the stone she erected. The Highland boy could not recover from his wounds. He was discharged from the Union Army in January 1865, and four months later he died at Buffalo, close to the Canadian border but far from Lochaber and his home. No one unscathed by experiences such as his can presume to imagine his suffering, but with the thought of his lonely passage across the Detroit River to that terrible war, I hope I have shared some of his emotions.

We may sail tonight. The decks of these landing-craft are alive with soldiers, the wind blowing their hair about their faces and their blouse collars turned up about their cheeks. I am sitting in the turret of the forward AA gun and every now and then someone else climbs up beside me, looks at the sea, at the sun shining on the roofs behind us, stands here for a while and then shivers in the wind and goes down below.

The gulls are going out to sea. All day they have been whirling and hanging low over the masts, while above them roar the Fortresses and Liberators on their way to France. But now the gulls are leaving us and going out to sea, floating with the tide, bobbing up and down on the waves like children's boats . . . Simple things interest us now, and as the sun sets men's faces seem to grow more sober. There's a strange intimacy between us all that did not exist when we left Cooksbridge. I don't know whether I am happy or sad.

On the distant evening when that was written I was at the beginning of a long road, both real and figurative, a highway we sometimes called the Liberation Road. The memory of it can return unprompted, and most strongly this morning when I came down the Great Glen. I was recording a radio programme on Wade's military road, and was in good conceit of myself, having discovered that I could still tramp some miles along a rough track without discomfort, although I panted too much into the microphone held by my companion, Mike Harding. A modern highway covers much of this old road from Inverness to Fort William, but some stretches of the original still exist along the eastern shore of Loch Oich, and by Loch Lochy to the Falls of Mucomir. Masked by trees, it crumbles in winter's hard grip every year, sometimes collapsing into the water and leaving gaps that must be waded rather than leapt.

Loch Oich is a narrow water, held by a crack in a great massif, no broader than four hundred yards or so at the widest, and in the manner of most Highland place-names there are variations of its meaning. It may come from *uisge*, for water, or *oig*, for the youngest, that is the smallest of the lochs in the Great Glen. But it is also said to mean awesome, and that too, at dusk or in the dark of a storm, can seem most proper. Studded with small islets of trees, it is a natural link in Telford's great canal, and the highest point above sea-level reached by that ambitious undertaking. I remember with delight an afternoon fifty-five years ago, when I stood on the foredeck of a paddle-steamer as it passed through the Laggan drawbridge and breasted the dark water of the loch with a bow-wave of glistening beads. Now there is little traffic but the holiday boats of summer, and it is long since I saw a chain of Peterhead trawlers going down to the Firth of Lorn and the herring harvest beyond the Hebrides. The only movement on the loch this morning was a sudden flurry of water-fowl and a consequent lap of ripples where a copse of birch soothed its twisted roots. Disturbed by our passing voices, the birds broke cover in alarm, moving low above the water before rising in a canting wheel about the stump of the MacDonells' castle.

All morning there was no alien sound greater than a murmur from traffic on the metalled road on the western shore of the loch. Such tranquillity could persuade a wishful mind that the peace it reflects has been timeless. For almost a century, however, from the eighteenth to the nineteenth, the Great Glen throbbed with occasional but energetic industry – the employment of axe, saw, hammer and lever, exploding charge and cracking stone, the rushing sigh of falling timber in the forests, the protest of wheels and the shouts of teamsters, and finally, towards the end of the age, the thump of monstrous steam-engines from Corpach on Loch Linnhe northward up the glen to Inverness. The large lochs were scattered with bellying sails of busy vessels, unaffected as yet by competition from the new roads. Twenty years before the death of the Gael at Culloden, the red mouth of an iron-furnace glowed on the shore at Invergarry, where the men of Clan Donald, pressed into its service by their improvident chief, still believed in talking-stones, water-horses, and an Evil Eye that could wither corn or dry up a woman's womb. The dominant sound in all this noisy industry was English, the voice of an English director, manager or overseer. The industrial exploitation of the Highlands has a longer history than might be thought, and the English were among the earliest to profit by it, even when Scotland was still an independent kingdom. In the sixteenth century, in the year of the Armada, Englishmen were in Wester Ross, far north of the Great Glen, organizing the felling and transportation of its ancient Caledonian pine. Highland lairds were eager for such contracts with the Saxon incomers, and took their own profit with an easy conscience. There were thus reassuring precedents for Hugh Fraser of Struy, once a Royalist captain, whose red forest supplied all the native wood needed for building the Cromwellian fort at Inverness.*

The climax of the remarkable surge of industry in the Great Glen was the building of the Caledonian Canal by Thomas Telford, who was not English but a Scot, born in a shepherd's hut on the Meggat Water in Eskdale. Other men had dreamed of such a channel before James Watt produced and later abandoned a plan to link the western and eastern oceans. In the early part of the eighteenth century a similar proposal had been thought worthy but impracticable. The force of the wind, it was said, sucked in from sea to sea and particularly fierce in the narrows at Loch Oich, would make navigation under sail impossible. In 1801, and in the rising age of steam, Telford had no need to concern himself with such objections. His vision was bold and energetically realized. Before breakfast on a September day like this, his friend Robert Southey watched the

* The Minister of Wardlaw (see p. 58) was witness to this transaction. 'I saw that gentleman receive 30 thousand marks at once for timber.'

building of the five locks at Fort Augustus. He was awed by the masonry assembled, by the size of the locks, each 180 feet in length, and by Telford's beloved steam-dredgers, devouring earth and drinking water. Above all, he admired the majestic industry of the undertaking.

Men, horses and machines at work; digging, walling and puddling going on; men wheeling barrows, horses drawing stones along the railways. The great steam-engine was at rest, having done its work. It drew out 160 hogsheads per minute; and two smaller engines (large ones, they would have been considered anywhere else) were also needed while the execution of the lower docks was going on; for they dug 24 feet below the surface of the water in the river, and the water filtered thro' open gravel. The dredging machine was in action, revolving round and round, and bringing up at every turn matter which had never before been brought to air and light. Its chimneys poured forth volumes of black smoke, which there was no annoyance in beholding, because there was room enough for it in this wide, clear atmosphere.

The Canal completed a revolution that had begun a century earlier with the building of the first military road. What remains of that surrenders each year to erosion and neglect, and it is hard to imagine the sweat and muscle, the invention and passion, which created it. As Harding and I passed by Loch Oich, upon what seemed to be a neglected lane of leaf-dappled sunlight, we walked upon stones that had been laid in the third decade of the eighteenth century by General Wade's road-makers. At one time there were more than a thousand soldiers and Highland militia at labour between Fort William and Fort Augustus, and this twenty years before Culloden. The lochside is the only route through the Great Glen at this point, and almost two centuries after the road was built a little railway company laid a track beside it, from Glen Spean to Loch Ness. The first train along the line left Spean Bridge in July 1903, upon a signal from a golden whistle, blown by the lady of Invergarry House. The rails kept a parallel course with the military road, never more than a few yards from it, even when plunging into the braeside for half a mile opposite Invergarry Castle. The entrance to this tunnel is still there, its red sandstone now black with grime and its mouth closed by a wooden gate. More in the imaginative spirit of *Ivanhoe* than the Age of Steam, it has castellated turrets and narrow

arrow-slits now choked with shrub and fern. This little venture, which bravely hoped to extend its track another thirty-five miles up the Great Glen to the Moray Firth, had a short if pleasing life and was closed to passenger traffic in 1933. When the war ended, its rails and sleepers were torn up, its embankments and cuttings left to nature and the lonely companionship of Wade's abandoned road.

The military roads of the Highlands were built by a succession of engineers, both civil and military, but all are sometimes referred to as Wade's roads. The error is excusable, even complimentary to the resolute old soldier who drove the first of them into the heart of Loch-aber. He was perhaps no great engineer, and no more than an indifferent field-officer, although at the age of seventy-four, and as a field-marshal and commander-in-chief, he led one of the three armies that pursued the Jacobites on their retreat from Derby. The military road he had cut into the mountains twenty years before made the Rebels' defeat and the suppression of the Highlands more decisive than they might have been had the only access to the glens been the cattle-trails and raiding-paths followed by Monck a century earlier.

The engaging chronicler of the building of Wade's road was his contemporary, Edward Burt. His *Letters from a Gentleman in the North of Scotland* have accompanied me during much of my travelling in the Highlands, carried in a box with Ordnance Survey maps and old guide-books. Burt was an Englishman and time has been flattering to his memory, for he is often described as an engineer, a road-maker on Wade's staff, and sometimes a captain of the army. In fact, he appears to have been a superior rent-collector, sent to Inverness in 1724 as a Justice of the Peace with the principal duty of securing payments due to the Crown from Jacobite estates attainted after the Rebellion of 1715. His repeated demand for respect as a representative of the King was finally answered by one nettled citizen of Inverness who told him that His Majesty was 'muckle better represented on a bawbee'.* Scots magistrates in the town complained of his 'haughtiness and flashes of passion', his arrogant contempt for Scots law which he frequently damned, and that he and his companions often threatened them with a whipping by the public hangman for insolence and lack of respect for English authority. If true, he was not a pleasing man but a little gauleiter, enjoying the small authority which better men had secured for him in battle. But his account of the Highlands in his time is a rich

* bawbee: a halfpenny sterling (sixpence Scots).

source of information, and allowing for its conventional assumption of English superiority it is largely free from the contempt and arrogance of which he was accused. His worthwhile pride is in the great road-building achievements begun in 1726, a year or so after his appointment to Inverness.* In one letter he warns his 'Friend in London' that the comfort now enjoyed by travellers should not give the impression that the construction of the roads had been effortless and easy. Although the work had . . .

. . . continued about eleven years in the prosecution; yet, long as it may be thought, if you were to pass over the whole work (for the borders of it would show you what it was) I make no doubt but that number of years would diminish in your imagination to a much shorter extract of time by comparison with the difficulties that attend the execution.

When its course can be traced on a good contour map today, George Wade's plan is simple and impressive. The roads he built or authorized gave rapid access to the Highlands, securing the march of Horse and Foot in the shortest time with the minimum of fatigue. They were strong enough to carry the wheel-drawn weight of carriage, bat-wagon and field-artillery. Branching from the Stirling plain, they resemble the veins of a broad leaf, or more graphically a finger-span turned obliquely across the mountains. The wrist of such a hand is the town of Crieff. Here the land soon rises in immobile waves, and here, Burt reminded his friend, the Romans halted the northward thrust of their roads, thus implying that General Wade was fulfilling a noble plan abandoned fifteen hundred years before. The grand objective was to drive the 'military ways' beyond Breadalbane to the wide strath of Rannoch and north-eastward to the upper valley of the Spey, over the hunched brown shoulders of the Monadhliath and down to Inverness. There the best known of the Wade roads runs straight in an arrow's flight along the shore of Loch Ness, down the Great Glen to Kilcumein, Fort William and the green water-gate to the Isles.

In past years, when I was younger, I walked some miles along these roads, from one agreeable point to another, in Breadalbane and Strathspey, Glen Albyn and the Rough Bounds, by Glencoe

* His *Letters*, seemingly written in 1736–7, were first published in London in 1754, by which time much of the Highland way of life they described had been destroyed by the defeat of the '45 Rebellion and the oppression which followed.

to Appin, Benderloch and the Firth of Lorn. In the beginning, when I was new to the seductive magic of the land and unaware of how deep my ignorance was, I leant upon the red-backed Ward Lock guides I carried with me. They told me nothing I wished to know about the military ways, and accordingly I felt no kinship with Wade's men or the battalions who later used the roads. I could not then, as I think I can now, hear the steady tramp of marching feet – ninety paces, one hundred paces to the minute, year by year for a century until the garrisons they served at Ruthven, Fort Augustus, Corgaff or Bernera were crumbling into rubble, manned by a few fragile pensioners. A deep attachment to the roads, and some companionship with those who once used them, came after I had myself been part of a great road-making venture, moving forward with the labouring wheels of a three-tonner or the cautious steps of an advancing foot-soldier. I took this road, the road both real and figurative, when I sat in the gathering dusk and summer chill of that forward AA turret in Newhaven harbour. Even earlier perhaps, when I was finally released from the camp at Kinmel Park, shouting joyous obscenities as the utility truck took me past the marble church at Bodelwyddan, by the castle at Rhuddlan to the railway station at Rhyl.

The principal supply route for the British Second Army in north-west Europe was sometimes called the Liberation Road, but its official designation was the number 240. Thus, according to the direction taken, the markers along its course said either 'Two Forty Up' or 'Two Forty Down'. It advanced almost daily, sometimes by miles, more often yards only, and at its furthest point was a forward platoon of infantry, or a section of Engineers clearing mines. Sometimes it passed along a highway that was as old as the history of man, but it also cut its own path across unharvested fields, through a shell-broken wood or over the stones of a dying village. The making and the holding of this road involved our Battery after dusk,* its cold moonlight illuminating a hostile landscape for armour and bulldozer, for field-ambulance and Bren-carrier, and for the most advanced, exposed and loneliest infantryman who quite properly did not always welcome our assistance. It was therefore natural that my novel – begun at the Lorelei, continued in Hamburg and finished in England – should originally be called *Two Forty Up*. It was a necessary book, I thought, both bitter and cathartic

---

* 474 Ind. S/L Battery R.A.

in gestation. The title did not survive Fred Warburg's disapproval, but my meaning was made plain in an introduction from which the subsequent title, *The Edge of Darkness*, was taken.

Of all things it will be the roads we shall remember best. They formed the circumference of our lives in a world that was as yet indeterminate, as much in process of destruction as liberation. Where the broad face of it was changing vividly beneath the emotions of battle and weather we were assured and comforted by the firm confidence of the roads.

They were strange roads for the most part, and in our memories they will transport our anecdotes from point to point along their route. Some were cut by bulldozers from the yellow earth of Normandy or the black mud of Holland. Some were old and ran for miles between long lines of friendly beeches. They were roads that carried us forward, and in our affection we swore at them and remembered them as friends by names and numbers that were our own invention. We made them part of our lives at the climax of our lives. They were roads that went forward, always forward. That was a great encouragement to us, although we knew that there was an end to them somewhere on the dark edge of the world where the infantry crawled forward and took the earth from the darkness . . .

The road was always there because we were making it, and whatever lay ahead in the wilderness yet to be cleared, the road itself was there, going forward, pushing back the darkness.

The two hundred and fifty miles of road built by George Wade were less than a quarter of all the military highways constructed in the Highlands that century, but they were the backbone and inspiration of all. This achievement, the most important of his life, perhaps, receives no acknowledgement on his florid monument in Westminster Abbey. Sculpted by Louis Roubiliac, it shows the robust figure of Time attempting to destroy the military trophies won by the General, an assault resisted by a buxom representation of Fame. The monument is above the door to the cloisters, but nobody in the Abbey has been able to tell me exactly where the General himself might be, except that he lies beneath an unmarked stone behind the altar. Most happily, however, on the floor below his monument, there is a stone covering the remains and bearing the name of Thomas Telford. Far northward at Aberfeldy in Strathtay, four hundred yards from the inn that was his headquarters, there is a more generous acknowledgement of Wade's great achievement – a tablet in Latin on William Adam's fine bridge. It invites the viewer to admire . . .

> . . . this military road stretching on this side and that 250 miles beyond the limit of the Roman one mocking moors and bogs and as you see crossing the indignant Tay. This difficult work G. Wade, Commander in Chief of the Forces in Scotland accomplished by his own skill and the ten years labour of soldiers in the year 1733.*

Summer was the only season in which those labourers could be usefully employed. Six hundred soldiers worked in the gangs, said Burt, assisted 'by detachments from the Highland companies'. The only clansmen in the crown's service at this time were the Independent Companies, later mustered as a regular marching regiment, the 43rd. Six of these companies had been raised a year before the first pick broke ground for the New Road, not far from the old Roman camp at Ardoch, to the north-east of Dunblane. Most of them were drawn from the Whig clans of Campbell and Munro and their duties, as described for another such levy half a century before, were 'to keep watch upon the braes'. From this, and by their dark tartan and their main purpose in suppressing *black*mail by lawless men, they acquired the title of Black Watch. Their role as navvies in George Wade's gangs – reluctantly, perhaps, and no doubt derided by other clansmen – is not mentioned in any history of the regiment that I recall. This is not surprising, for all accounts of its early years depend heavily upon *Sketches of the Highlanders*, published in 1822 by Colonel David Stewart of Garth.† He undertook this work at the Regiment's request because most of its records had been lost by shipwreck and by enemy action. He therefore relied upon the memories of old men, none of whom may have wished to recall a time when soldiers of the Black Watch worked as labourers on George Wade's roads.

Private soldiers of the gangs were paid sixpence a day above their normal pay, also sixpence. Corporals received eightpence and sergeants a shilling. But this was for a day worked, and the labour was often interrupted or halted by storms, by wind, rain or flood.

---

* Translation from *Aberfeldy Past and Present*, N. D. Mackay, 1954.
† Its full title was *Sketches of the Character, Manners and Present State of the Highlanders of Scotland with Details of the Military Service of the Highland Regiments*. Stewart served in the Black Watch during the Napoleonic wars.

The small red detachments, stretched along a surveyed route, were commanded by subalterns who received half-a-crown a day 'to defray their extraordinary expense in building huts,' said Burt, 'making necessary provision for their tables from distant parts; unavoidable though unwelcome visits; and other incidents arising from their wild situation.' Private soldiers supped on cheese, ale and ammunition loaf and sometimes, on rare occasions when the General arrived in his great brown coach, they roasted an ox whole in the dust or mud of the road he came to inspect.

Whatever Burt's title or duties, whatever his involvement beyond an admiring curiosity, his account of the road-making is graphic and authentic. He enjoyed the sight, the sound and the success of the work, and was often one of the first to pass along a new section when it was completed. He rode at speed, galloping with no admitted fear of a fall. One ride was as smooth as Constitution Hill in London, he said, and he was able to travel 'in great tranquillity' where before there had been discomfort and hazard. The great tracts of moorland in the Highlands, their treacherous sinking ground, had always been awesome, and now he triumphed in their defeat.

When one of these bogs has crossed the way on a stoney moor, there the loose ground had been dug out down to the gravel, or rock, and the hollow filled up in the manner following, viz. First, with a layer of large stones, then a smaller size, to fill up the gaps and raise the causeway higher; and lastly, two, three, or more feet of gravel, to fill up the interstices of the smaller stones and form a binding surface. This part of the road has a bank on each side to separate it from a ditch, which is made withoutside* to receive water from the bog, and, if the ground will allow it, to convey it by a trench to a slope, and thereby in some measure to drain it.

There was no such sophistication when I saw the makers of Two Forty Up breaking new ground beyond the ruins of Overloon, the lurching bulldozers following the reinforcing files of 3rd British infantry. When our lights moved up at dusk the highway was already a muddy ditch, its ruts filled by the malevolent water that lay so close to the surface of Holland. That night we were torch-

* withoutside: on the outer side.

bearers to the road-makers and at dawn, when we withdrew, we took their abuse in good humour.

It is foolish for a sedentary man to romanticize manual labour, and there is perhaps an uneasy guilt when I write of it. My father was proud of his manual skill, the strength of his shoulders and arms, a physical endurance which he over-estimated in time and which accordingly shortened his life. Trained in sail, almost a hundred years ago now, he could walk like a tree-cat on the yards and rigging of the training-ship *Impregnable* before he was sixteen. Later in his life, and at a hard time when no work could be refused, he was one of a select group of riggers, 'old ships' he called them, past seamen who were employed to raise and make fast the ceilings of coloured cloth above the arena at the Olympia. He had also been a sail-maker, and kept his needle, awl and palm in a bag of chamois leather until he died. He was obliged to be a tailor as well, for in his youth seamen were still expected to make their own dress uniforms. He cut and sewed the white duck-suit in which he was married, posing proudly for a photograph with my mother, his naval straw hat dipped forward on his brow. In that picture his neck and shoulders are strong, his hands large. In others, taken when he served aboard the *Perseus* in the Persian Gulf, he is a slim young man erect, an able-seaman in charge of a coaling-boat for the day. He remembered those times with gentle amusement as well as pride, and I was a silent listener, already inspired by the stories of W. H. G. Kingston. The *Perseus* was a black-hulled, yellow-funnelled sloop on anti-slavery patrol, pursuing Arab dhows at sea, her boat's-crews sometimes going ashore with Martini-Henry and belted cutlass, chasing slavers into the rocks and on one unbelievable occasion ending a battle between two villages by kicking a football through their line of fire.

My mother's father was also a manual worker, a skilful scaffolder, although he had served no apprenticeship that might have earned him more than a casual labourer's wage. On both sides of my family there was rarely a man who did not work with his hands, with spade, pick, hammer, saw, scythe or hedging tools. One of the strongest memories of my father is the sight of him at work, the movement of his body taking the strain upon sinew and muscle. In his eighth decade, until his stroke, he worked tirelessly in his garden within the smell if not the sight of the sea. He took long, slow walks in the lanes of West Sussex, picking stalks, seed-pods and roots from the detritus of other gardens and bringing them to miraculous life in his own. I am a poor successor of such men, but not one of them, I think, would have hesitated before exchanging his hard life for my own.

I would not say that familial recollections make it easy for me to understand the builders of Wade's roads, but I hope they give me some empathy with the soldiers of the gangs. My own experience of cruel and unremitting labour was mercifully short, and salutary. For a brief while in the mid-summer of 1944, pursuing my dogged efforts to reach Normandy, I was forgotten in a work-shop on the northern fringe of London where my continued applications for an overseas posting lay ignored in the company office. England was now under attack from the V-1 rocket, the small, black flying-bomb that droned across the summer sky, hovered for a moment in awesome silence and then plunged earthward. In the efforts to defeat it, the work-shop at Sawbridgeworth (and others elsewhere perhaps) was instructed to produce gun-platforms, easily mobile and capable of bearing a light anti-aircraft weapon. Short sections of railway line were cut to a prescribed length and then mounted on a box-like frame of sleepers. Each mounting, we were told, would be long enough to permit the rapid movement of a Bofors or a 3.7 to anticipate and destroy a rocket in flight. I am not sure that we believed this possible, but at the end of the day or night we were soon too weary for debate. At first, when a rocket passed above us, we looked up and waited for its fall, but in time it became commonplace and our work was unrelenting. I learnt to cut iron and spot-weld with adequate skill, to bore holes in sleepers and mount shoes, to carry impossible weights upon my naked shoulders, and to sleep deeply in the little time allowed us. The days were dry, airless and excessively hot, and the sweat of our stinking flesh brought black clouds of insects from the farmlands beyond. I remembered this work some weeks later, when the Second Army over-ran the launching-pads closest to Britain, and the empty shells of rockets were used as swill-bins at the château to the south of Abbeville. I also remembered that summer's labour during winter nights when we looked eastward to the rim of Germany and watched the rapid ascent of the deadlier, white-tailed rocket that succeeded the flying-bomb. It is now a bad memory of a horrid season.

Winter washes over us in icy rainstorms. It grips our vehicles as they bog down in the mud. At stand-to, a mug of tea and rum is cold before it touches our lips. We hunch our bodies about our souls and curse irritably. We stand over petrol-fires as the wind drags out the flames, long petals of bronze chrysanthemums. We are black with the rain, and long for snow which we will also hate. We move on – moving on 240 Up, moving on to a windmill, to a butter-factory, to a slit-trench and the winter grip of night again. Night is the proper time for warfare, distances compressed, contact with familiar things lost, and anonymity preserved. The adders' tongues of gunfire flicker at the end of 240 Up. The war is sincere at night, and at night we know that it will never end.

At that time I knew nothing of Wade or his roads, nor would have given a cigarette-end for the knowledge, perhaps. But now all I learn about them deepens and strengthens my interest. The customary breadth of a Wade road was sixteen feet, wide enough for the passing of two wagons, two companies of men three abreast, or two troops of Horse in column of twos. The route was determined by inadequate maps and difficult surveys. It largely followed existing droving-trails and the advantageous alternatives offered by the land, but occasionally – as if in frustrated impatience – it climbed a mountain brae with the undeflected boldness of a bayonet-thrust. The men of the gangs followed a course indicated by widely spaced camp-colours, the markers normally used to identify the lines of a tented battalion. Fragments of red, blue, white or yellow, they could be seen from a considerable distance. Burt's occasional sensitivity is sometimes illuminating. He was intrigued by the harsh colours which the flags, the raw earth and broken stones painted upon the virgin landscape, and by what appeared at first to be a whimsical disorder.

Now, let us suppose that where you are, the road is visible to you for a short space and then is broken off to the sight by a hollow or winding among the hills; beyond that interruption, the eye catches a small part of the side of another hill, and some again on the ridge of it; in another place, further off, the road appears to run zig-zag, in angles, up a steep declivity; in one place, a short horizontal line shows itself below, in another the marks of the road seem to be almost even with the clouds &c.

It is easy to share his delight in such a prospect, his joy as he puts his horse to a gallop along a highway as smooth as any fine prospect in the City of Westminster. The road he knew best, during and after its creation, was that which ran along the shore of Loch Ness to Foyers, climbing then to Whitebridge and the mantle-skirt of the Monadhliath before coming down by Glen Tarff to Fort Augustus. Access to the road from Inverness was easy, and he could canter to the most forward gang, exchange civilities with its hospitable subaltern, and be back in the town for dinner at four o'clock. His admiration was unrestrained when he wrote of the building of the Loch Ness road, the most hazardous in design, demanding in labour, and triumphant in completion. It can still alarm a motorist coming to it for the first time. Although now widened and strengthened, the tall rise of the rock upon its eastern flank, and the omnipresence of dark loch-water upon the other, can work upon an uneasy imagination. There was already a track southward from Dores in 1724, but most of Wade's road was made anew, dug, cut or blasted from the land. For twelve miles it was built out into the loch, upon a sturdy foundation of rocks blown from the sheer escarpment above. This was the hardest of the roadmen's tasks, asking more from muscle and spirit than any moorland bog or wild stone ford. The long cliff-face they attacked with strength and courage was known as the Black Rock, a name given to it by the gangs, or by the Gaels before them.

> There [said Burt] the miners hung by ropes from the precipice over the water (like Shakespear's Gatherers of Samphire from the Dover cliffs*) to bore the stone, in order to blow away a necessary part from the face of it, and the rest like wise was chiefly done by gunpowder; but when any part of it was fit to be left as it was, being flat and smooth, it was brought to a roughness proper for a stay to the feet; and, in this part, all the rest of the road where precipices were like to give horror or uneasiness to such as might pass over them in carriages, though at a good distance from them, they are secured to the lakeside by walls, either left in the working, or built up with stones to a height proportioned to the occasion.

The old cutting marks can still be seen, it is said, rough signatures of the English foot-soldiers, the Munro and Campbell clansmen who worked in the dust, the heat, and constant risk of bloody

---

* The reference is to *King Lear*, Act IV, Scene vi. Samphire, Saint Peter's Herb, is an edible cliff-plant used in pickling, and also, as glasswort, in the making of glass. Shakespeare called the gathering of it a 'dreadful trade'.

injury. Fifty years after the completion of this lochside road, its military need now obsolescent, Samuel Johnson rode down it astride a Highland pony and later remembered it as 'a source of entertainment'. The narrow shelves that had been left as stays for climbing feet now supported an active plant-life from which the Doctor's Highland guides – John Hay and Lachlan Vass, whose names are rarely mentioned – brought him edible nuts. It was on this road that Boswell saw his friend in the saddle for the first time and contrasted this 'interesting object . . . jaunting about at his ease in quest of novelty and pleasure' with his literary life in London. Sarah Murray, a woman not easily frightened, thought the journey along 'a very narrow shelf blown out of the Black Rock' required courage and a steady team of horses. She had both, and the view beyond the leather curtains of her coach, across the choppy water of the loch to the ivy-green stones of Urquhart Castle, was compensation for the 'little palpitations' she experienced.

Edward Burt's greatest praise for the new roads was perhaps to be expected from one whose English conceits so angered the Scots of Inverness. He recalled the wretched lodgings which were all a traveller could once find in the Highlands. Now, he said, the roads had removed that evil. Where once there were but huts of turf for a hundred miles, there were 'houses with chimneys, built with stones and lime, and ten or twelve miles distance one from another', and although they were not large they were well adapted for occasional travellers. They survive only as a Kingshouse here and there, as rare now as the marker-stones that were erected every five miles along the way. Burt praised them for easing the boredom of a journey, and for telling a traveller where he was 'in point of time, in rain, snow drift or approaching night'.

Few Highland chiefs were enthusiastic about the New Roads, even those willing to have their clansmen used in the undertaking. Burt probably knew these touchy gentlemen better than most Englishmen of his time, and was certainly the only one to write with experience of Highland society. The discontented chiefs, he said, complained that . . .

. . . an easy passage is opened into their country for strangers who, in time by their suggestion of liberty, will destroy or weaken that attachment of their vassals which it is so necessary for them to support and preserve. [They complain] that their fastnesses being laid open, they are deprived of that security from invasion which they formerly enjoyed. That the bridges, in particular, will render the ordinary people effeminate, and less fit to pass the waters in other places where there are none.

In the context of this objection, wiser men would later see the roads as a great civilizing force, and the building of them a moral obligation of compelling inspiration. These sentiments later enthused the self-esteem of the Improvers, the land-owners old and new who repaid the earth for its wondrous harvest of wool and mutton with the noble gift of roads. Thus George Granville Leveson-Gower, Marquess of Stafford and later first Duke of Sutherland, authorized the building of thirty-four bridges and four hundred and fifty miles of roads in the county of his ducal title. At the same time his commissioner and factors were removing or re-settling its native people and replacing them with two hundred thousand True Mountain Sheep. In that knowledge it is easy to believe that George Wade's New Road was the forerunner of Clearance and Eviction.

Edward Burt's *Letters* are rarely concerned with the men who laboured with spade, pick and axe, or hung from the Black Rock with bags of gunpowder slung about their necks. He sought the company of officers, and although he implies that this was as agreeable to them as it was to him, there is room for doubt. His assumption of a common bond of gentility and education is implicit in his writing, but he could be angry on behalf of the soldiers who had no literate spokesman. He was appalled by their lodgings in Inverness. They were so squalid, so mean and miserable, that none of the soldiers he knew had experienced such quarters before. One grenadier – with tears in his eyes, said Burt – begged his commanding officer to see for himself the sparse pallet of straw, close to the door of a hovel which the owner had given in response to a billeting order. In the days before military barracks, and the corruption of barrack-masters, soldiers endured worse conditions than this, and the story exposed Burt's inexperience, if not the grenadier's duplicity, perhaps. However, he was no doubt right in declaring that insanitary lodgings resulted in the prevalence of Bloody Flux, dysentery so fierce and inexorable that 'hardly a day passed but a soldier has been buried'. Disease, more than death in battle, was the great killer of all armies until this century, and the fevers of the West Indies could devour a battalion and its replacements three times in less than half a decade. As an alternative, hard but healthy work on the roads, the torn canvas of a tent or leaking branches at night, must have seemed a welcome relief from the risk of an abominable death in Inverness.

A lack of true concern for the private soldier was so commonplace that one wonders why Samuel Johnson could declare that any man must think ill of himself for not having been a soldier. Civilian hearts have always quickened to the beat of a drum, and a trumpet call can arouse those who have no need or wish to answer its summons. The spiritual nature of the common soldier, from the establishment of a standing army until this century, has been a maze of contradictions – resentment of service and pride in its achievements, suspicion of rank and loyalty to it, fear of death, of shame and unwelcome courage. He has soldiered on with patience, with occasional violent protest, and with a steady belief that those who can despise the military man know nothing of what they condemn. In 1847 an ageing Chelsea Pensioner – a cavalryman who had served in such diverse engagements as Waterloo and Peterloo – wrote his memoirs, or had them written by a hack. 'No beings on earth,' he said, 'are subjected like the military to the whims and caprices of their countrymen.' I was a soldier in the ranks for six years, and I did not serve my time without inner wounds which I alone was obliged to heal. In this experience I was one among a great many. Nor am I the only man who cherishes a confusing remembrance of military life – pride, revulsion and ridicule, perverse affection and unforgiving hatred, but above all an abiding and I hope compassionate comradeship with all who have soldiered throughout history.

When I came to Kinmel Park as a conscript in 1940 I had not heard of the camp's dark history, and could not know how that would affect my own service. It was dusk when the train arrived at Rhyl. Almost all its passengers were men of my own age, born in that seminal year 1915 and now called into the Royal Regiment of Artillery. There were trucks awaiting us in the station yard with their engines running, dull green and black in their camouflage, like grazing pachyderms breathing gently. Their young drivers, indolent in washed denim, studied our clumsy indecision with the arrogance of men who had easily survived all the humiliation now awaiting us. Junior NCOs shouted encouragement, directing us to 'embus', carefully adding 'please', and we were too self-concerned to recognize that small politeness as a valediction to our lives until now. We were mostly silent during the short journey from the coast to the camp, but one man who had been an undertaker's assistant described in detail the embalming of a corpse, to impress us or subdue his own nervousness. I have mercifully forgotten what he said, but I have an unkind memory of his appearance. He had pink, pale skin, pale hair and pale-lashed eyes. The evening darkness, quickly thickening below the canopy of the truck, soon hid our faces. For the first time since I received my call-up papers, I was truly alarmed. I was no longer the helmsman of life and I was afraid. Cravenly, as I swayed against the shoulders of the men beside me, I encouraged myself with the thought that my school cadet corps had tutored me in the skills of soldiering, and this distinction would surely be recognized and rescue me from anonymity. When we turned into the camp and debussed at a large garage, we were politely directed inside to a line of cook-house tables. Here a sergeant or a bombardier mechanically completed our attestation, a few questions, smiling indifference to my experience in the Latymer Upper School Cadet Force, a broken fingernail pointing to where I was obliged to sign away my life. That night the windows of the barrack-room were closed and boarded, and the air was soon thick with smoke and the odour of sweat. As I lay awake like others and waited for dreamless sleep, I had no thoughts deeper than a nagging irritation. In time I would know this to be the mind's defence against the spirit-numbing pressures of the Army. The bombardier taking my attestation had described me as a printer because he did not understand what I meant by journalist. In the space allowed on the paper for a declaration of religious faith he wrote C of E instead of Atheist, as I replied. By morning this seemed of no importance, and in time I took perverse pleasure in the theatrical church-parades to which the attestation had committed me. A year or two later I 'lost' my Army paybook, and when allowed to fill in a new one by a tolerant officer I correctly recorded my non-belief. The point I made was meaningless, for I knew that should the occasion arise the Army would nonetheless bury me as a member of the Church of England.

That noisy, exhausting and relentless camp, which has dominated so many of my memories here, and even now can arouse thoughts that are anachronistic and absurd, was less than two years old when I came to it. It was built for the training of the Militia in 1938, the first conscription of youth hastily assembled in the wake of Munich and in the certain belief that war was now inevitable. Some of those young boys had remained as drivers, clerks, mech-

North Wales, 1940. The friends of my training days have gone down the Ruddlan road to the war, and I await a summons to an Officer Selection Board.

anics and junior NCOs, but most had been lost in the collapse of France or were now in Africa and the Far East. The great camp was sprawled on a gentle slope rising from the Rhuddlan plain to the Clwyd hills, dust-white streets of harsh stones, and barrack-blocks of creosoted wood, a parade-ground large enough for two or three battalions to perform close-order drill, lorry-parks, work-shops, and garages like aircraft hangars. The barrack-blocks were known as spiders, each with six long huts, like insects' legs attached to the central body of an ablution room. The spaces between the huts were often cultivated by defaulters, growing vegetables that were rarely enjoyed beyond the officers' or sergeants' mess. The newly turned earth attracted flights of nervous finches, sometimes enticed through an open window of the hut and therein pursued with manic delight by bored soldiers. Entry to the camp was by the vehicle-gate on the St Asaph to Abergele road, or by the Main Guard on the country lane that went over the hills to the Elwy Valley and the cool stones of Ma's public in the Dolben Arms. I have discovered that little of the camp remains – no spiders, but a few isolated huts crouching on a slope above a four-lane highway that has been driven through the parade-ground and over the site of work-shops, garages, the NAAFI, garrison theatre and Captain Fereday's little chapel-hut. The rest of the area is an industrial estate. Only by stationing myself in the lane, wher' the Main Guard had been and with my back to the old flint wall of Bodelwyddan Park, was I able to fit fading memory into present reality.

To the west of the camp there was a plantation of conifers, tall, green and straight-stemmed, soothing to the eye when seen from the door of a spider or down the bleak-white glare of a Battery street. Beneath the trees were vestigial ruins of the vast camp built here during the First World War and used as a holding centre for Canadian soldiers landed at Liverpool or waiting for the voyage home to demobilization. Recovered from wounds and declared 'fit for garrison duty', Robert Graves came here towards the close of that war. As a stores and transport officer, he commanded several thousand men in an administrative chaos that required an insane mind to rationalize. He was gone from Kinmel Park before the camp erupted in mutiny, violence and bloodshed.

I knew nothing of that when I mounted the first guard of my training – 'Outlying Picket Ammo Store', the watch on a sand-bagged magazine in the centre of the plantation. I was conducted to it by the NCO Marching Reliefs. It was a gentle, melancholy evening, the sun sinking in a red mist beyond the Conway range. In the silence of the trees the NCO Marching Reliefs told me that he would visit me once before I was relieved. 'So be here, right?' I could move about at ease, but I should remember that I had four rounds in the magazine of my bundook and one up the spout. 'You know? Right. So why innit the safety catch on?' He stared at me briefly with a despair intended to stiffen my morale, and then left me with a mordant warning. 'No smoking, right? If you see any bleeding Canadians with bayonets fixed carry on, never mind. Got that?'

The dusk of that summer evening passed gently into the solace of a full moon. I stood for some time beside the ammo store and then walked with rifle slung along the streets of the old camp. My boots made whispering trails on the auburn carpet of needles, and in an occasional clearing the milky light drew long, black shadows from the trees. I was lonely without loneliness, curiously detached from the thousands of young men who had passed through here on their way to the obscene horror of that old war. I was standing by the store again when I heard steps approaching, lightly and in a muffled run, it seemed. They halted abruptly, a sudden shuffle, then movement again. When the sound came closer, and there was no reassuring whistle from the NCO Marching Reliefs, I was alarmed. I brought my rifle to the port and hoarsely shouted the old challenge. There was no response, and my thumb was on the safety catch when the footsteps moved into the moonlight. The stag and I stared at each other for a moment only before he turned his splendid, antlered head and walked into the darkness of the trees.

The mutiny was never mentioned in our indoctrination lectures. What we discovered for ourselves we heard in the public houses of St Asaph and Abergele, or the Ty Fry Café on the Towyn road. Four months after the November armistice, it was said, and angered by arrears of pay and delays in their own repatriation, the Canadian soldiers decided to make their own way home. The local residents told the story with understandable hesitation. What happened then? 'It was bloody slaughter, man, wasn't it?' For proof of this there was some tangible evidence in the burial-ground of the Marble Church, the cool white building that dominates the little village of Bodelwyddan. Among the headstones of soldiers who died in the terrible influenza epidemic following the war are three or four with laconic inscriptions – 'Killed in action 1919'.

The story we were told over a glass of ale or a mug of the Ty Fry's insipid tea, was graphic and heroic. The Canadians turned upon their officers, took weapons from the armoury, trucks from the vehicle park, and drove towards Rhyl. At Rhuddlan bridge, a mile from the sea and in the shadow of the old medieval castle, they were halted by machine-guns. 'Many were killed, but it was all hushed up, see? Not the sort of thing to have talked about, was it?'

The truth, as far as it can be known, is more savage than heroic, more distressing than tragic. Most of the twenty thousand waiting men were indeed Canadians. Their barrack-huts were squalid and neglected. The march of winter from the sea to the Clwyd hills can be bitterly hostile, as I remember, and that year it was particularly harsh. By March the earth was bogged and the camp-lines deep in undrained water. Many soldiers were sick, and influenza was rife. And their food . . . their food, it was said, was the worst of Army food. The Ty Fry Café, where we heard garbled stories of the mutiny, was all that remained, I think, of a collection of civilian sheds and shops known as Tin Town, a meeting-place for soldiers out of camp, for boasting and wild threats. They had no information about their repatriation and they were further angered by the rumour that the ships which should be carrying them home had been offered to the Americans. Protest began with disobedience, followed by the looting of camp canteens and the buildings of Tin Town (where the mutineers were joined by some civilians). Finally there was arson and an assault on administrative buildings of the camp. Armed with sticks, stones and a few rifles, and led by a sapper corporal with the inappropriate name of Tsarevitch, the mutineers advanced on the forces sent against them. Some waved red flags, and some shouted the signal for the assault, 'Come on the Bolsheviks!' There was savage fighting before the red flags were lowered, four dead men and twenty-one wounded from bullet and bayonet. Fifty men were charged, of whom twenty-seven were sentenced to imprisonment by a court-martial, the report of which is still secret. Before a coroner's inquest, an officer said he thought the cause of the mutiny had been partly due to Russian influence, and partly drink.*

The knowledge of this mutiny, little more than twenty years before, must sometimes have occupied the thoughts of our commanders at Kinmel in 1940, and no doubt influenced the judgement of the Lancashire Fusilier when he considered the behaviour of 1576980 Lance-Bombardier Prebble J.

When the friends of my training days were gone down the Rhuddlan road to the War, I awaited a summons to an Officer Selection Board. In time I appeared before a panel of ageing officers

---

* There is a brief but illuminating account of the affair in *Mutiny in the British and Commonwealth Forces, 1797–1956*, Lawrence James, Buchan & Enright, 1987.

at the holiday camp in Prestatyn. They sat behind a barrack-room table upon which was laid a grey blanket, with paper, pencils and pencil-sharpeners dressed in regimental line. On the wall behind were brightly coloured posters, taunting reminders of the uncaring years – blue seas and scudding clouds, a curling surf, long-legged girls and yellow sand-castles. I stared longingly at these lies as the members of the panel studied the papers before them. When they questioned me it was with courtesy and earnest concern, but I was inwardly hostile. I prejudged their opinions, and in youth's impatience with middle age I felt superior to them. I remember that with shame. None had fewer than two rows of ribbons above the left-hand pocket of his tunic, and each had at least one decoration in addition to the campaign medals. All, no doubt, had dark memories and sad agonies of which I was carelessly ignorant. My Army record so far, my schooling, my cadet experience and my father's lower-deck rank in the Royal Navy, my quick response to questions of cunning simplicity, the well-boned shine of my boots and the pale green perfection of my webbing belt, all these were strong qualifications for selection, but none stronger than the pressing need for officers at this time. When I was dismissed, I rose and took a loud pace to the rear before saluting. They smiled at me with reassurance and called me Prebble, not Bombardier.

Some weeks later I was told that I had passed this unexacting test, and later still I was sent to an officer training-school in Wiltshire. My departure from Kinmel was organized by Regimental Sergeant-Major Mulvanney who, until this moment, had seemingly been unable to distinguish me from any other soldier in the mudcoloured ranks that came under his inspecting eye on the paradeground. But this morning, as we waited for transport on the verandah of the regimental office, he told me that he had been watching my performance as a junior NCO, as a fugleman during arms-drill, and as an instructor in foot-drill. 'You'll be the right stuff, Bombardier. Squad . . . by the right, change direction right. Eh?' He grasped my hand and shook it warmly before I boarded the truck, and the touch of his cane upon my shoulder was like an accolade.

The officer cadet school at Shrivenham was an assembly of redbrick blocks of depressing similarity, with an untidy growth of garages, work-shops, pre-fabricated huts and vehicle parks. There was a large drill-square, glistening with small quartz fragments, like unwelcoming snow they seemed as the truck that brought me from

Swindon station slowly circumnavigated the parade. My short time here was a recall of my initial training, more demanding if possible, seeking the ultimate endurance of body and spirit. Each day began with the half-light of dawn, physical training on the square or a cross-country run over cruelly designed obstacles. This was followed by foot-drill and arms-drill, with an indigestible meal at mid-day and an afternoon in hot, unventilated lecture-rooms. The hours of drilling were more bearable than the suffocating atmosphere of the classrooms. Once I mastered it, I enjoyed the stamping performance of drill and the perverse joy of executing every order with mocking bravura. There was also an extraordinary freedom of mind as the body responded in clockwork motion. Marching, turning, wheeling into line . . . open order, march . . . close order, march. Slope arms, present arms, order arms, as you were . . . order arms, as you were . . . order arms stand still you dozy gentleman sir! Released from directing responsibility, the mind was able to watch the body with calm detachment, waiting for the slam of feet, the slap of hand to the butt of a rifle, the answering rattle of a halfpenny cunningly placed in an empty magazine. Enjoying yet despising this childish, ancient ritual, only half-believing that it served some purpose now, not caring to think that it might have some horrible reality in the future.

A soldier's existence is perhaps the reverse of a civilian's life, and may be judged only if that is understood. The liberty of a civilian can be seen as licence in a soldier. Independence of thought and action, the right to disagree, are the gifts of history to a civilian. For a soldier they are impermissible, and that too is the legacy of history. He is no soldier at all if his commanders cannot expect an immediate and unquestioning response, and the first sacrifice a soldier makes to his country is the surrender of his mental and physical independence. To survive he must maintain an inner self-respect while enduring humiliation, abuse and ultimately fear. I learnt part of this lesson at Kinmel and I was taught it again at Shrivenham.

But from the week of my arrival I knew that I did not wish to be there, that I had made a mistake. My reasons may now appear callow, but at the time they were fierce and insistent. I had allowed the Army to make a decision for me that I should have made myself. I thought it was too soon to become an officer when my only experience was the life of a training-camp. I believed I should be tested by the War before I was given the right and power to command the lives of other men. If this now seems both naive and impracticable, it should be considered within the context of the time, my age, my emotions, the social and political beliefs that controlled my thoughts. I was also afraid. I was aware of that even then, although youth helped me to thrust it to the back of my mind. I was afraid of the war, of how I would face it, and I knew that I should have that experience before I was granted a commission. All this, of course, was in conflict with the Communist Party's line and my expected obedience. But the Party at that moment was standing upon its head in opposition to the War, and would remain in that absurd position until Russia's entry would make it a People's War again. It did not occur to me to ask its permission to change my mind, then or later when I finally left it.

I gave myself time to think about what I should do, which is perhaps a euphemism for cowardice. There was no one with whom I could discuss the matter. My companions did not debate why they were at Shrivenham. They were where they wished to be, and where most of them thought they should be. They spent their evenings, the short hours between Tattoo and Lights Out, boning and polishing the leather of the Sam Browne belts they had bought in confident expectation of a commission. As their fingers directed the rubbing-cloth in small circular movements, they discussed the advantages there would be in returning to their civilian employment with a commissioned rank. Occasionally there was argument over the reasonable sum that should be paid to a venal staff-sergeant in exchange for the questions to be asked at the next test. I do not think I was angry with them. I did not despise them. They depressed me and I was eager to be gone from them and from Shrivenham.

At last I presented myself to the Troop Officer before morning parade and asked to be returned to my unit where I wished to volunteer for overseas service. He was younger than I and was embarrassed by the request and by the reasons I gave. He called me 'old chap' with appealing emphasis. 'Sleep on it, will you, old chap, and see what we think tomorrow, eh?' I did so and made the same request in the morning. Now he dismissed me abruptly from his mind and passed me to his superior. He was a white-haired major, with a healthy face and a friendly smile below his clipped moustache and direct blue eyes. He wore the ribbon of the Military Cross and as many medals as the Lancashire Fusilier, but there the resemblance ended, for he was plainly disturbed and paternally concerned. He undoubtedly thought I was foolish, as perhaps I was, and that I could be persuaded by arguments that would convince him. When he was satisfied that my intention was serious there was a moment of silence as we looked at each other. I was aware that he was older, and more tired than he appeared on parade. He asked – not ordered – me to sit down. He wished to tell me a story. 'From the other war, y'know?' His company had been in the line for a long time, subject to artillery and mortar bombardment, sniper fire and occasional trench-raids. It was early winter, he said, and the muddy water in the trenches was sometimes as high as a man's thighs. His company's losses had included all of its subalterns and some senior NCOs. Morale was thus very low. As I now recall it, his voice became softer at the close of his story, and his words are among the few I can remember with fidelity in the whole of this incident.

A new replacement of subalterns came up the line and in the evening, when the Company Sergeant-Major reported to me, I said to him, 'Well, sarnt-major, how are the men now?' And he said, 'They're all right now, sir, they've got their officers with them.'

He asked what I thought, whether I understood the story. Later I would see that it justified my argument as much as it proved his, but at the time I could say no more than repeat my request. He acknowledged it with a disappointed tilt of his head and a dismissive lift of his hand. 'I'm sorry,' he said, 'in that case I must pass you on to the CO.'

The Commandant, to whom I was now sent, was a lieutenant-colonel of the Royal Artillery. Although I must have seen him at other times, he was a stranger when the Regimental Sergeant-Major marched me into his office like a defaulter on parade. He did not order me to sit, or stand at ease. Holding the position of attention, back straight and chin lifted, it was not easy to answer his questions until I relaxed and looked at him rather than the wall beyond his head. He filled his chair with the green khaki of good barathea, shining leather and rainbow ribbons. His face was florid, I think, and nondescript rather than patrician. It has sometimes pleased me in the fifty years since to confuse him with the commandant of another OCTU whose martinet views and idiosyncratic behaviour brought him the ribald attention of the *Daily Mirror*. It was his custom, said that soldier's friend, to ride a white horse to the morning parade, to greet the steady ranks of cadets with the holiday-camp cry of 'Hi-de-hi!', to which they responded with 'Hi-de-ho!' The man I now faced would perhaps have considered that excessive, but I have no doubt he approved of the spirit behind it. He stared at me for a long time without speaking, or so it seemed, and I had time to measure the heavy breathing of the RSM who stood behind my shoulder, as close as he could without touching.

When the Commandant spoke, moving the papers on his desk as if emphasizing a word, he did not ask me to explain my request. He began a brisk interrogation. What were my politics, what was my *trade* before the war, my membership, if any, of a trade union, and why did I believe such organizations were necessary? When an ambiguously phrased question permitted me to say that I thought I should have some field-service before taking a commission, the only response was a suppressed sigh from the Sergeant-Major behind me. The Commandant's obvious distaste increased as I explained, under direct questioning, why I would vote for a Labour government after the war, why I thought it was necessary to nationalize major industries, and what I meant when I used the word Fascism. In wiser years I would have been more circumspect, but the Commandant heard no more than he suspected. He made no critical comment, and ended the interview with a nod to the RSM. 'March him out, and have him wait, if you please.'

In the outer office the RSM took and lit one of the clerk's cigarettes and studied me through its smoke. As if I needed a lesson in understanding, he began to talk of hardship in East London where he lived before becoming a boy-soldier. 'Well, then, you know, don't you?' he said when I told him that I once collected rents there. Recalled by the Commandant, I was shown the authorization for my RTU. I was to read his note at the bottom, he said, and then sign it where indicated. I signed upon reflex, I suppose, although I did not see what he could do if I refused to acknowledge his added comment.

Cadet Prebble is being returned to his unit at his own request. In view of his beliefs about the rights of the working-class and of the trade unions, he is no longer considered fit for officer training.

I would like to think that I realized immediately, and with amusement, that the Commandant's obvious expectation of political and social conflict at the close of the War was remarkably similar to that of the Communist Party. At the time I did not realize that the implied caveat of his note must travel with me for the rest of my Army life, and indeed beyond it. With subsequent additions, the substance of the small dossier I inspired no doubt reached Lord Beaverbrook. When I was discharged from his employment, I crossed the street to the news editor of the *Daily Mail*, who had been a captain and the editor of *Soldier* in Hamburg. With condescending good humour, he offered me work as a reporter. 'Starting at the bottom, the very bottom, mind, and no more than the basic rate, with the understanding that I'll have no bolshie behaviour.' I needed the work, but it seemed proper for me to save us both from the risk of that embarrassment.

Released from Shrivenham, I came back to Kinmel Park, arriving after Lights Out to a dark hut and the good-humoured derision of recruits I had once trained. Their course was almost over and they were now confident enough to be jovially abusive, prefacing or ending each taunt with an emphasized 'Sir!' In the morning I reported to the Battery Office, waiting on the verandah until I was called before the Lancashire Fusilier. We were alone. Acknowledging my salute with a nod of his bowed head, he said, 'Stand at ease.' He took the Commandant's note from its envelope and studied it slowly, although he must have read it before. I admired the skill with which his one hand opened the paper, then smoothed and flattened it with his cane. He had not yet looked at me. A gulf separated us, of rank certainly, and age of course, class no doubt, but above all the uncrossable chasm of what he considered to be true soldiering. I think I knew that he was a just man, and though I would have liked his sympathetic understanding, I did not expect it. He would not persecute me for my apparent indifference to the things he thought most important, but he would not forget and he would grant no favours. When he looked up to me, it was from the memory of his young manhood to the reality of mine. He touched the Commandant's note and asked if I had any comment. 'No, sir.' 'You are satisfied with it?' 'Sir, I wish to volunteer for overseas posting.' 'You don't want to comment on this?' 'No, sir.' 'Very well, the CO has decided to deal with you.' He put the note into a brown folder and thus into my records. 'That's all,' he said, as if surprised to find me still there. I came to attention, took a noisy pace backward, saluted and left.

The Commander was Lieutenant-Colonel Bell, inevitably known as Tink-a-Bell, a retired officer brought back into service from his work with the Royal Artillery Benevolent Association. He was a gentle, concerned man, sincerely perplexed by events that had no solution in decency and fair play upon a common ground. The exception to his goodwill towards all was The Enemy. Within a week of their arrival, every intake of recruits was assembled in the garrison theatre to hear his lecture on 'Morale and the German Army'. I remember but one fragment of it, the first sentence as he looked up from the lectern. 'When they're born, there's not much difference between German babies and British babies, except the Germans have less hair.'

I was marched into the Colonel's office by Regimental Sergeant-Major Mulvanney, who did not understand my reasons for returning from the OCTU, but was certain they were contrary to good order and military discipline. Thus he too chose to regard me as a defaulter on parade, muttering beneath his breath as we entered the office. 'Lef-ri, lef-ri, lef-ri . . . Halt. Stand ssstill!' The Colonel smiled at me pleasantly. 'Stand at ease, Prebble, will you?' When he asked me why I had returned, and why I wanted an overseas posting, he listened sympathetically with his head to one side, nodding occasionally. But when I said that I should have some experience of active service before I was given command of men, he appeared distressed. 'But you were a lance-bombardier, you had a degree of that command, didn't you?' 'Sir. I meant as an officer, sir.' 'Should this apply to everybody, do you think?' 'I can't say, sir. Perhaps it should.' Behind my shoulder the Sergeant-Major cleared his throat gently. The Colonel then told me what he had decided. I was a good soldier, he said, no doubt of that. My stripe would be returned to me and I would be sent on an instructor's course – which he was confident I would pass – and on my return to the permanent staff I would be promoted to lance-sergeant. 'Then we'll see what can be done about your posting. All right? Good. Carry on, Mr Mulvanney.' Outside on the verandah, the Sergeant-Major said, 'Straighten your cap.' He leant towards me. 'Who's a lucky man, then? But I'm watching. I can see through doors, Prebble. Through walls I can see. March off !'

This is a story of logical improbability. The school of instructors to which I was sent was part of the military establishment at Shrivenham, and the Commandant of the OCTU was also commander of the school. When our paths crossed during the following weeks there was nothing in his expression or manner to acknowledge our recent encounter. On occasions when he inspected us, erect in his well-brushed khaki and lemon-green blanco, he passed me with no more than a customary tug at a webbing-strap, or a peremptory tap on my rifle to demand examination of its barrel. The course was exacting, in classroom theory, field-practice, foot- and arms-drill. However successful a student was in all these, fail- ure to deliver a satisfactory ten-minute lecture meant failure of the whole course. Secure in my success until then, I gave my lecture to a panel of tutors, among whom the Commandant sat silently and impassively. I failed.

The night train that took me back to North Wales was delayed by air-raids in the Midlands, and halted for an hour and more at times. The coaches were dimly lit and crowded, the corridors blocked by sleeping bodies. The windows were sealed against blast and masked with black blinds. The air was rank. Sometimes, in the long silences, there was soft, nostalgic singing from down the train, the haunting notes of a mouth-organ, the crying of a child. Outside in the darkness, the thudding of a distant raid was the knock of an impatient caller beyond a heavy door.

The Lancashire Fusilier was surprised by my failure. His anger was restrained, his sallow skin darkening as he read the report. Putting it aside abruptly, he told me that I was a bad soldier. I could keep my stripe, remembering always that it was not a rank, only an appointment. But I should know that I could expect nothing from him, no favours, no allowances. He kept his word, to himself and to me. Promotions were almost automatic for junior NCOs; as one stepped on, another stepped up, but I remained a lance- bombardier. I challenged his decision to grant no favours as often as I could. I applied for any transfer that might release me to any new service or formation, but without his approval they were all unsuccessful.

Summer that year in the Clwyd hills was rich and disarming, dusty sunlight hanging like gossamer on the leaves of the Elwy valley. Winter came in strong contrast, deep, drifting snow along the Conway range, isolating the hill-farms. We were sent in trucks to dig white-walled approaches in the choked lanes, to rescue stock and carry children down to the valley-floors. There was a joy in that work, of being young, healthy and self-reliant.

I had time to reflect that I had brought my misfortune upon myself. It had made me a prisoner, safe from the War.

September the Eighteenth

Now that my companion and I have reached it, the pier at New York is almost a disappointment – a few black stumps and sun-grey boards standing out to the narrows of Loch Awe. Eight hundred yards across the oil-smooth water the shore rises abruptly in a blunt hill at Portinnischerrich, like an aged head above the autumn shawl of the Eredine Forest. Four months ago, when I came by east Lochaweside, the earth beneath the branches of that ancient woodland glowed with young fern and the purple bloom of foxgloves. Here on the western shore at New York there are no more buildings than there are words to its name, and like the pier they are abandoned. It is a quiet part of a sometimes tranquil loch, but its history was once crowded and noisy. This was a drovers' ferry-point long before the York Buildings Company erected a pier in the eighteenth century, its pack-horses carrying charcoal over the water to the iron-furnaces on Loch Fyne. There are small islands scattered off-shore along the snaking length of Loch Awe, most of them with the ruin of a medieval chapel or a castle built by the Campbells when they took the lochside from the MacDougalls. Half a mile northward from Portinnisherrich is Colin's Isle. The first stone of its dour keep was laid six hundred years ago. Towards the end of the sixteenth century the Campbells brought a prisoner here, an infant MacDonald, heir to the dying lordship of the Isles. They held the child for fifteen years, unknown to his kinsmen until he was discovered and released by raiders from Glencoe.

We watch the water moving gently against the rotting pier and I talk of serendipity and the chance link between this quiet shore, the York Buildings Company, and a moment in my youth. After the Jacobite defeats of 1715 and 1719, English opportunists came to lease and exploit the estates of attainted rebels, greedy for the ancient timber and mineral richness of the mountains. The York Buildings Company was among the most energetic and survived longer than others, whose life-span was as brief as their enthusiasm.

Its woodsmen felled oak and ancient pine across the breadth of the Highlands, taking sixty thousand trees from the Abernethy Forest alone. There the timber was floated or carried down the Spey to the coast, and when trimmed, planed and fashioned it went to sea in the sloops, frigates and line-of-battle ships of the Royal Navy. The York Company also penetrated deep into the Rough Bounds beyond the Great Glen, to the sea-lochs of Moidart and Ardnamurchan in search of lead, barytes and quartz, and on Loch Sunart at Strontian – 'a filthy clachan', their manager said – they discovered and discarded an element that survives as strontium. The narrow glen where it was found twists northward to a mountain-flank, and the spoor of the Company's labour is found on the green floor of timber and upon the lower braes – vestigial huts, smithies, washing-floors and the dark adits of abandoned mine-shafts.

The York Buildings Company was already old when it came to the Highlands in 1719. It was established in 1675 by two Londoners who were granted Letters Patent to erect and operate a water-house within the grounds of York House, between the Strand and the River Thames. The mansion was built by Nicholas Heath, Archbishop of York, upon land granted by Mary Tudor, and was later a gift from James I and VI to his favourite, George Villiers, first Duke of Buckingham. Time has long since removed it, but the memory of it survives in the streets now upon the ground, in York Court and the eponymous York Buildings, in Villiers Street and Buckingham Street. Until recent years there were also Duke Street, George Street, and a narrow passage named Of Alley. The first of these ran briefly from Villiers Street into John Adam Street and up the slope to the Adelphi. It was here that I entered journalism, in a modest way, and believing that what I wished to be, indeed all that I had the talent and wit to be – *A Writer* – could now be realized.

In 1934, having composed a successful answer to an advertisement in the *Daily Telegraph*, I came to Number Two Duke Street to be a 'junior reporter' on a proposed trade paper, a competitor to the well-established *Draper's Record*. During my time as a rent-collector and clerk in the Stockwell estate agency I had written many applications for different employments, most of them in journalism, and this was the only response I received. I was interviewed by Mr Head, who was to be the publication's news editor, a bright-eyed, nervously active man in his thirties, stunningly dressed in a double-breasted grey suit and a yellow silk tie. I remember him with gratitude and with regret, for later, I was told, he died a prisoner of the Japanese on the Burma Railway. I came for the interview after a morning of rent-collecting in Bermondsey, and in the trusting confidence of youth I deposited my music-bag, heavy with coins, in the left-luggage office of Charing Cross Station. Head was not interested in the examples of my literary success so far – a short story in the *Daily Herald* and another in the *Evening News* – but he placed them respectfully to one side of his desk. After a few brief questions he gave me a small cutting from an American newspaper. It was undated and announced the coming departure for London of a departmental buyer, from Sears Roebuck, I think. 'Find out when he's arriving, where'll he be, and let me know,' said Head, dismissing me with an encouraging lift of his hand.

I retrieved the music-bag and walked down Villiers Street to the Embankment Gardens, where I sat and looked at the neat beds of flowers, the foraging pigeons, and the tram-cars swaying past. Incompetence, and a growing panic therefrom, immobilized my mind until I saw the red cap of a telephone-box beyond a hedge of laurel. I knew nothing of retail department stores and their buyers, but this was an age when telephone directories were left unmolested in call-boxes. I found the London office of Sears Roebuck in the L–Z section. I laid a few pennies in pairs upon the shelf and dialled the number. The buyer, I was told, was already in London at the Hyde Park Hotel, which I then called. I have long since forgotten what I said, and remember a few words only from the buyer. 'Come right over, mister reporter, and take tea.' I made a third, and I hope restrained, call to Head who said, 'That's quick. Given up, have we?' And then, when I told him, 'Go and see him. Get a story, and start on Monday, can you?' I stepped lightly from the call-box, intoxicated by self-esteem.

The three or four years I spent with Century Press were instructive but unfulfilling. Until the office was moved from the decaying Georgian house in Duke Street I enjoyed working in that commemorative enclave below the great shoulder of Charing Cross Station. The narrow crevasse that was Of Alley was filled with garment shops, renting dinner-jackets to the waiters of Soho and the Strand. The façade of each, from its narrow street-window to the first or second floor, was draped with black coats and trousers, hanging from poles or wires like the heavy fronds of funereal vines. They sometimes came to life in the dusty winds that blew from the river, arms and legs twisting and turning in an insane dance. In Villiers Street there was one of London's few Chinese restaurants, owned as some were by a Japanese who watched his customers from behind a beaded curtain. Here, in a darkened room with scarlet wallpaper and yellow dragons, I acquired an enduring taste for chicken chopsuey, sweet and sour pork, and special fried rice, all for less than a florin. When the Sino-Japanese War became a deep and passionate issue for radical Britain, many restaurants so owned were deserted by their customers. Those of us who made this sacrifice now paid two shillings for a simple bowl of rice at a lunch organized on behalf of Aid for China, our self-satisfaction sometimes honoured by the smiling presence of the Soviet Ambassador, Litvinov. Towards the top of John Adam Street was a theatre where I first saw a performance of Wycherley's *The Country Wife*. It was a benison for past travail. I had studied Restoration Drama in one of several attempts to matriculate, at school and later. The memory of them is still chilling, nine set subjects, all papers to be taken within five days, matriculation depending on a high achievement in *all*. After my third failure to pass in Chemistry, I abandoned the dispiriting effort.

Few of the southern adventurers who exploited the subject Highlands (with the earnest co-operation of some of its lairds) could equal the initial success of the York Buildings Company, but one which did also survived a century and more. Six years after Culloden, the Newland Company established an iron-furnace at Bonawe on Etiveside, at the river's mouth where visitors to Ardchattan Priory were once ferried across the loch. Its owners were ironmasters from Furness in Lancashire – Michael Knott, Richard Ford and his son William. Hard, resolute and ambitious men, they took a lease for 110 years on thirty-four square miles of forest and water-runs belonging to Sir Duncan Campbell of Lochnell. For this they gave him £1500, and a yearly rental of £415 for the land upon which they built their furnace and sheddings. The contract was signed five days after the trial and condemnation of James Stewart of the Glen for being party to the Appin Murder, and his skeleton still hung upon a gibbet at Ballachulish, a day's walk from Bonawe, when the first iron was smelted in 1753. Thus were Campbell vengeance and Campbell business acumen theatrically linked in time. But old Lochnell was not a typical laird of that clan. If he were not himself a declared Jacobite and Catholic in the year of the 'Forty-five, two of his brothers fought for the Pretender at Culloden, one known as *Papanach Mor*, the Big Papist, and another the Prince's Catholic chaplain who died of his wounds.

The ruins of the Bonawe Furnace, inactive since 1876, have been restored and preserved as a pleasant museum, re-creating some of the texture of its past, if not the fire, the heat, smoke, debris, noise and confusion of a vibrant industry. A small boat makes summer trips from the quay to the lochhead, a serene and consoling voyage even on days of mist when water and hills merge in a fine gauze. When sunlight touches the great shoulders of Cruachan with yellow fire, and shines on the rocks where grey seal lie in languid trust, it is easy to believe that the stark slopes of Glen Noe, Glen Liever and Glen Kinglass were ever thus, and that the eye is sharing sight with men long dead. But when Duncan Campbell sold the lease of Loch Etiveside these eastern braes were a great woodland of oak, birch and ash and the tall, red-shanked, black-bonneted Caledonian pine. In 1845 the *New Statistical Account* recalled their savage rape. Except for a few alders clinging to the river-banks, and some brushwood on the lower braes, there was little to sustain the memory of a great forest. To fire the furnace at Bonawe, 'Glen Kinglass is almost bared of wood, though it was once adorned with firs. They have levelled a great proportion of the trees to dust and converted them to charcoal. The axe has since recklessly felled what remained.' In summer droughts the scars left by the woodsmen are sometimes visible on the hills. Resurgent saplings which might have replaced the trees were long since devoured by the deer and sheep.

The Newland Company built a substantial village about its iron-works, with cottages, store-houses, a church and a school. The dominant inhabitants were mostly incomers, Lowland and Border Scots, Englishmen from Lancashire, Cumberland and Northumbria. They had little sympathy for or understanding of the indigent population, and were thus more a colonial settlement than part of a nation. In time the Knott family became the principal owners, ruling from a grand house on Coniston Water, ten miles to the north of their parent iron-works on the Furness peninsula. In summer – like the Smiths, Astleys, Sellars, Clarks and all the Improvers – they enjoyed long holidays in a Highland home. George Knott, the most resolute of the family in the eighteenth century, tirelessly bullied his managers at Bonawe, advising the wretched men to be just as relentless with their workers and with the small farmers on the Company's land. Knott had no respect for Highlanders, lairds or people. The former he described as 'hawks and birds of prey', remembering the terms of Lochnell's lease perhaps. The latter were 'the commonalty', their labour or their small crofts accepted on sufferance and only if they obeyed the Company's power without question. If they did not, George Knott called them 'weavers, taylors etc. and such like useless people . . . grazing on common land and breeding mischief'. Those who would not or could not be of service to the Company were dispensable. The manager was told to dismiss them and drive them away, their empty cottages to be destroyed lest they be unlawfully occupied by other vagrants. Widows and dependants were also evicted. 'Those that are able and do nothing but stroll about,' the manager was told, 'turn them out entirely, as mischief is the certain end of that profession.'

Firm in the religious faith of redeeming labour, the iron-master was also hard in moral judgement of his managers. These unfortunate English exiles, as remote from their homes as their countrymen would soon be in imperial outposts, took to drink as their only solace among a hostile people and an awesome landscape. In 1781 one manager – who seems to have been an agreeable fellow despite his weaknesses – received a threatening ultimatum from the big house at Coniston. There was not, he was told, such a drunken hole as Bonawe in the whole of the kingdom. He was to reform his ways, to work not gossip, to kill all his sporting dogs, serve the Company not self-interest, keep the Knotts regularly informed and not chatter idly with shippers, but above all he was to 'stop drinking and drink-trafficking'. He had carried these practices to such an extent that he was now . . .

> . . . a disgrace to your employers by your retailing whisky out by bottle. I look upon it as beneath the dignity of an agent and a shame that the House should become a whisky shop . . . Though you have money at your command, think not that you are able to roll in it, you ought to be attentive and not drink and chatter among a great deal of common people, but look above them with a proper decency and respect at the same time; for the mode you are going on must infallibly be the death of you.

When told of one 'refractory' Highlander at Bonawe, a man called MacFarlane and a breeder of mischief no doubt, George Knott said he should be 'put on board some vessel for the Clyde, with directions to the master to give information to a press-master to impress him'. Whether the manager did this or not, he did protest that he 'could not wish to make widows' hearts ache nor the orphans cry', and he hoped the Company had not sent him there to persecute the fatherless. He was told to practise such 'mortification in order to learn them Industry, Attentiveness and Gratitude'. The harsh realities of that time have no echo today on the treeless slopes of Glen Kinglass, or the well-cut grass, gravelled pathways and restored buildings of what its guide-book rightly calls 'one of the most notable monuments of the iron industry in Britain'.

On the road that comes through the Pass of Brander to Loch Etive and the Firth of Lorn, the village of Taynuilt grew with the neighbouring furnace. At its centre, masked by houses on the small rise of *Cnoc Angeal*, Angel's Hill, there is a rough finger of untooled granite, twelve feet in height. It was erected by the iron-men in January 1806, three months after the victory of Trafalgar, the first monument to it and its dead hero. Such enthusiasm was not entirely disinterested. The Newland Company smelted iron for the gun-makers of Carron below the Kilsyth Hills, and in one year alone its works supplied the Navy with two hundred and forty tons of shot for small-bores and murderous carronades. Pitted relics of the iron balls it cast are now pyramidally sited at grass edges of the Bonawe museum. Before the workers manhandled the stone to its present position, it lay on the loch-shore not far from the mouth of the River Awe. It was once the only remaining stone of a prehistoric circle, perhaps, but beguiling tradition believed it had been carried across the water by an old woman, bound to her back by withies and abandoned when it broke free as she came ashore.

There had been no successful precedent for the charcoal blast-furnace at Bonawe, only the fierce ambition and dismal failure of Thomas Rawlinson and the Invergarry iron-works on Loch Oich. He came first to the Great Glen in 1727, a Lancashireman from Whittington, and although he was a Quaker, said Edward Burt, he was 'a man of polite behaviour', a quality that would in time almost kill him at Invergarry. His family had prospered as land-holding gentry under the first Tudors, and from property and its rights, which one of them defended as a captain of Parliamentary Horse at Marston Moor, they moved to trade and the noble production of iron. Thomas Rawlinson was the senior partner among nine men of like interest in his county who formed a company to practise the 'Trade, Mistery and Business of making Pigg Iron and other Iron' on the shore of Loch Oich. They took a lease on the ground of John

MacDonell, *Iain MacAlasadair Dubh*, 12th Chief of Glengarry and
2nd titular Lord MacDonell in the Jacobite peerage. In return for
£320 Sterling, a tack duty of twelve shillings Scots every Whit
Sunday, and a mutual penal sum of £2000 Sterling, he gave the
men of Lancashire . . .

> . . . peaceable ingress and regress with men horses carts and car-
> riages of all sorts to cut down and root up cord saw and make
> [char]coal pits and do everything necessary for felling cutting
> cording sawing [char]coaling carrying and disposing of the same or
> any other commoditys belonging to them and in places to erect iron
> works of any kind . . .

Rawlinson had surveyed the land a year before, when he was thirty-
seven, and had been delighted with it and with the cautious welcome of its gentry. The company was also given the right to make
dams, weirs and other works, to cut turf, erect houses and store-
rooms, to create wharves and harbours, ferry iron ore, charcoal,
wood and other stores on the water of the loch. In his generous
surrender of these rights, John MacDonell also agreed to the employment of his children, his clansmen, as casual labourers in support of an experienced, greedy and contentious labour force from
outwith the Highlands. This Glengarry, like his great-grandson
eighty years later,* was a clown in the arena of his ancestors, but
in this mercantile venture, which had little success from its beginning, he was the only principal who received anything like profit,
since his land, his castle and the fabric of the iron-works were
eventually surrendered to him. He lost it all, of course, nine years
later in the '45 Rebellion to which, he said, he 'had not the least
accession', although twelve hundred men were mustered for the
Prince under the Glengarry banner. Indeed, he aroused little
admiration and some healthy contempt among the Jacobites. John
Murray of Broughton, the Young Pretender's secretary, called him
'an indolent Creature, and entirely given up to Drink'.† One should
not believe everything written by that equivocal man, but Mac-

---

* Alasdair Ranaldson MacDonell, 15th Chief, a caricature of the past he tried to
recreate in dress, manners and conduct, all embodied in the theatrical Society of
True Highlanders, which died with him when he was mortally injured leaping
from a sinking steamer on the Caledonian Canal.
† Written in the Tower of London in August 1746, when Murray was turning
King's Evidence.

Donell certainly enjoyed Rawlinson's spirituous hospitality, having allowed the Englishmen to repair and occupy his castle while he, said Edward Burt, 'inhabited a mean hut'. And there Burt was exaggerating hearsay, for this second house was stoutly built and well roofed, and in time Thomas Rawlinson occupied that too.

The belief in a successful furnace was based on hope and dubious chance, and the argument that it would be cheaper to carry ore to the woodlands than transport fragile charcoal out of them. The ore came by sea to the old burial-shore of Corpach on Loch Linnhe, sometimes carried as ballast in the holds of Baltic traders. Thence it went overland to Loch Lochy and by land and water again to Invergarry, where it passed into the blast-furnace fuelled by the felling of MacDonell's forest trees. The plugs of iron were carried southward by the same route to England. The furnace, sheddings, stores and stock-pens, houses and cottages were built with fabric brought from the south, and by masons from Edinburgh under the direction of an English engineer with the felicitous name of Penny. The furnace-men were Lancastrians, the charcoal-burners came from Ireland, carpenters and sawyers from the Lowlands, carters and wainers from the Borders. There were also thirty-five men of Glengarry's clan, some with useful trades but most to clear and clean the ground in return for their food and £6 (Scots?) at the half-year. These labourers lived in thatched or turfed huts near the mouth of the river and were called 'The Family', by the partners of the Company at least. Fed and fostered by a redoubtable English-woman from Hawkshead, Elizabeth Armistead, their appetites were as great as their skill and muscle. In addition to vast quantities of beef, mutton, chickens, butter and cheese, they also ate six tons of oatmeal and nine of malt in one year. Their supplies and working material came by wagon and pack-horse along the Mine Road, a highway they had built from Corpach to Loch Lochy. At that water's end the loads were transferred to small boats or to a sloop of thirty tons, the *Nightingale*. It cost the Company twenty-five shillings to launch this vessel, and Cameron of Lochiel, the chief whose ground this was, was granted a passage-fee of eight shillings and sixpence for every ton of ore carried through to Laggan at the lochhead.

At no time was the Invergarry venture in profitable competition with furnaces in England. When it finally ceased operation in 1736, having been idle for seven weeks for want of ore, it had processed less than 2,500 tons of pig-iron, of such poor quality that it realized little more than half the sum earned in Lancashire. The only traces now of this noisy, wasteful decade may be a discarded plug of iron below the grass headland of the hotel at Invergarry, or a rusted grave-marker on the old burial-ground of Mucomir at Gairlochy. At the centre of progressive failure, Thomas Rawlinson's self-esteem in time approached manic grandeur. He saw himself as a Highland laird, and MacDonell, perhaps, as his mirror image. Like many English incomers later, he dressed himself in tartan, wearing kilt and plaid to entertain those whom he called 'The Company's Friends' – the gentry of surrounding clans, and officers from the garrisons of the Great Glen. The latter were particularly favoured, for the Army took much of the Invergarry iron, though it was laggard in payment. The foolish generosity of Rawlinson's table made the attendance of such men certain, and he was lavishly generous to those whom he needed to impress, the gift of a good riding-horse to one and a silver decanter to another.

Neither he nor his noisy crew of Lowlanders, English, Irish and Welsh were liked by the Gaelic people of Lochaber. It is doubtful whether he ever understood the Highlanders or their hostility. Some complained that he was not employing their skills as smiths or foresters, but the true animosity was perhaps deeper in ancient fear and suspicion. He struggled against horse-stealing and cattle-lifting, theft and petty arson, and ultimately the attempted murder of an English blacksmith and the actual killing of a Lowlander who prevented it. Soldiers from Fort Augustus pursued and captured the murderer in the hills above Loch Garry, and his execution in Inverness was watched with critical detachment by Edward Burt. The condemned was a blacksmith, he said, sturdy and small 'but a fearless desperado of the Camerons' who became impatient with the fumbling incompetence of the hangman and decided to end matters himself. 'He cried out upon the Trinity, which I dare say he had never heard of before he was committed . . . and then jumped off the ladder.'

Rawlinson's self-created image – ironmaster and Highland laird – destroyed itself when his guests and drinking companions began to sense the inevitable failure of the enterprise. At what must have been the last of his hospitable evenings he greeted them in a traditional Highland way. They were welcome, he said, to everything in his house. Burt thought some of them had come to make trouble and were now given an excellent excuse. 'God damn you, sir!' said one. 'Your house? I thought it was Glengarry's!' There were angry words and then blows, the candles were overturned, and in the darkness it seemed that every Highland gentleman was struggling with another for an opportunity to beat their host about the head. He escaped from them into another room where he locked the door, opened a window and called to his workmen for help.

The memory of Rawlinson survives thinly in the contentious claim that he, an Englishman, was the inventor of the *feilidh-beag*, the little kilt now popularly worn. The argument, or at least the reason given, is persuasive. Having watched his Highland labourers struggling to work within the encumbrance of a belted plaid – many yards of tartan swathed about shoulders and hips – he ordered the cloth to be cut in two and the top half discarded. Although this proposal may not have been original, it is the earliest record of the little kilt. The dispute is almost as old. In 1785, when there was some discussion of its English provenance in the *Edinburgh Magazine*, there was a contribution from Evan Baillie, merchant of Inverness, a city officer and a lawyer who acted for many influential Highlanders of the district. Moreover, his family had held land for two hundred years in the hills above Loch Ness at Abriachan. He told the magazine that Rawlinson 'being a man of genius and quick parts, thought it no stretch of imagination to abridge the dress'. And so might any man, perhaps, but Baillie said he had known the Englishman and he rejected any suggestion that the little kilt was in use before the ironmaster came to Invergarry.

I certify from my own knowledge, that till I returned from Edinburgh to reside in this country in the year 1725, after serving seven or eight years with writers to the signet, I never saw the felie-beg used, nor heard any mention of such a piece of dress, not [even] from my father, who was very intelligent and well-known to the Highlanders, and lived to the age of 83 years, and died in the year 1738, born in May, 1655.

The earliest, if not the first, illustration of the little kilt dates from the middle of the eighteenth century. It is not worn by the principal figure in the painting, but by what appears to be a servant or henchman in the background. The subject is Alasdair Ruadh MacDonell, 13th Chief of Glengarry, a literally intriguing figure in the shadows of history, part Jacobite and part Hanoverian spy and still awaiting a novelist's inspiration. He was the son of that indolent drunkard John MacDonell, in whose castle Thomas Rawlinson wore the little kilt as if he were born to it. The truth about its invention is of little consequence, except to the sensitivity of some Scots, but the story entertains a mischievous mind amused by paradox, for there is much that is theatrically absurd in Highland dress as now worn, and historically false in its assumption as a national costume.

When I first came to Invergarry, on foot and scarcely into my majority, I crossed the river by the old bridge at its mouth, half a mile downstream from the present highway and where there was once an ancient ferry. Replacing an earlier bridge built by the furnace-men, perhaps, it was first constructed at the beginning of the last century when Perthshire contractors cut a road through Glengarry to the sea-water of Loch Hourn, thus serving drovers from the Isles, woodsmen hauling MacDonell's timber to the builders of Telford's canal, and carters of birch-wood for the coopers in coastal fisheries. I remember with clarity that idle pause on Invergarry Bridge, sunlight fragmenting the surface of Loch Oich and clothing the hills behind me in saffron. Almost any bridge across living water can calm my mind if I stand long and patiently enough mid-stream. There is sometimes the recall of other bridges, and the occasional wish for tangible contact with the past, my own or what I know of the bridge's history. And so I place a palm upon the reassuring stones of Whitebridge, of Aberfeldy and Shiel Bridge, and even on the wall of a culvert on the climb by Ratagan to the fort at Bernera, *feeling* always the passage of weary soldiers. In the thoughts of other bridges I visualize none more nostalgically than the iron and timber of the railroad span over the Saskatchewan. I respond to the remembered tug of water below, brown spume and leaping ice, and the terrifying bravado of frightened boys. And, of course, there is that other railway bridge, over the Firth of Tay to Dundee, the manifestation of one man's doomed dreams. For a few months only it was the admiration of the world. 'Beautiful Railway Bridge of the Silvery Tay', wrote the Dundee weaver William McGonagall, self-styled poet and tragedian, and master of bathetic verse,

> That has caused the Emperor of Brazil to leave
> His home far away, *incognito* in his dress,
> And view thee ere he passed along *en route* for Inverness.

My account of the building and destruction of this bridge was the first of my books about Scotland and its history, and had I not written it I might not have been bold enough to attempt the others. It was a cautious introduction to a land, a nation and its past that is now more familiar to me than my own. At first the subject was intended to be an article of fifteen hundred words to acknowledge the seventy-fifth anniversary of the collapse of the bridge in a winter gale. My agent, Colin Young, to whom the book is dedicated and whose great talents were extinguished by his early death, advised me to write at greater length. After some cowardly hesitation I did so, finishing a first draft in two weeks in that room above the Windrush at Minster Lovell. I did what research I could in Dundee, crossing the Tay by the present bridge and looking down from a carriage window to the seaweed stumps upon which the first spans had rested. I also stayed in the same travellers' hotel where the designer of the bridge, Thomas Bouch, had lodged during its construction and the dark days after its fall. Like the massacre of Glencoe, the collapse of the Tay Bridge and its relatively few casualties could have been obscured by greater disasters which now have no hold upon public memory. In a foreword to a later edition of the work, I tried to explain why there should be this enduring remembrance.

It is not the loss of seventy-five lives, an engine, five carriages and a brake-van, one thousand yards of iron girders. Nor yet the loss, within eighteen months of its completion, of the longest and the greatest bridge in the world. Something more was destroyed in the darkness of those terrible seconds: the Victorians' smug pride in their industrial supremacy, their belief in their creative infallibility. Disasters on a colonial battlefield, at Kabul, Cawnpore or Isandhlwana, could be reversed by the punitive victories that always followed, but the self-conceit of the age never recovered from the fall of the Tay Bridge and the unnerving revelations of a Board of Trade Inquiry.

Those revelations, of a bridge 'badly designed, badly constructed and badly maintained', demanded a culprit to carry the blame and the shame. There was no doubt who this should be. Not the contractors who followed the design without much protest. Not Fergus Ferguson, the foreman-moulder who cheerfully admitted that he had directed his workmen to plug holes in the cast iron with Beaumont's

Egg, described by him as 'beeswax, fiddler's rosin, and the finest iron borings melted up, and a little lamp-black'. It was not one of the locomotive engineers who drove their trains through the High Girders at greater speeds than good sense and the regulations required. It was not the Astronomer Royal, whose advice on wind strength and pressure was dangerously inaccurate, and who saw nothing odd in the fact that he, an *astronomer*, was almost the only authority consulted on such matters. Not these, and many others, but Thomas Bouch, his recent knighthood disgraced when he was held to be entirely or principally responsible for the faults in the design, construction and maintenance of the bridge. When these charges were published in the Inquiry's report, Bouch went gently out of his mind. He had risen from a humble beginning in Cumbria to great eminence as a railway engineer and bridge-builder. He had constructed more than three hundred miles of railway in Scotland and England, and by a harsh irony the fall of his bridge brought back into operation the train-ferries he had designed for crossing the firth at Dundee. I think I responded honestly to his tragedy.

> He lived for four months after the Report destroyed him . . . The maddest of men would not now have asked him to design a kitchen wall . . . He had nothing to do now, and having nothing to do had no reason to go on living. So he died, with the least disturbance possible.

My research for the book included a meeting with Bouch's grandson. He was a courteous, softly spoken man, living in a Warwickshire house, of Georgian brick, I think, facing a yellow drive and a semi-circle of excellent grass. He could tell me little about the engineer, and sadly confessed that the Tay Bridge, its fall and his grandfather had never been discussed in his presence when he was a child, and never at all by his father. He was more interested now in writing and in poetry, and when I left he gave me a privately printed volume of his own verse.

Although the confusing circumstances of the day are only dimly recalled, I have a lasting memory of the Nijmegen Bridge as I saw it during the brief time I was in the town, lost or abandoned by a driver who had delivered me to the wrong troop. As I lay beneath a truck with two young companions, I looked up the slope of the street to the startling ceramic blue of the sky, to a great parabola of iron and the body of a German sniper, a grey bundle caught in the fork of a girder. Months later, and south of the charred ruins of Xanten, there was another bridge, a long chain of pontoons which the Engineers looped across the Rhine within hours, it seemed, of the first boat assault. It rippled with the remorseless traffic of support vehicles and it brought the last of the Luftwaffe upon us. They came at night, Junkers and Heinkels from zero to six thousand feet, and were engaged by light AA guns and the beams of two troops from our Battery. They came to bomb and machine-gun the bridge and the banks, and of those we destroyed the four that I remember were shot down after illumination, each falling upon a burning scream to the darkness of the water. At dawn, the mist over the river was dense, muting the throb of vehicles on the pontoons and the long bursts from distant Spandaus in the east where German paratroopers were still resisting.

In a lull towards midnight on the day the bridge was opened, I came over the river from the far bank where I had been dealing with a reluctant W/T set. Carrying a rifle and tools upon my back, I rode a collapsible Airborne bicycle that had no gears, no brakes, and a cruel saddle no wider at best, I am sure, than three inches. The sickening movement of the pontoons, the menacing sound of water, the reptilian eyes of masked headlamps, and the knowledge that no driver could see me as he passed, at last unnerved me. I dismounted, still in fear and closer now to the edge of the board-walk, but successfully reaching the bank and mounting the machine again. Riding between the white tapes of a lane, in the glow of our beams and against the orders of a beachmaster, I was suddenly pedalling against a tank column, lurching saurians throwing up waves of gritty soil, the turret-men shouting cheerful obscenities. I threw the machine away, and until dawn I tried to sleep against a Bren-carrier with young infantrymen sprawled about me, some sleeping, others tired-eyed and white-faced. At Troop HQ an infuriated TSM sent me back to recover the machine, but it had been crushed under the tracks of the armour. Traffic on the bridge was now immobilized by a breakdown, and Bofors gunners turned and turned their weapons, nervously searching an empty sky. Amphibians that could not wait for the bridge to be cleared plunged into the swift water on the far bank, slapping white waves with their flat bows. They came ashore like heavy seals, and there was blood and black water and wounded on their decks. Field Security Police had erected a cage for prisoners, no more than a looped perimeter of barbed wire inside which grey young men hugged their bodies with tightly folded arms, or crouched on the ground to defecate. I hate the thought of that night and that dawn, and I am sometimes ashamed of the elation I felt. But this memory of the Xanten bridge is balanced by another, six weeks later.

We knew, as everybody knew, that the War had ended early Monday morning. We knew that the German delegation in Rheims had signed at 2.41 a.m. On Monday evening we told ourselves that the War was over. It was getting dark and the sharp triangles of our tents were slipping into the ground mists. You might think that when peace comes the guns stop and you listen to the song of a bird, but as darkness dropped a Bofors began firing, a high stream of tracers that drooped over us. And then another and another, and down by the Rhine the multiples began to send up their scarlet curtains. One by one along the river bank the searchlights exposed and their beams slipped gracefully through the ack-ack fire. Joining in the celebration, the REs on the Xanten and Rees bridges began to burn piles of gun-cotton and the dark blue sky turned crimson. This went on for an hour, until one by one the guns stopped and the beams went out.

When that was written, on a May evening above the Rhine, the thought of another bridge had slipped from my mind, but it returns more frequently now, and with sadness. I have forgotten where it was; in Holland, beyond the Maas and towards Kleve perhaps. It was early spring, a dawn frost glistening like quartz on the canvas of the trucks. Further movement ahead was interrupted by a surly artillery dispute, and we were halted on the far side of a small river, no wider than could be crossed by two Bailey spans. We would not be operational until dusk, and the troop's vehicles were therefore pulled into the side of a narrow track, tilting on the soft shoulders and breaking the white tape. One man from each truck stood by it, as was the rule, to wave on more urgent traffic, and with this weary duty I leant against the radio-truck where Frank crouched over his set, headphones crackling on his ears. He occasionally responded in singing monosyllables, returning then to gentle mockery of the driver who had worked at Bournville and now, in nostalgic misery, was making a sandwich from a chocolate bar and white bread. I was tired, but should not make that an excuse for my indifference to the body in the river a few feet away. It was a girl, face down in the water and perhaps killed earlier in the morning gun-fire. As each vehicle crossed the spans and mounted the bank, the pontoons sank and then rose upon a buoyant wave. When this washed against the body of the girl, her arms moved gently and her dark hair flowed from her head and caressed her shoulders. No one spoke of her then or later. We could have done nothing, perhaps, but one of us should have said *something*.

That memory, like others, usually returns when I am tired or dispirited, but one unexpected recall was almost absolution for the sin of omission. A few years ago in Edinburgh, where I was observing the duty a writer owes his publisher, I was told by the hotel that a girl had been asking for me and would return. She was Dutch, and it would be a literary pretence to say that she was perhaps the same age as the girl in the water, nor at that moment did I make that comparison. She was reading history at the University, and at school in Holland, she said, she had taken my work as an English set-book for her matriculation. We talked of places in her country known to us both, although at different times and in different circumstances, and also briefly of the War, which had been over long before she was born. She had brought one of my books for me to sign, and she gave me a small ceramic bottle, shaped like an eagle and containing whisky. When we parted at the door of the hotel, I thanked her for coming and for the gift. Thank you, she said, and thank you for the Liberation.

It was the Liberation that finally freed me from the malign force that repeatedly drew me back to Kinmel Park and held me fast, but it was long in coming. The German invasion of Russia in June 1941 released the British Communist Party from its comic head-stand, setting it upon its feet and more or less facing reality. With almost its first breath, it demanded the immediate opening of a Second Front in Europe to relieve the intolerable pressure on the Soviet Union, and however impracticable the proposal was at that time the memory of it is still emotionally persuasive. For me, and for many servicemen I think, there was an uncomfortable shame in being idle witnesses of the suffering of the Soviet people. The Organizers in King Street cynically or idealistically exploited this, of course. We were told that in view of the new alliance, Party members in the Forces could and perhaps should openly declare their political allegiance now, and demonstrate that Communists were leading the workers' struggle for a Second Front. In the security and ordered life at Kinmel there seemed to be one solution only for my unease, and that an old familiar. On leave in a London now wounded and shabby, I was told by King Street that I was to 'do nothing so bloody stupid as volunteering for the Front. Stay where you're useful'. I did not tell the Organizer that on the day of the German assault I had again asked for an overseas posting. The Lancashire Fusilier had listened without change of expression, and briefly refused the request.

It was again a summer of beguiling beauty. The Elwy Valley was richly green in a heavy heat, and seaward from the camp, beyond the Rhuddlan plain, distant convoys moved slowly through the haze. Our group – the *faction* in Party idiom – met frequently in a barrack-room or the Ty Fry Café, where we argued at length about the conduct of the War, the political situation and of course how far it was in our power to affect the course of both. We were now joined by *delegates* from the Driver Training Regiment to the west of the camp, and sometimes from a Signal regiment in Prestatyn. One of the gunners was Harry Stratton, a taxi-driver from Cardiff who had fought with the International Brigade in Spain. Gentle and grave, without personal hatred, he was perhaps the only one among us who was selflessly sincere, and not intellectually drunk sometimes with the spirit of our own rhetoric. When post-war reality betrayed us all, he held fast to his beliefs, I think, but no fault should be charged against the compassion that inspired them.

That September, in a café room where the Canadian mutineers may have met, we agreed that we should organize a petition urging the government to open a Second Front immediately. We were not wholly simpletons and knew the Army well enough to expect difficulties, and a further resolution proposed that I should ask my Troop Officer whether the petition would be within the bounds of King's Regulations. He was a small, round-bodied lieutenant, once a schoolmaster I think, and a declared Liberal who had enlivened one ABCA discussion period by speaking fervently in support of a People's War and a People's Government. He listened sympathetically to my explanation of the petition – which we wished to send to the local MP for transmission to the House – and then warned me that it would be impermissible without the approval of the Commanding Officer. We ignored that advice, and somewhat unhinged by excitement we decided to call a camp-meeting at which the petition would be read and signatures invited. I wrote the draft, a wordy document, but fifty years later its sincerity is still clear, I think. It referred to the current agitation for the Front 'by workers through their Unions, by journalists in their newspapers, by Members of Parliament and the spokesmen of political parties . . .'

. . . and yet the Government hesitates. We appreciate the gravity of the step advised, but the gravity of procrastination is greater. Civilisation depends upon our boldness and our actions at this hour. So far the Army, upon whom the awful responsibility of an offensive must fall, has said nothing, being content to prepare itself for the day when that offensive comes. But the soldiers who sign this letter to you now, Sir, wish to state emphatically their sympathy and unity with those persons and organisations in civilian life who are earnestly advocating the opening of an immediate front against the Nazis. We believe that active assistance beyond that already given should be sent immediately to the Soviet Union, that Britons should take their rightful share in the defence of democracy at this hour; that we should not, in our own conscience, be accused of being, once more, too late!

The attendance at the camp-meeting surprised us. The barrack-room was crowded, and the door was finally locked against late-comers, thus cutting off any tactful retreat by the Troop Officer who had come by his own wish or on orders from Regimental Office. In the chair, flanked by Harry and my friend Elwyn, I read the petition and called for debate, which was noisy, good-humoured, sometimes obscenely sceptical, and occasionally impassioned. Before the meeting ended, and by a resolution agreed, I believe I added a sentence declaring that every signator would be willing to serve in the Front when it was opened. During that evening, and on following days when it was taken through the camp after Tattoo, the letter was signed by two hundred and fifty soldiers, fifty of them NCOs. At a triumphant meeting of the faction in the Ty Fry we agreed that six of us should each write a letter to a national newspaper, describing the petition and its support. I think one only was sent at that time, mine to the *News Chronicle*. We were careless and light-headed, and our knowledge of the risk was salted by the excitement of danger. The initial lack of response by Regimental Office is still puzzling and may be attributed to the shock of the attack on the Soviet Union and the sudden and numbing alliance with that country. My own feelings, as remembered long after, were strongly subjective, a renewed impatience to be gone from Kinmel, a joy in that release of body and spirit which was surely probable. Whatever happened, there could be no wish to keep me there after this.

At its beginning, the collapse of the petition was comedy. A gunner working in the Quartermaster's Stores – the misanthropic old soldier (excused boots and parades) known to all servicemen in all camps – returned from the NAAFI one morning to tell the QM that Lance-Bombardier Prebble had been 'talking sedition'. The Warrant Officer acted without consultation, reporting the matter officially to Battery Office. I was at a training-site on operational duty, near a hill-farm below Moelfre, and the ration-truck brought me back to camp that evening before we exposed. The QM had made alarming accusations of incitement to mutiny, but the Battery Sergeant-Major, despite his ill-temper at being called so late from the mess, formalized them into something less melodramatic. I was placed under open arrest with Elwyn, whom the splenetic storeman had included in his complaint.

I was at liberty within the camp, although accompanied everywhere by a junior NCO of equivalent rank, and the following evening I was able to do something which, I thought, might prevent the affair from going beyond the camp and the confused patience of its commanding officer. The *News Chronicle* had not yet published my letter, and it now seemed imperative to dissuade it from doing so. There was one public telephone in the camp, a red sentinel at the crossroads where Badgie the trumpeter sounded his daily calls. Every evening, from Tattoo to Lights Out, there was a waiting queue of soldiers by the box, the flare of cigarette sparking the dusk, and the sound of anxious voices calling distant homes in bombed cities. It was understood that Badgie had a pre-emptive right to the telephone after he had sounded a call, and his conversations were never brief, his long and insolently indolent figure leaning against the glass, trumpet bright upon his shoulder and the bugle turning, turning on its lanyard. When I spoke to the night desk of the *Chronicle* the answer I received was reassuring but deflating. 'All right, old son. Don't worry. Sorry. It's been spiked. We've had a lot like it.'

The Lancashire Fusilier dealt with me briefly, expressing no censure or opinion, but telling me that I must be remanded for the Commanding Officer. In the Driver Training lines that morning, Harry and nine of his companions appeared before their Adjutant, were sternly questioned and then dismissed. When I was marched before him, Colonel Bell was clearly distressed. He told me that he did not understand why there should be this excitement in the ranks, but since he was sure that I might be acting with the best of intentions it would be a good thing all round to have a Court of Inquiry to sort the matter out. At this I could hear, perhaps *feel*, the incredulous exhalation of breath from the Regimental Sergeant-Major behind me. The Colonel smiled at us both. 'Do think carefully about all this, will you, Bombardier? Good. That's all, Mr Mulvanney.'

The Court of Inquiry was an enlightening experience. Had it not been called, had the CO been less sympathetic, and had I been charged with any number of offences, I have no doubt that I would have been sentenced to detention in a military prison, with embittering and ineradicable consequences. What fear I had of this at the time did not, I think, deeply influence me, beyond a conscious need for care and concern. But it must be said that with the change in the War and political feelings it would have been foolish for the Army to have taken such punitive action. The Court met in the Regimental Office, in a clerks' room cleared for the purpose. It consisted of three, perhaps four field officers, Battery commanders whom I knew by sight only. I sat with them, on the right of the President at a blanketed barrack-room table. Before the proceedings began, my rights were briskly explained. I could question any witness I wished. I could dispute or correct any evidence that was demonstrably and factually inaccurate. Any other observation I made was to be my stated opinion. The evidence was recorded in longhand by one member of the Court and passed to me for reading before the next witness was called, and in this unhurried way the proceedings travelled throughout the morning and the afternoon. Almost all the witnesses had been present at the camp-meeting, and most had signed the petition. They were asked for an account of one and their reasons for the other, the purpose of the petition as they saw it, and whether or not they believed it had been permitted by Regimental Office. I was invited to put any question I wished, and I remember one only. Did the witness agree with the need for the petition and for a Second Front? The replies were balanced, and those who said that their original sympathy had been hasty and was now regretted were understandably NCOs. When the long business was over, I was civilly dismissed and my escort took me back to the barrack-room.

At first parade on a following morning I reported to the verandah of the Regimental Office. Mr Mulvanney made good theatre of the occasion, in a voice that brought grinning faces to the window of the guard-room opposite, and the expressive closing of the Adjutant's window at his elbow. His exhortation was delivered without punctuation and in an effortless monotone.

Cap Off Straighten up Right turn As you were Right turn As you were Get those men away from the window Guard Commander Right turn Smarten up bombardier Quick march Lef-ri lef-ri lef-ri . . .

When I stamped into his office, the Colonel welcomed me with his weary smile. 'Stand at ease, will you, Prebble?' He fingered the written evidence of the Court with a poor pretence of reading some of it again. He could see no way to begin except through the RSM. 'Has he been told anything, Mr Mulvanney?' The RSM was surprised. '*Sir?*' 'I mean, does he . . . do you know, Bombardier, how serious this could be?' '*Sir.*' 'I'm glad, but I don't think there's any serious offence under King's Regulations, just an excess of zeal. But these things can be very serious if they get out of hand, do you see, Bombardier?' '*Sir.*' 'Good man. I'm just making it a reprimand, but do try and understand, not too much zeal, eh, Bombardier? And don't worry. This sort of thing, the War you know, is in good hands. March him out, Mr Mulvanney.'

I left on the storm of the Sergeant-Major's voice, at a quick pace through the outer office to the verandah where I was kept at the mark-time for a salutary period. When he had called '*Haltstandstill!*' he studied me carefully, leaning from the waist, cane straight beneath his left arm-pit and his face close to mine. He held this position silently before speaking in an unexpected mild tone. 'I've only one thing to say to you, Lance-Bombardier Prebble. What know you of England who only England know? Cap on and clear off.'

Despite this potentially dangerous incident the group continued its activities with self-satisfied vigour. We published the wall-newspaper weekly, organized more discussions under the umbrella of the Army Bureau of Current Affairs, conducted mock elections and held Parliamentary debates. When the ban on the *Daily Worker* was lifted, copies of it were delivered to us at the Ty Fry and sometimes sold with other publications from a table near the wall-newspaper. There was no regimental effort to restrain this activity, but I was marching-reliefs on more guard duties than the rota would justify, and sometimes, on the excuse of 'clearing up this mess', the RSM or the Provost-Sergeant sent a fatigue-party of defaulters to remove the chairs and tables and clean the floor of the room where we were about to hold an approved meeting. Dogged and often dispirited, I continued my efforts to be posted from the camp. With some bizarre solemnity, the group took a vote on whether I should leave so influential a station, and concluded that I should not. There were times, probably therapeutic, when I almost believed that I should wait for that revolutionary moment for which I would be a right man in a right place at the right time, but this pretension was invariably dissolved by the acid of self-ridicule. When I proposed that all in the group should volunteer for posting to units that might take part in a Second Front, this too was discussed at length but never resolved.

Escape was sudden and miraculous, like the opening of an unsuspected door. Mechanics were now urgently needed to maintain and repair radar equipment for guns and lights. The announcement of this on Daily Orders did not encourage me to volunteer, for I had no qualifications or experience in electronics. All was changed in one moment. It was a Sunday morning, the first of a white winter. I was returning to the Main Guard with a small squad, my body tired under the weight of great-coat, steel helmet, full equipment and weapons, sleepless from a night of marching-reliefs, and ten hours yet before Stand Down. There were few men on the barrack-streets. Badgie was returning from his second call of the day, his long strides leaving a measured track in the frost. Old Soldier was on his way to the garrison theatre where the Anglican service was regularly held. Like the surly QM storeman, he was a time-serving man with bad feet. The theatre was his war effort, and he kept it clean with broom, mop and duster. Every Sunday morning at this hour he drew a large wooden cross from the stores and took it to the theatre where he mounted it upon the stage beside a lectern. He carried it on his shoulder, his back bent, his pace slow, and the comparison was amusing, irreverent, and deeply sad.

As we passed the Battery Office the BSM leaned from the window. 'Stand those men at ease, Bombardier, and come inside a moment.' He was taking Church Parade later and his belt and gaiters were freshly blancoed, his trousers and sleeves pressed to a knife-edge. The brass crown and laurel on his cuff gleamed as he pushed a copy of yesterday's Orders across the desk. 'What've you done about that, then?' 'I have no qualifications, sir.' 'You don't

need them. Any bod who's got the education, we've got to release.'
He smiled at me unexpectedly. 'I'll be glad to see the back of you,
Bombardier.'

I left Kinmel with the hope that I would never see it again, an
exhilaration sobered by the knowledge that nothing in a soldier's
life is certain, and that pessimism is his strongest defence against
despair. The training-course for radar mechanics was held in civilian schools, technical instruction first in Doncaster and theory
later in Huddersfield. Our instructors were also civilians, and
the only military presence in our lives for four months was the
occasional appearance of an administrative staff-sergeant of the
RASC. We came from all regiments and corps, with a perverse and
obstinate attachment to them, so intense and influential that for
some months after we had passed the course we were allowed to
wear the cap-badge or collar-dog of our original units. Like myself,
most men had been glad to escape from them, but even I jealously
maintained a right to wear the cannon or bomb of the Royal Regiment of Artillery. In such a contrary manner, perhaps, was reason
taken from us and replaced with an ancient, deceiving loyalty that
still lingers half a century later.

It was the winter of a new year, and I have yet to rid my mind
of the irrational belief that for all of its existence Yorkshire has been
the prisoner of snow, frost, pitiless winds or wounding rain. The
endurance of such weather in Doncaster, ringed by its satellite
pit-heads and white-capped pyramids of slag, was compensated by
my billet, the little terrace home of Mr and Mrs Washer, a miner
and his wife. One of its two small bedrooms accommodated three
soldiers, and we lived, ate, studied, laughed and sang in the kitchen,
beside a black-leaded, red-mouthed range and against a wall covered
with the cap-badges of men who had been quartered here before.
The front parlour was never used, its curtains drawn even against
the thin light of a winter's afternoon, shadowing the shining spear-
blades of an aspidistra and the sepia photograph of a soldier of the
Great War. Three men were undoubtedly more than should have
been billeted upon the Washers, but though we were welcome for
the money the Army paid them, there was also kindness and concern, warm affection for some of us and a wish to make the lives of
all more pleasant. In the first week of February I was ill with gastric
influenza, and Mrs Washer walked to the school office to summon
a doctor. The young RAMC officer who eventually came offered
some casual advice and left quickly. For a week and more I was

nursed as if I were the son of the house, weakness and the rage of delirium being cured by her selfless care. On the day of my departure I repaid this with the only things she wanted, a kiss upon her lips, a cap-badge and a scrap of red and blue cloth for its backing.

In Huddersfield another staff-sergeant of the RASC sent me to a large Victorian house upon the wind-struck heights to the south of the city. At the one upper window from which I was later privileged to look I could see rain and fog, the yellow mud of a polluted river and a frozen sea of roof-slates. The householder was one of the owners of the *Huddersfield Examiner*, and during the weeks I was there he also appeared to be editing the paper. Although the house was large and empty enough to have accommodated many soldiers, there was only myself and a corporal of Engineers. We shared one room and the same double bed. When we arrived we were told – by the cook, I think – that, apart from this bedroom, the stairway and the kitchen where we would eat, we were to go nowhere without permission. The cleaning of our boots and webbing was to be done outside in a stone-paved court at the rear, its door to the house being our only entry and exit. On Sundays, however, we would be invited at least once to take mid-day dinner with the master and mistress. Our meals during the week were no more and probably less than could be wisely bought on our service ration-cards. If breakfast one morning was a slice of streaky bacon, the fat from its frying was used for the next day's meal of fried bread. Now and then, so rarely that I seem to remember each occasion clearly, there was a small boiled egg, its yolk copper-green and hard. Supper was sometimes a sausage or a thin slice of corned beef, but more often a root-vegetable pie of impossible description.

The corporal was an uncommunicative man, and the most he ever spoke was an incoherent rambling during his sleep. Although I was his bedfellow for two months I can remember little about him. At mid-day on our first or second Sunday, wearing our best battle-dress, we came up from the kitchen to the dining-room where a half-bottle of ale was set by our places. We were served roast beef and Yorkshire pudding, portions of meat as meagre as rationing allowed but introduced by a patriotic encomium from our host. Conversation was stilted and patronizing, not unkindly but constrained by an assumed lack of common interests, although I thought the ageing owner-editor would have liked to talk to me about our mutual craft. His wife had difficulty even with small-talk. We learnt later, elsewhere in the town, that she had accepted our

billeting with great reluctance, having expected two young subalterns at least, but she was bearing it bravely as her sacrifice in the
war effort. When dinner was finished we went down to the kitchen
and she retired to the study where, surrounded by the week's
national newspapers, she wrote the 'London Letter' for the
Examiner.

The weather in February was fiercely cold, the yard outside the
back door entrapping a northern wind in whirling coils of snow.
Refusing to go into this Arctic world one morning, I cleaned my
boots in the bedroom, spreading a protective copy of the *Examiner*
on the floor before the gas fire, its jets locked to a frugal height. I
was discovered by the cook, reported at once to the mistress, who
complained to the principal of the school, who passed the matter
to the RASC staff-sergeant, who begged me to do nothing more to
prejudice his agreeable posting and permanent sleeping-out pass.

I spent every evening I could away from that sad, cold house
and its lost occupants, leaving the Engineer corporal to write his
notes at the bed-side by the light of a twenty-five-watt bulb. I
joined other men in their happier billets, in particular a red-haired
Lancastrian with a taste for Sibelius, Mozart and Tchaikovsky,
a mocking Trotskyist whose imminent revolutionary moment, he
thought, was much closer than mine. He was billeted in the house
of a successful provision merchant who had a plump daughter, an
expensive radio-gramophone and a collection of classical records.
In that welcoming home, seduced by abundant heat, strong lighting
and an amoral indifference to the diktats of the Ministry of Food,
I found the strength to pass the course. Very little of my training
at Doncaster or Huddersfield is now remembered. I retain incon-
sequential memories only – how to fire a blow-lamp and heat a
soldering-iron, to make a scriber, assemble a rudimentary wireless
set, and improvise a resistance from a lead pencil. When the course
was over we were told that we were now Radar Mechanics and, if
it was of interest to us, we were also honorary members of the
Amalgamated Engineering Union. The staff-sergeant told us this
with suitable gravity.

Our dispersal throughout AA Command was unpredictable, but
we were asked where we wished to go. No soldier believes that his
response to this question is ever seriously considered, but he
answers truthfully as if it were a lottery in which chance must surely
be favourable one day. I asked for a posting to the 1st AA Division,
the defence of London, to be near my home and family perhaps,

but also because it was the most active and was *in the War*. This was not foolish vainglory, I hope, and in any case the request was ignored. When I was given my orders I was posted to an AA division in Wales. The Battery HQ, when I came to it by truck from Barmouth station, was in a large house above Bala Lake. It was early spring and almost dawn, stand-down for the searchlights in the Berwyn Hills across the water. I stood in the vehicle park, a Victorian lawn darkened by foreign conifers, full-pack and kit-bag leaning against my legs as I watched each pencil of distant light falling to the earth. Called into the office, I drank rich tea and ate a bacon sandwich until the Battery Clerk came from his blankets. He looked at my movement order, ran a finger down papers of his own, cleaned his front teeth with the tip of his tongue, and found the troop and the site where I must go. 'Dog Three over the lake. Wait outside for the ration-truck.'

To eyes wearied by a Yorkshire winter, this land had a crystal beauty, sun-bright and rain-washed, the sky cleansed of the night's alien visitors. The ration-truck went by the lake-shore to a grey village not yet awake, and then eastward into the hills by rough lanes and cart-tracks, the grass of the lower slopes changing to a brown pelt of scrub and rock before we went over a saddle and down to Dog Three, at a place with the ubiquitous name of Ty-nant.

The focal centre of the site was an old ninety-centimetre projector, its green barrel crowned with the dipoles of radar aerials and its bearing-arm stretched out in mute supplication. It was a cumbersome instrument, clumsily mobile on tracked feet, a dead thing during the day but starting into miraculous life at nightfall. On the crash and spit of a successful arcing, it could thrust a milk-white tube of light into the sky as far as the stars it seemed, and for a moment after it was extinguished it left a faint reflection of itself upon the clouds. Nine men were the minimum needed to operate it, but with supernumeraries like myself, the cook and sometimes a driver-mechanic, the full strength of the site could increase to twelve. There was a Nissen hut, a latrine, a small cook-house and a canvas shelter for the Lister engine, a long cable's length from the projector it fed with power. The site's only defence was an old Lewis gun a few running paces from the hut, the drain-pipe barrel and round ammunition-pan of the trenches. This morning it was loosely draped in a ground sheet that snapped and twisted in a wind which, I would soon discover, never ceased.

The little detachment was the most bizarre unit I knew during my six years as a soldier. The men had been there so long that they appeared to have lost contact and interest in anything beyond Ty-nant. They wore a mixture of service and civilian clothing and few of them, I was told by the driver of the ration-truck, took their short-leave, preferring to lie on their blankets in the Nissen hut, maliciously enjoying their idleness while others worked. They were uncommunicative, introspective and at all times sullen. They could have been the original of all the bawdy or despairing anecdotes told about remote service units. I was neither welcomed nor ostracized. I was asked no questions and was not expected to have any of my own. Each man seemed to work in silent, frowning protest, and off-duty or in the waiting that followed Stand To at dusk, the sense of dull hostility was almost tangible. All the customary conversation was absent – no autobiographical information, no professional concern for the War. All boasts of physical or sexual achievement had long since been reduced to code-words and catch-phrases of unintelligible brevity. Privacy was almost impossible, and available only to the bombardier who built a cubicle of blankets at the end of the Nissen hut. When the entrance to this was drawn, no one disturbed him.

The cook was perhaps the most important man on the site, substantial food being the fundamental requirement of morale. He was not a good cook, but what he supplied was usually hot, its taste improved or disguised by Daddy's Sauce. He was the product of the war's early months when those who did not pass the test of their basic training with the Royal Artillery, and inspired no confidence in their future progress, were given the briefest introduction to a field-kitchen and mustered as site-cooks. Like many of his trade, the man at Ty-nant had a dog, a beloved mongrel and less than loving companion. Understandably, it was grossly over-fed and slow in all movement except lightning dashes at food dropped or thrown. No one else liked it, its sycophantic whining, its fleas, its occasional biting, its foul habits inside the hut, but all were ready to defend it against threat from outside. Some yards from the site was a small sheep-farm, a white house and decaying sheds. Soon after the dog was acquired, the farmer complained that it was worrying his sheep, a familiar charge which the detachment ignored. He made several complaints to the Battery Commander which, when they were deflected to the detachment, were again disregarded. The farmer then declared that if the dog came near his sheep again, he would shoot it. The cook's response was characteristic and unanimously approved. If the dog were shot, he would open fire on the farm-house with the Lewis gun. He emphasized the intention occasionally by aiming the weapon at the farmer's door, and making the sound of rapid fire with his tongue and teeth.

I was on the site for two weeks only, and every waking hour I tried to think of ways of leaving it. The detachment slept until noon after a night's operation, but I could not. With my newly acquired knowledge I passed the morning in earnest but largely unnecessary maintenance of the SLC, the radar transmitter and receivers mounted on the projector. This esoteric activity distanced me further from the detachment, most of whom were uneasy about the equipment, believing that if its high amperage did not electrocute them, it would certainly rob them of their virility. We were placed on Stand To every night, and were frequently operational in the defence of the littoral between Anglesey and the Wirral. In the darkness above us there was an aerial road from Barmouth Bay to Merseyside along which winged armadas came and went, leaving the northern sky flushed with crimson. Sometimes the bombers were tactically ignored, and sometimes our beam leapt upward to join others and engage an enemy we saw only as trembling blips on the green face of a cathode-ray tube. Once the planes had passed over us, there was a long wait for their return, bearing and elevation operators slumped in weariness, the spotters turning slowly in their reclining chairs, studying the empty sky through their glasses. When the bombers came homeward, they were engaged again, and this time with gunfire sparking our beams, and the occasional silver gleam of a pursuing night fighter.

Towards the end of my time with the detachment, on the last night it seems to me now, the customary routine of 'Stand to . . . Engage . . . On target . . . Expose . . . Douse . . . Stand down . . .' was broken, the brooding passion of the site exploding in a moment of comic and hazardous insanity. Before dawn a wounded or lost bomber came suddenly upon us from the hills, perhaps searching for the long glen that leads down to Barmouth from Bala Lake and Wrexham beyond. Its engines and fuselage screaming, it was briefly held by three lights, one of them ours. Two were doused as it slipped below the hills, and thus it came towards us at Ty-nant, 'down the beam' it might have seemed to those who believe that possible. The incident was over before comprehension could grasp it. The cook was standing by the Lewis gun where he had brought a dixie of tea, and now he pulled back the bolt of the weapon and fired in a wild traverse. I remember the sudden burst of unbearable sound, the smothered barking of the dog and a startling clang as the aircraft's fire struck the corrugated iron of the Nissen hut. Then the plane was gone, but the cook continued to fire, the trajectory of the tracers dropping towards the roof of the farm. The door of the house opened, a long bar of yellow light slanting, an angry yell and two retaliatory explosions from the shotgun. On the far side of the site one of the spotters laughed hysterically.

The Troop Officer arrived in a utility soon after first light, to inspect the damage to the Nissen hut and to mollify the farmer with an assurance that the dog, as if it had been responsible for the disturbance, would most certainly be destroyed. To my surprised pleasure, he also brought my movement orders, posting me out of the troop, the Battery and the Division. I returned with him later that morning to the big house on Bala Lake, and the further we got from Ty-nant the less I believed in its existence. The Troop Officer was cheerful and talkative, placing one brown boot on the dashboard to the disgust of the driver, and shouting over his shoulder to me as I bounced on my kit-bag in the back. He said I must be a soldier of some importance, for I was going to the SAAD. In the Battery Office I was told that this was the School of Anti-Aircraft Defence, newly formed and based at Kinmel Park.

The camp seemed unchanged when my transport approached it from Rhuddlan – the familiar brown and grey sprawl on a gentle green slope, the distant sound of vehicles, of marching feet and shouting voices. When we turned in at the Garage Gate I saw a line of new projectors on the square, 120-centimetres two or three times as large as the old nineties, and mounted with canvas shelters for the operators. More than this, the drilling-squads were not men but women, as stiff-legged and awkward in skirts or ballooning trousers as any male recruit. Kinmel Park was now a training-camp, a *school* for young ATS girls who were to be the new radar operators for the Royal Artillery. Many of the old permanent staff were gone, including the Lancashire Fusilier, but some of my friends remained. There was also Regimental Sergeant-Major Mulvanney. He came from his office and across the camp-street to the Guard Room when I alighted, gently tapping his leg with his cane as he looked at me. He lifted the cane and touched the mechanic's badge on my sleeve and then the divisional sign on my shoulder. 'Take that one down,' he said. His voice was more weary than hostile.

'Bad penny, eh, Bombardier? Or Lance-Corporal, is it? Bit of a cammylone, aren't we? Behave yourself. I'm watching.'

Thus began another, the longest imprisonment in Kinmel. There were old friends in the spider and new ones in the radar work-shop. There was the production of another wall-newspaper, more ambitious, more talented. There were gravely concerned meetings of the faction in barrack-rooms or the Ty Fry, more discussions, musical concerts and plays broadcast by cable, and again my persistent requests for posting elsewhere. There was the Dolben Arms, the sweet sunlight of that valley and the joy of the good friendships it nurtured. And the writing of *Where the Sea Breaks*. When I think of that slender book, with all its faults, I long for the effortless energy that produced it. It is true that I was occasionally released from the camp, brief postings on loan to operational Batteries in mid-Wales and East Anglia, but these deepened rather than eased my frustration. In Norfolk I was on the periphery of an insane and mercifully short attempt to oppose the night bombers with searchlights sent out to sea, thus creating a new and deluding coast-line. All the political, artistic and organizational activity with which I occupied my mind only deepened a guilty despair. I remember much of that time in fragments or disconnected words, a smile on a face that has lost its name, a voice that recalls nothing of the speaker. Memory rarely holds the door, and too often calls silently beyond its panels. But some incidents can remain clearly in the mind, unaltered, indestructible. There was a September evening still warm at nine o'clock with the heat of noon. I was orderly-NCO in the work-shop when RSM Mulvanney came in with the Provost Sergeant, wanting a favour, he said, but with no shame in making it sound like an order. I had heard of the surrender of Italy that day, he supposed. 'Well, the Eyeties here don't believe it. Got a set that can pick up Rome or some place?'

The Italians in the camp were prisoners-of-war, young men and old wearing chocolate-brown battle-dress, diamonds or squares of yellow on their backs. They were employed as labourers about the camp, sweeping, washing, gardening and window-cleaning. The more fortunate were taken each morning to one of many hill-farms, and they sang merrily on their departure and sadly on their return. They were amiable and unobtrusive and usually ignored once the eye became accustomed to them. I found a large receiver and carried it to their lines, marching rather than walking between the RSM and the Provost Sergeant. The prisoners were assembled in one hut, standing against the walls, sitting on the floors and on the two-tiered bunks. A few lay on the beds, their backs turned and their heads covered by a blanket, but most watched me intently as I plugged in the set, flung the aerial wire over a roof-beam, and crouched on the floor at the dials. When I found a station that was acceptable, they shouted and clapped their hands. The RSM tapped my shoulder with his cane. 'Got it, have we?'

As an excited voice flooded from the set, at almost full volume, the prisoners responded emotionally, repeating words and phrases in joy or disbelief. The RSM and the Sergeant prudently retired to the door, leaving me on my knees by the receiver where I turned a dial now and then, not from need but from a belief that I should appear concerned and professional. The Italians pressed upon me, touching my shoulder gratefully or leaning to reach the volume knob. I slapped their hands away and they cheered. The grief of some was as theatrically manifest as the joy of the majority. There were emotional embraces, angry words, kisses and glancing blows, an attempt to sing the Fascist hymn, and another to drown it with an old song from the Risorgimento. The intense, sweating atmosphere was soon unbearable. The RSM pushed his way to me and dragged me up. 'Get up, lad. Leave them the set. *Get out!*' As I walked away from the hut, the airless warmth of the evening seemed cool and refreshing. Entering my spider, I could still hear the prisoners' song, and the guitar that was now accompanying it.

In time there was another radio voice, the Kansas twang of Eisenhower on a Tuesday in June. The whole camp was still, quieter than a Sunday morning before parade, only that military voice and others marching from the barrack-room windows. We did little else but listen that day, in the radio work-shop where responsive argument was incessant. Before noon, I reported to Regimental Office and told the RSM that I wished to volunteer for Normandy. 'That's something new, isn't it,' he said, with a nod to indicate that he was being heavily ironic.

This time there was no refusal, no evasion. As regulations required for those posted overseas, I was issued with new clothing and new equipment. I also received a new rifle with a dark chestnut stock, the whole coated in protective grease. We made a solemn ritual of its cleaning in the work-shop, the boiling-out of its barrel and the long pull-through with slightly oiled four-by-two. While some were demanding their right to use the pull-through, others were blanco-ing my new webbing, laying it on the hut steps to dry in the night air. When all this was done, we went absent, walking over the hill to the Elwy Valley, knocking on the door of the Dolben and waking Ma from her bed. We came back to the camp before reveille, in the glorious gold of an early dawn, intelligently drunk and acknowledging every hedgerow sound as a valediction for Lance-Corporal Prebble J., *bloody fool*.

In the morning after first parade, I reported to the Regimental Office, wearing great-coat and full marching-order, back-pack with steel helmet strapped, side-pack, water-bottle, bayonet and rifle, my kit-bag on my shoulder. Mr Mulvanney took command of my departure, inspecting my appearance with a concern unnaturally paternal. When I went into the office for my papers, he guided my arm, and again when I came out. His farewell was brief. To secure this posting I had been obliged to surrender my rank, my *appointment* as a lance-corporal, a stripe I had cherished and fiercely defended. Mulvanney did not know how to address my naked sleeve. I had been bombardier or corporal for so long, and to call me Prebble now must have seemed too formal. He put my kit-bag into the back of the utility for me, and touched my shoulder briefly as I got into the cab beside the driver. 'Take care of yourself, lad.'

My orders posted me to a REME work-shop in Swansea, and I was not alarmed by this, believing it would be a staging-point only. During the peripatetic railway journey through the Marches I sat within the ramparts of my kit, watching the unfolding beauty of this land and enjoying the sentimental sadness of leaving it. At Swansea station an ATS driver was waiting with a fifteen-hundredweight to take me to the work-shop. She was perhaps nineteen, chewing gum with calculated defiance and speaking in an American accent recently acquired. For the first time I heard an inane phrase that was to sour the course of conversation for years. To every answer I gave her questions, she replied 'Fair enough'. Before the work-shop had been reached, the comfort of that melancholy journey through the Marches had been destroyed.

The base work-shop was large – pre-fabricated huts, garages and sheds. It was a soulless labour prison, and within twenty-four hours I realized that nobody knew why I was there, or cared where I wished to go. This indifference was favourable, however. On the second day I volunteered for service in Normandy, and before a week had gone I was posted. The clothing and equipment I had received at Kinmel were taken from me and replaced with others equally new. The QM was not hostile, only puzzled. Impressed by my assurance that I was indeed a volunteer, he supervised the clothing issue and instructed one of his staff to boil and clean the rifle he had selected for me. I was taken to the railway station through the empty streets of Sunday observance. The driver of the utility was the same ATS private. 'Didn't stay long; did you,' she said. 'Good riddance, eh?' 'Fair enough,' I said.

Nobody in the work-shop at Sawbridgeworth, where I arrived late in the evening, knew why I had been sent there. My request for an immediate posting, beyond Hertfordshire, beyond the Channel, was ignored by the staff-sergeant clerk. Frequent applications later were sometimes sympathetically received, but the response to them was always evasive. My spirits now flagging, I let the unit absorb me. I wrote for its excellent wall-newspaper, and I was worked to exhaustion in the construction of those gun-platforms. As often as I could, however, I presented myself at the work-shop office, correctly dressed and with my application properly worded and written. The irritation of my regular appearance, less than the power of argument, finally persuaded the Adjutant, and later the CO, to approve my posting.

I was quickly dispatched, and this time I knew the course was directly set. Once more I was issued with new clothing, equipment and arms, but hope was most encouraged by a pass for embarkation-leave. There had been no mention of this at Kinmel or Swansea. Upon the conclusion of five valedictory days I was to report to a reinforcement holding-unit at Cooksbridge in Sussex. During that leave I was of course troubled by doubt, by occasional fear, and certainly by shame for what now seemed to be my absurd posturing. A morning separation from my wife and sons at Weston-super-mare, where they had been recently evacuated, was a cinematic cliché – craning from a carriage window and waving to figures soon lost as the train took the bend of the platform.

The RHU was a great encampment in the grounds of the big house at Cooksbridge two miles to the north of Lewes, a canvas web of fly-tents held together by treacherous guys and stays. There were perhaps twenty or thirty thousand men in the lines, moving aimlessly throughout the day, half-dressed in defiant idleness or over-clad for the guards, pickets and fatigues by which a bewildered camp-office hoped to exhaust the minds and bodies of confused men. The mess-tents were four or five great marquees of black and green canvas. The cook-houses adjoining were always noisy with the sound of voices and angry metal, and so wreathed in steam from bubbling soyers that they sometimes appeared to be floating in a mist. After one picket-duty patrolling the woodlands and a twenty-four-hour guard of throbbing tedium, I decided to have no more. I volunteered for permanent fatigue-duty in the mess-tents and cook-houses. Here we worked hard, but on our own choosing, and were excused all other duties. We ate when others had been fed, but we ate with the cooks and thus we fared well. There were hours of freedom in the afternoons, lying under the fly and watching sunlight moving through the sequin leaves of tall trees, and there were moments of rough comradeship, sitting at a mess-tent table long after Lights Out, drinking sweet cocoa laced with rum.

But this was not escape from the camp, only surrender. NCOs from the administration tent sometimes strolled through the lines, holding impressive sheets of paper and calling for men of this or that regiment. Those who stepped forward were swiftly gone. In this way, most wonderfully, I left Cooksbridge, but not because my name, my corps or my trade had been called. The summons that day was 'Fall in Normandy wounded!' for those early casualties who were now thought fit enough to rejoin their units in France. On a providential impulse, but with no faith in its success, I crawled from beneath the fly and *limped* to the NCO. I gave him my name and he looked at my leg. 'All right, that?' he said, and I nodded. He did not ask for my unit, but looked at my greasy denims with disgust. 'Get cleaned up, then. On parade with your kit in half an hour.' At dusk I was sitting in the forward AA turret of that landing-craft at Newhaven.

The crossing was dark and rough and long. The vessel was holding three times the number of soldiers it was built to carry, and most of them were soon sick. I stayed on deck, away from the fetid air and retching noise below, sustaining myself with self-heating soup, hard biscuit and Spam. I was joined by a seaman wearing a steel helmet and a duffle-coat. I wished to be friendly, remembering my father's affectionate observation that the Navy carried the Army to war on its back, but he had clearly come to frighten me. This 'ugly little bastard', he said, was spot-welded, built for a brief life of three landings only, and this, after Anzio and others, was its fifth. When the vessel slapped its shuddering bows against the hard water, he nodded wisely. 'Spot-welded. Can't take much of that.' On my firm advice, he left me to frighten someone else.

At Arromanches I was one of several hundred disembarked on the loop of pontoons that would eventually become Mulberry

Harbour. As we moved inland towards Bayeux, to a field where we were told there were tents to build a camp, there was a sudden sound of gunfire to the east, and the mocking music of Glenn Miller from the camouflage netting of a laagered tank troop. The rain that had begun as we disembarked was now heavy, and roadside mud flooded over our gaiters and into our boots. In the darkness of the field we abandoned the erection of tents and slept where we fell. Dawn was fragile and beautiful in the mist, and by its light I saw that I was lying near the grave of a Highland Light Infantryman, aged nineteen. Someone had built a low wall of apples about it, the small green apples of Normandy, bitter to the taste.

Later – a week, perhaps; time has no definition in such memories – I rode the flat-car slowly eastward along the railway line to the fallen bridge at Rouen and the sullen murmur of gunfire beyond the distant Somme. When the truck took me away from the château near Abbeville, and the horror of its bloody well, I did not know where I might be going. The pretence of seeking my unit could be maintained only if I remained in advance of my following papers, but how it must end I could not know. There was yet another RHU to the south of Brussels. It had been established a day or so before. Its tents, hurriedly pegged on a slope, ballooned and snapped in a fierce wind. The rain was thickening when I alighted, at night again, and I crawled under the nearest fly, laid my ground-sheet upon the grass, and slipped into sleep without thought or discomfort. I awoke to sunlight, to the barking of a penetrating voice and the thumping beat of feet. From above the rim of my great-coat and beyond the edge of the fly I saw a platoon of legs, no higher than the knee, immaculate in polished boots and newly blancoed gaiters, rising, falling and turning in the splattering mud. I moved to the edge of the tent and saw the accusatory eye of a divisional flash, the visored peak of a drill-sergeant's cap, and realized that I had gone peacefully to rest in the lines of a Guards holding unit. I gathered myself and my equipment and moved away as discreetly as possible.

Under another fly across the camp, with a mess-tin of tea and another of bacon and bread, I watched the rain and reminded myself that it was on such a day in such weather, and perhaps across this field, that Wellington's army had retreated from Quatre Bras to Waterloo. The thought was too theatrical and gave no comfort. The morning was empty of movement and decision. A senior NCO, an old man he seemed then, stopped at the tent-door, bending to enquire if we were all 'wet and comfortable'. The phrase would stay in my mind, to be remembered occasionally, but not until I read the letters of Private Wheeler, soldier of the Peninsula and Waterloo, would I discover its military antiquity. He said it was 'an expression of one of my old comrades'.

The rain stopped at noon, and the canvas steamed in the sun. The unexpected warmth encouraged a great drowsiness, a brooding silence as men slept with their dreams. Now and then we were dragged into the present by the cries of runners, calling for men by the names of regiments and corps. Since no one could be wanting me, I lay with my eyes closed and within reach of sleep. I stirred to one voice, without sharp understanding, raising myself on an elbow. A REME corporal was walking down the line. He wore a new leather jerkin of shining sorrel. On his shoulder was the white shield of Second Army Troops, and behind the badge on his cap was the blue, red and yellow flash of the tradesmen's corps. He chanted rather than called, and with no evident expectation of an answer. 'Any SLC mechanics . . . SLC radar mechanics . . . ?' I rolled from beneath the fly and stood up. 'Corporal?' I said, and pointed to the insignia on my arm.

His fifteen-hundredweight took me from the holding unit within the hour, northward to Brussels. He was a vain man, I think, conscious of his smart appearance, his good battle-dress and that splendid jerkin, and I was yet to discover that such sartorial vanity did not survive beyond the Battery's base work-shop. Sounding his horn incessantly, he drove skilfully on roads crowded with trucks, ambulances, half-trucks, armour and civilian vehicles. Shouting above their clamour, and in fragmented sentences like Jingle, he told me that the Battery had been in Europe since the morning of D-Day, that it was no longer employed in anti-aircraft defence but as an artificial moonlight unit, and he did not explain what that meant. I was to go up the line, he said, to one of the troops. 'Wherever it is. We're over the Escaut so they must be beyond Eindhoven now that the Airborne's in Arnhem.' The names were already new to the ear, awesome and exciting. He knew that his casual familiarity with them was impressing me, and that I was perhaps afraid.

We entered Brussels through a lilac dusk, along wide avenues and past tall houses with mansard roofs like Napoleonic shakoes. At the gates of the Saint Jean Barracks the Corporal went inside to speak to the Military Police. 'They'll give you a night's kip if you've got twenty Players.' I gave him the cigarettes, and in growing wisdom I knew they might go no further than his pocket. This small service done, he drove away to the house of a Belgian where, he said, he had got his feet under the table during the city's liberation.

In a large, vaulted chamber of the barracks I was given two blankets and told to make my bed on one of the mattresses along the wall. During the Occupation, German soldiers quartered here had painted a sentimental mural, the flow of the Rhine from Basel and the Schwarzwald, by Strasbourg, Mainz and Cologne, the prosperous smoke and fire of the Ruhr to Holland and the sea. Beneath this nostalgic evocation and in Gothic letters was the legend, '*O, du wunderschönes Deutsches Rhein!*' Kilroy had already pencilled his boast beneath it. My blankets were thin and holed, and the mattress was browned by stains of blood. I spread my ground-sheet over them and slept gratefully until I was awoken by angry shouts and a sobbing scream. A prisoner had been brought in and was held now against the wall until a cell could be found for him. He was a German soldier in civilian clothes, a sniper, one of his guards explained. He was tall and young, and his jaw was bloody and broken. He had resisted capture on the high floor of a house by the Jardin Botanique, using his teeth when his arms were held. A Military Policeman, enraged by a lacerated hand, struck back with the revolver it held. The prisoner was shortly taken away, and his agonizing cry echoed in the chamber long after it was silent.

The Corporal's utility left at eight-thirty, northward and eastward in a stream of traffic towards Holland. Near the Escaut Canal he stopped, turning the vehicle onto the pavement of a small town. There he left me, to visit another family under whose table, he said, he had recently placed his feet. I know that the street was full of dust, movement and noise that morning, but in the memory of it I am alone, standing beside the vehicle and hearing nothing but the music of an old gramophone and a husky, sensual voice singing *La vie en rose*. It comes from a café at the top of a gentle rise, and I walk towards it. It is closed, despite the notice on its door. I copy that down on the back of an envelope and I have it still. As I finish reading it now, the noise of that eager, relentless day returns, mocking the illusion of silence.

A tout va bien. Every morning many soldiers come to my house where they are very happy. Centrally heated English spoken. Egg

278

chips vegetables bread and afters. Fifty francs. By the light of the door you shall know us. Thank you for the 6 June 1944 and I wish you a good return to England.

We found the Battery HQ with difficulty at dusk. It had gone forward from the Escaut into the Dutch corridor with the Third British Infantry Division and was now at Eindhoven, the Leyland trucks laagered near the Philips radio plant. I remember no daylight hours there, only night, white houses grotesquely luminous in the flash of gunfire on both flanks of the corridor. I remember the hospitality of the Dutch with whom I spent the night, a factory worker and his family, his elderly parents, all sitting stiff-backed and drinking the coffee I brought. They had nothing but gratitude for our wounding presence in their town, and I was humbled by the intensity of emotion in that small room. I was in Eindhoven for one night only, I think, and in the morning I was sent northward to one of the troops as a replacement for a radar mechanic wounded in the advance from Normandy. The troop I was meant to join was somewhere on the line by Nijmegen, where the Airborne survivors from Arnhem would come. This was all the driver knew and he was reluctant to discover more.

And that day he would go no further than Grave, the light of a westering sun burning on its steep gables and deepening the orange glow of marigolds in its gardens. The low ground about it had been a landing-area for American airborne, and the water-bright grass was littered with broken gliders, fragile wings and perspex canopies shimmering like dying moths in the falling light. Along the banks of the Maas a battery of five-fives was maintaining a remorseless, rhythmic fire upon the German support lines. The driver was fearful of an inevitable response from a counter-battery, and at his insistence we took shelter within the seventeenth-century walls of a Franciscan monastery. After the heat, the dust, the noise and sour apprehension of the day, this house was cool and comforting. Towards midnight, all was silent and the close anger of the war strangely at rest. There was a strong smell of formaldehyde, and for a brief moment harsh voices, a shout of pain from the room where the medics worked. The sympathy and concern of the monks, confusing newcomers like myself with the worn and the wounded, was shamefully embarrassing, and perhaps that made me unable to sleep. My back against a wall, I wrote instead.

The brown brothers showed me their great fishing-nets, their tobacco plants, their large washing-bowls and the seals the Germans had placed on the brewery four years ago. They walked around us in great delight, puffing happily at the cigarettes we gave them. In their clean, flower-lined garden, the contrast between their clothes and ours was bizarre. They spoke of the Nazis in an odd, detached tone, even when they told me of another monastery where the Germans had established a Gestapo HQ.

In the morning we looked at Nijmegen across the flat plain, sunlit and shining like a view from a Vermeer window, but with puff-balls of dirty smoke where shells were bursting beyond its bridge. The driver thought we had come far enough. He had talked a lot about Normandy and his fear, and he told me again that he had nightmares about the shelling. He explained in detail how the impact of the explosions weakened the limbs, crushed the chest and watered the bowels. Could he not leave me in Grave until someone from troop came for me? While I was considering this, he swore upon Christ, kicked a wheel of his vehicle and said, 'Get in!' We moved slowly towards Nijmegen, along a road crowded with vehicles and between the trudging march of infantry files. There was a nagging delay, waiting on more urgent traffic at the Maas-Waal Canal, and then suddenly we were in Nijmegen, its wounded houses, the smell of fire and dust. The driver found the HQ of A Troop and left me there, where nobody wanted me, and where there had been no signal from Battery. I was told to find what shelter I could, and wait until a message came. There was an air of weary unease at the HQ, raw nerves and eyes that were direct but uncommunicating. I had arrived at the end of the troop's duty here, and my memory of it is unclear, although I wrote of it in the Battery history.

They were under the control of the infantry brigade holding the bank. Once their observation post was even in advance of the infantry, and Recce men had laid mines across their path. The detachments prepared themselves for infantry as well as AA work. They dug their projectors into the field on top of the bank, and scraped billets from the sand below. They dug graves and buried the three Yankee paratroopers they found in the field.

In the early afternoon of the second day, and after a night spent in a cellar with a silent Dutch family, I was told that I should be with

C Troop. 'And they', said a detachment sergeant, 'are at some flaming railway station on the Jerry border. So sit on your arse out of the way until they care to send for you.' I waited for the transport in the unnatural quiet of the autumn day. Two children, whom I remember year by year when their flowers bloom, came to me with garlands of marigolds and put them about my neck. I talked to them in fragmentary German until the shells struck the road and I dragged them under a truck. Even in my experience of air-raids in London and Liverpool I had known nothing like this. The fierce sunlight, the clang of metal upon cobbles, whirling dust, stone splinters, and all those bodily reactions the driver had graphically described.

A ration-and-post truck from Battery took me to C Troop, down a long, long road it seemed, bordered by splintered trees and hasty signs: 'Enemy fire Keep moving!' It was past dusk, the eastern sky already illuminated by the moonlight of the beams, when I was roughly welcomed at the station. A strip of floorboard in the waiting-room was cleared for me, between Corporal Alec and Chappie, the Don R, an unshaven Tynesider who wore a Wehrmacht belt and nursed a dirty-white puppy inside his jerkin. It was a foul, crowded billet, soon shuddering with the fire of battery and counter-battery and the occasional spite of mortars. I saw with my back against the wall, breathing deeply. Alec was reading *Lilliput* by the light of a small bulb wired to a car battery. Encouraged by his calm, I rested a diary on my knee and wrote. I said nothing about the incongruous relief I felt, the peace at being here.

> Move up to Mook, nine kilometres from Nijmegen. Troop HQ in a railway-station. Sixteen filthy men and a puppy called Dempsey in the waiting-room. Infantry moving up to-night, characterless shapes in the dark. Mortar-fire now heavy. Large ammunition dump in the rear just hit.

In the morning the TSM told me to dig a slit-trench, beside the line or between the sleepers. The station was masked from the Germans by a high dune of sand and scrub, but half a mile or less beyond it the land fell and the line was open to their fire. Before Groesbeek, in the timbered high ground, there were said to be three battalions of German infantry facing one of ours. But there was no apparent threat this morning. The sun was bright and the sky quiet now that the last wave of Lancasters had passed over into

Germany. The trees where the disparate battalions lay under arms were rich in seductive colours, and I paused in my ludicrous digging to enjoy them. For the first time, not in days but years, I felt a great ease of mind and heart, and also a shameful pride. In this mental idleness I watched a figure carefully crossing the line below the saddle in that protective dune. He wore a steel helmet and a jerkin, a Sten upon his back, and he carried a large dixie with difficulty, pausing to change hands. He fell as all power left his body. I did not hear a distant shot, and my eye was held by the yellow wave of tea which flowed from the dixie. He lay unmoving and unaided, until a Bren opened fire on the saddle and two men ran from a screen of trees to take him away.

I had never seen a soldier killed. As I stared down the rusting iron of the tracks to that damned, abandoned dixie, Chappie dropped into the trench beside me. 'Poor sod,' he said, and then, looking at me, 'What're you crying for, Johnnie?'

June the Third

I t is within an hour of midnight and there is stillness in Waverley
Station. The Euston train waits, its engines not yet throbbing,
yellow light falling from the open doors of the sleeping-cars. I
remember the days of steam, the panting of a potent locomotive,
the glow of its open mouth, the driver leaning from the cab as he
wipes his hands on cotton-waste, the smell of sulphur and an arched
roof fogged with smoke. It is an old man's privilege to be nostalgic
about past pleasures that were in fact often unpleasant, but now
that they are gone there is warmth in the thought of a steam-train
rocking on an uneasy line, the engine's throaty call against the rush
of night, even the cinders that spun like gnats through an open
window. My memories of the night train to or from Waverley span
six decades, and are linked with others more emotional. For I was
a mature man, set in middle age perhaps, before air travel – which I
hate – satisfied the stultifying desire to reduce the time of travelling.

The first railway sound I seem to remember with any intensity
is of course the slow clickety-clack of wheel on track and the lonesome whistle of the emigrant train, sobbing across the prairie.
There are boyhood afternoons set eternally by the engine-house in
Sutherland, watching a great monster come slowly onto the turn-
table and wheel there to join its tender, like old friends at a rendezvous. There is the far horizon and my uncle's freight, a long black
thread stitching yellow wheat to a blue sky, and smoke rising to the
sun. There is the Liberation Train pulling eastward out of Bayeux
for Rouen and the distant guns, hungry and excited men burning
the timbers of their flat-cars. When we left Mook station, going
south to give moonlight for the bloody fight at Overloon, I did not
think I would ever see it again, or believe that trains would one day
go down the line where the dixie fell. But after the Rhine was
crossed, I was granted a short-leave to Belgium, and sent back to
Mook for transport thence by train. I did not recognize the station
at first; spring and the industry of the Dutch had almost disguised

the stain of war. Nor could I or any of the men gathered there have expected what we found. I wrote about it much later, in an unpublished story or an unfinished book which I called *Long Ago and Far Away*.

The leave-train was on the far track waiting for them. The rails had not yet been re-laid at the platform. The shallow slit-trenches where Robert Lockyer had been afraid were still there, but full now with the wet and abandoned containers of mortar-bombs. Bitter cinder-weed was growing between the sleepers and grass was moving in from the dunes. Children had made a swing of Don Eight, looping the signal-wire over the arm of the water tower. Two bright-haired girls swung on it gently as they sang, and in the eternity that children inhabit the passage of war through their village had been so long ago that they now had little interest in the soldiers.

But there it was – the miracle of an English railway carriage. Soldiers were standing beside it, touching it and laughing incredulously. It was a bright green jewel strung among the black coaches of the Reichsbahn and the Chemin de Fer. Its brass hand-rails shone in the sun, and the golden letters SR and First Class had been newly painted. It was an old coach, older than many of the soldiers, but it was here, for them, for their brief journey. Someone had signed the order that sent it across the Channel to prove that nothing was too good for the lads out there. Before they climbed aboard, the soldiers treated it with sincere mockery, removing their caps in a half-bow to let others of higher rank precede them. In every compartment the seats had been re-upholstered in dappled red, and smelt strongly of disinfectant. Between the winged head-rests were brass studs for antimacassars. The pictures above were old, from a past long, long gone, before that other war and now dead in a sepia mist. Lockyer read the captions aloud in whispering disbelief. Polperro . . . Lulworth Cove . . . Bournemouth . . . Torquay . . .

I never finished the story, and perhaps this was the best part of it. Many years later I took its title and one sequence – that search for Christmas paper – and turned it into a television play that came to nothing. I do not regret this. To read what I have written about my life is difficult, but tolerable. To see it enacted would put a distressing strain on patience and credulity.

A year after that journey from Mook to Diest another became an enduring memory. The train waiting at Hamburg station on the day of my demobilization was sadly disreputable, a dozen black carriages of the Reichsbahn, their swastika badges scraped away or roughly modified with paint, and the eagle that once clutched the crooked cross now hung absurdly in the air. We left in the evening for Tournai where, we were told, motor transport would carry us to Calais. The journey took twenty-six hours, the train moving slowly and perversely, sometimes immobile at long, unexplained halts. We were crowded together on the seats of every carriage, on the floor, in the aisles, mixed inextricably with equipment, cigarette-ends, heels of bread, torn paper from 'unexpired rations', and empty wine bottles. We slept as we could, or resisted sleep with tobacco, brandy or schnapps. For ten hours there was darkness beyond the dirty windows, sometimes relieved by the flicker of a distant light or the glow of a track-side fire. I do not remember the daylight hours, only the night, the heavy irony of our occasional songs, the brief quarrels, fierce words subsiding abruptly into the maudlin emotions of soldiers mustering-out. The train seemed to travel eastward as often as to the west, north as much as south, seeking a track undamaged or repaired. The halts in shadowy towns, among the gaunt monoliths of ruined cities, grew longer with the night. There was no explanation given, or no one to explain, but from a window we could look up the train to the engine, to the glow of its fire, and see the fireman tossing coal to the dark figures that struggled below the embankment.

In the boredom of a long wait, and aroused by the noise, I cleaned the window with the ball of my hand. I saw children's faces below, reaching hands, and heard the insistent piping of their voices. *'Habt ihr Brot . . . ? Habt ihr Brot . . . ?'* It was perhaps inevitable that this, my last memory of Germany, on the last day of six years' soldiering, should become the last words of the novel I had begun at the Lorelei.

When the train stopped, the untidy clamour of the children's voices swirled about it again. There must have been scores of them down there in the darkness, scrambling and fighting on the loose earth. The shrill insistence of their voices had one cry only, *Habt ihr Brot*. He could not see them, he could only hear their odd voices, and as he looked along the side of the train he saw the heads of other soldiers projecting uncomfortably. Here and there an arm joined the heads, tossing a white bundle. Then the new day held his attention. Sensing an enemy in the fine, glowing optimism of the dawn, the children

The author, Belgium, 1945.

swarmed up the embankment into its light, their voices rising in a desperate treble. *Habt ihr Brot . . . ?*

Have you bread? We had bread and we threw it to them. None of us, I think, would have believed that this cry would become louder, more despairing in every part of the globe with every decade that followed.

Index

The New Emperors
Mao and Deng: A Dual Biography

Harrison E. Salisbury

'A fascinating story . . . enlivened by personal anecdotes and
packed with splendid reports of the two "New Emperors" that
will make addictive reading not only for diplomats, scholars and
their colleagues, but also for businessmen and tourists.'

Clare Hollingworth, *Daily Telegraph*

Harrison Salisbury's knowledge of China and its leaders – based
on twenty years of study and first-hand research – has produced
an epic narrative history of the new Communist dynasty. As he
surveys the convulsive events that shaped modern China – the
Nationalist–Communist civil war, the Communist takeover, the
mass famine following the Great Leap Forward, the Cultural
Revolution – Salisbury focuses on Mao and Deng and their
complex relationship.

How Deng won Mao's favour by building Mao's secret Third
Line, a gigantic industrial redoubt whose crippling cost was in
inverse proportion to its ultimate strategic value, and rose to
power; how he was ousted and persecuted by Mao during the
Cultural Revolution; how he was recalled by Mao and then
toppled by Mao's wife; and how General Ye Jianying plotted to
overthrow the Gang of Four and install Deng as the 'new
emperor' – all are sketched in dramatic detail.

'A stunningly detailed account of two enigmatic figures'

Financial Times

ISBN 0 586 21864 5

The Honourable Company
A History of the English East India Company

John Keay

'The first accessible narrative history of the English East India Company which has appeared for some time . . . Keay recounts his story with the sweep of a James Michener, but one anchored in the meticulous scholarship of historians . . . Commercial successes and failures, battles and politics from Table Bay to Tokyo Bay are treated with verve and clarity.'

Christopher Bayly, *The Observer*

Over two centuries, the East India Company grew from a loose association of Elizabethan tradesmen into 'the Grandest Society of Merchants in the Universe' – a huge commercial enterprise which controlled half the world's trade and also administered an embryonic empire. A tenth of the British exchequer's total revenue derived from customs receipts on the Company's UK imports; its armed forces exceeded those of most sovereign states. Without it there would have been no British India and no British Empire.

ISBN 0 00 638072 7

The Scars of War

Hugh McManners

'Absolutely not for the squeamish. This book lifts the veil of the "forget factor" which we all lower over the horrors of war once the fighting is over. It is not a happy story, but it needs telling.'

General Sir Peter de la Billiere

War is by far the most traumatic 'life event' any human being can experience – a devastating combination of danger, uncertainty and horror. What really happens on the modern battlefield? How do today's professional soldiers prepare for, and cope with, the physical and psychological hardships of combat? And what happens when the combatants return to normal life?

In a work of remarkable and revealing candour, Hugh McManners has gone beyond the history books, autobiographies and regimental diaries to talk to scores of servicemen. He shows how the power and range of today's weapons make modern war more stressful than ever before, and he looks at the long-term mental and emotional effects of combat. *The Scars of War* carries on where John Keegan's classic *The Face of Battle* left off. It is a powerful and wide-ranging report from the front, which will have a profound impact on many aspects of military thinking.

ISBN 0 586 21129 2